MASERATI CARS
Ultimate Portfolio
1999 - 2007

Compiled by R M Clarke

ISBN 9781855207608

BROOKLANDS BOOKS LTD.
P.O. BOX 146, COBHAM,
SURREY, KT11 1LG. UK
sales@brooklands-books.com

www.brooklands-books.com

Printed in China

Brooklands Books

ROAD TEST SERIES

Abarth Gold Portfolio 1950-1971
Alfa Romeo Giulietta Gold Portfolio 1954-1965
Alfa Romeo Alfasud 1972-1984
Alfa Romeo Alfetta Gold Portfolio 1972-1987
Alfa Romeo Spider Ultimate Portfolio 1966-1994
Alfa Romeo Spider & GTV Perf. Port. 1995-2005
Alpine Renault Ultimate Portfolio 1958-1995
Alvis Gold Portfolio 1919-1967
AMC Rambler Limited Edition Extra 1956-1969
AMX & Javelin Gold Portfolio 1968-1974
Armstrong Siddeley Gold Portfolio 1945-1960
Aston Martin Gold Portfolio 1921-1947
Aston Martin Ultimate Portfolio 1948-1968
Aston Martin Ultimate Portfolio 1968-1980
Aston Martin Ultimate Portfolio 1981-1993
Aston Martin Ultimate Portfolio 1994-2006
Audi Quattro Gold Portfolio 1980-1991
Audi Quattro Takes On The Competition
Audi TT Performance Portfolio 1998-2006
Austin-Healey 100 & 100/6 Gold Port. 1952-1959
Austin-Healey 3000 Ultimate Portfolio 1959-1967
Austin-Healey Sprite Gold Portfolio 1958-1971
Bentley & Rolls-Royce Portfolio 1990-2002
Berkeley Sportscars Limited Edition
BMW 6 & 8 Cyl. Cars Limited Edition 1935-1960
BMW 700 Limited Edition 1959-1965
BMW 1600 Collection No. 1 1966-1981
BMW 2002 Ultimate Portfolio 1968-1976
BMW 6 Cylinder Coupés & Saloons Gold P. 1969-1976
BMW 316, 318, 320 (4 cyl.) Gold Port. 1975-1990
BMW 320, 323, 325 (6 cyl.) Gold Port. 1977-1990
BMW 3 Series Gold Portfolio 1991-1997
BMW M3 Ultimate Portfolio 1986-2006
BMW M5 Gold Portfolio 1980-2003
BMW 5 Series Gold Portfolio 1988-1995
BMW 6 Series Ultimate Portfolio 1976-1989
BMW 7 Series Performance Portfolio 1977-1986
BMW 7 Series Performance Portfolio 1986-1993
BMW 8 Series Performance Portfolio
BMW Alpina Performance Portfolio 1967-1987
BMW Alpina Performance Portfolio 1988-1998
BMW Z3, M Coupe & M Roadster Gold Port. 1996-02
Borgward Isabella Limited Edition
Bristol Cars Portfolio
Buick Performance Portfolio 1947-1962
Buick Muscle Portfolio 1963-1973
Buick Riviera Performance Portfolio 1963-1978
Cadillac Performance Portfolio 1948-1958
Cadillac Performance Portfolio 1959-1966
Cadillac Eldorado Performance Portfolio 1967-1978
Cadillac Allante Limited Edition Extra
Chevrolet 1955-1957
Impala & SS Muscle Portfolio 1958-1972
Corvair Performance Portfolio 1959-1969
El Camino & SS Muscle Portfolio 1959-1987
Chevy II & Nova SS Gold Portfolio 1962-1974
Chevelle & SS Gold Portfolio 1964-1972
Camaro Muscle Portfolio 1967-1973
Blazer & Jimmy Limited Edition Extra 1969-1982
Blazer & Jimmy Limited Edition Extra 1983-1994
Camaro Performance Portfolio 1993-2000
Chevrolet Corvette Gold Portfolio 1953-1962
Chevrolet Corvette Sting Ray Gold Port. 1963-1967
Chevrolet Corvette Gold Portfolio 1968-1977
High Performance Corvettes 1983-1989
Chrysler Imperial Gold Portfolio 1951-1975
Valiant 1960-1962
PT Cruiser Performance Portfolio
Citroen 2CV Ultimate Portfolio 1948-1990
Citroen DS & ID 1955-1975
Citroen DS & ID Gold Portfolio 1955-1975
Citroen SM Limited Edition Extra 1970-1975
Shelby Cobra Gold Portfolio 1962-1969
Crosley & Crosley Specials Limited Edition
Cunningham Automobiles 1951-1955
Datsun Roadsters Performance Portfolio 1960-71
Datsun 240Z & 260Z Gold Portfolio 1970-1978
DeLorean Gold Portfolio 1977-1995
De Soto Limited Edition 1952-1960
Dodge Limited Edition 1949-1959
Dodge Dart Limited Edition Extra 1960-1976
Dodge Muscle Portfolio 1964-1971
Charger Muscle Portfolio 1966-1974
ERA Gold Portfolio 1934-1994
Facel Vega Limited Edition Extra 1954-1964
Ferrari Limited Edition 1947-1957
Ferrari Limited Edition 1958-1963
Ferrari Dino Limited Edition Extra 1965-1974
Ferrari 308 & Mondial Ultimate Portfolio 1975- 85
Ferrari 328 348 Mondial Ultimate Portfolio 1986-94
Ferrari F355 & 360 Gold Portfolio 1995-2004
Fiat 600 & 850 Gold Portfolio 1955-1972
Fiat Dino Limited Edition
Fiat 124 Spider Performance Portfolio 1966-1985
Fiat X1/9 Gold Portfolio 1973-1989
Ford Consul, Zephyr, Zodiac Mk. I & II 1950-1962
Ford Zephyr, Zodiac, Executive Mk. III & IV 1962-1971
High Performance Capris Gold Portfolio 1969-1987
Capri Muscle Portfolio 1974-1987
High Performance Fiestas 1979-1991
Ford Escort RS & Mexico Limited Edition 1970-1979
High Performance Escorts Mk. II 1975-1980
High Performance Escorts 1980-1985
High Performance Escorts 1985-1990
Ford Thunderbird Performance Portfolio 1955-1957
Ford Thunderbird Performance Portfolio 1958-1963
Ford Thunderbird Performance Portfolio 1964-1976
Ford Fairlane Performance Portfolio 1955-1970
Ford Ranchero Muscle Portfolio 1957-1979
Edsel Limited Edition 1957-1960
Ford Galaxie & LTD Gold Portfolio 1960-1976
Falcon Performance Portfolio 1960-1970
Ford GT40 & GT Ultimate Portfolio 1964-2006
Ford Torino Performance Portfolio 1968-1974
Ford Bronco 4x4 Performance Portfolio 1966-1977
Ford Bronco 1978-1988
Shelby Mustang Ultimate Portfolio 1965-1970
Mustang Muscle Portfolio 1967-1973
High Performance Mustang IIs 1974-1978
Mustang 5.0L Muscle Portfolio 1982-1993
Mustang 5.0L Takes On The Competition
Goggomobil Limited Edition
Holden 1948-1962
Honda S500 • S600 • S800 Limited Edition 1962-1970
Honda CRX 1983-1987
Hudson Performance Portfolio 1946-1957
International Scout Gold Portfolio 1961-1980
Isetta Gold Portfolio 1953-1964
Jaguar and SS Gold Portfolio 1931-1951
Jaguar C-Type & D-Type Gold Portfolio 1951-1960
Jaguar XK120 • 140 • 150 Gold Portfolio 1948-1960
Jaguar Mk. VII, VIII, IX, X, 420 Gold Port. 1950-1970
Jaguar E-Type Gold Portfolio 1961-1971
Jaguar XJ6 Series I & II Gold Portfolio 1968-1979
Jaguar XJ6 Series III Perf. Portfolio 1979-1986
Jaguar XJS Gold Portfolio 1975-1988
Jaguar XJ-S V12 Ultimate Portfolio 1988-1996
Jaguar XK8 & XKR Performance Portfolio 1996-2005
Jeep CJ-5 Limited Edition 1960-1975
Jeep CJ-5 & CJ-7 4x4 Perf. Portfolio 1976-1986
Jeep Wagoneer Performance Portfolio 1963-1991
Jeep J-Series Pickups 1970-1982
Jeepster & Commando Limited Edition 1967-1973
Jeep Cherokee & Comanche Pickups P. P. 1984-91
Jeep Wrangler 4x4 Performance Portfolio 1987-99
Jeep Cherokee & Grand Cherokee 4x4 P. P. 1992-98
Jensen Interceptor Ultimate Portfolio 1966-1992
Jensen - Healey Limited Edition 1972-1976
Kaiser - Frazer Limited Edition 1946-1955
Lagonda Gold Portfolio 1919-1964
Lancia Aurelia & Flaminia Gold Portfolio 1950-1970
Lancia Fulvia Gold Portfolio 1963-1976
Lancia Beta Gold Portfolio 1972-1984
Lancia Stratos Limited Edition Extra
Lancia Delta & integrale Ultimate Portfolio
Land Rover Series I, II & IIA Gold Portfolio 1948-71
Land Rover Series III 4x4 Perf. Portfolio 1971-1985
Land Rover 90 110 Defender Gold Portfolio 1983-94
Land Rover Discovery Perf. Port. 1989-2000
Fifty Years of Selling Land Rover
Lamborghini Performance Portfolio 1964-1976
Lamborghini Performance Portfolio 1977-1989
Lamborghini Gold Portfolio 1990-2004
Lincoln Gold Portfolio 1949-1960
Lincoln Continental Performance Portfolio 1961-1969
Lincoln Continental 1969-1976
Lotus Sports Racers Portfolio - covering 1951-1965
Lotus Seven Gold Portfolio 1957-1973
Lotus Elite Limited Edition 1957-1964
Lotus Elan Ultimate Portfolio 1962-1974
Lotus Elan & SE 1989-1992
Lotus Europa Gold Portfolio 1966-1975
Lotus Elite & Eclat 1974-1982
Lotus Elise & Exige Gold Portfolio 1995-2005
Marcos Coupés & Spyders Gold Portfolio 1960-1997
Maserati Cars Performance Portfolio 1957-1970
Maserati Cars Performance Portfolio 1971-1982
Maserati Cars Performance Portfolio 1982-1998
Maserati Cars Ultimate Portfolio 1999-2007
Matra Limited Edition 1965-1983
Mazda Miata MX-5 Performance Portfolio 1989-1997
Mazda Miata MX-5 Performance Portfolio 1998-2005
Mazda Miata MX-5 Takes On The Competition
Mazda RX-7 Gold Portfolio 1978-1991
McLaren F1 • GTR • LM Sportscar Perf. Portfolio
Mercedes 190 & 300 SL 1954-1963
Mercedes S & 600 Limited Edition Extra 1965-1972
Mercedes S Class 1972-1979
Mercedes S Class Limited Edition Extra 1980-1991
Mercedes 230 • 250 • 280SL Gold Portfolio 1963-1971
Mercedes-Benz SLs & SLCs Ultimate Port. 1971-89
Mercedes SLs Performance Portfolio 1989-1994
Mercedes G-Wagen Gold Portfolio 1981-2005
Mercedes 190 Limited Edition Extra 1983-1993
Mercedes CLK & SLK Limited Edition 1996-2000
Mercedes AMG Gold Portfolio 1983-1999
Mercedes AMG Ultimate Portfolio 2000-2006
Mercury Gold Portfolio 1947-1966
Mercury Comet & Cyclone Lim. Edit. Extra 1960-75
Cougar Muscle Portfolio 1967-1973
Messerschmitt Gold Portfolio 1954-1964
MG Gold Portfolio 1929-1939
MG TA & TC Gold Portfolio 1936-1949
MG TD & TF Gold Portfolio 1949-1955
MGA & Twin Cam Gold Portfolio 1955-1962
MG Midget Gold Portfolio 1961-1979
MGB Roadsters 1962-1980
MGB MGC & V8 Gold Portfolio 1962-1980
MGC & MGB GT V8 Limited Edition
MGF & TF Performance Portfolio 1995-2005
Mini Gold Portfolio 1959-1969
Mini Gold Portfolio 1969-1980
Mini Gold Portfolio 1981-1997
High Performance Minis Gold Portfolio 1960-1973
Mini Cooper Gold Portfolio 1961-1971
Mini Moke Ultimate Portfolio 1964-1994
Mini Performance Portfolio 2001-2006
Starion & Conquest Performance Portfolio 1982-90
Mitsubishi 3000GT & Dodge Stealth P.P. 1990-99
Morgan Three-Wheeler Gold Portfolio 1910-1952
Morgan Plus 4 & Four 4 Gold Portfolio 1936-1967
Morgan Cars Portfolio 1968-2001
Morris Minor Collection No. 1 1948-1980
Nash Limited Edition Extra 1949-1957
Nash-Austin Metropolitan Gold Portfolio 1954-1962
Nissan Skyliner GT-R Limited Edition Extra 1989-02
NSU Ro80 Limited Edition
NSX Performance Portfolio 1989-1999
Oldsmobile Muscle Portfolio 1964-1971
Cutlass & 4-4-2 Muscle Portfolio 1964-1974
Opel GT Ultimate Portfolio 1968-1973
Opel Manta Limited Edition 1970-1975
Pantera Ultimate Portfolio 1970-1995
Panther Gold Portfolio 1972-1990
Plymouth Limited Edition 1950-1960
Plymouth Fury Limited Edition Extra 1956-1976
Barracuda Muscle Portfolio 1964-1974
Plymouth Muscle Portfolio 1964-1971
High Performance Firebirds 1982-1988
Firebird & Trans Am Performance Portfolio 1993-00
Pontiac Fiero Performance Portfolio 1984-1988
Porsche Sports Racing Cars UP 1952-1968
Porsche 917 • 935 • 956 • 962 Gold Portfolio
Porsche 912 Limited Edition Extra
Porsche 365 Ultimate Portfolio 1952-1965
Porsche 911 1965-1969
Porsche 911 1973-1977
Porsche 911 SC & Turbo Gold Portfolio 1978-1983
Porsche 911 Carrera & Turbo Gold Port. 1984-1989
Porsche 911 Ultimate Portfolio 1990-1997
Porsche 911 Takes On The Competition 1990-1997
Porsche 911 Ultimate Portfolio 1998-2004
Porsche 914 Ultimate Portfolio
Porsche 924 Gold Portfolio 1975-1988
Porsche 928 Gold Portfolio 1977-1995
Porsche 928 Takes On The Competition
Porsche 944 Ultimate Portfolio
Porsche 968 Limited Edition Extra
Porsche Boxster Ultimate Portfolio 1996-2004
Railton & Brough Superior Gold Portfolio 1933-1950
Range Rover Gold Portfolio 1970-1985
Range Rover Gold Portfolio 1985-1995
Range Rover Performance Portfolio 1995-2001
Range Rover Takes on the Competition
Riley Gold Portfolio 1924-1939
Rolls-Royce Silver Clould & Bentley S Ultimate Port.
Rolls-Royce Silver Shadow Ultimate Port. 1965-80
Rolls-Royce & Bentley Gold Portfolio 1980-1989
Rover P4 1949-1959
Rover 2000 & 2200 1963-1977
Subaru Impreza Turbo Limited Edition Extra 94-00
Subaru Impreza WRX Performance Port. 2001-05
Avanti Limited Edition Extra 1962-1991
Sunbeam Alpine Limited Edition Extra 1959-1968
Sunbeam Tiger Limited Edition Extra 1964-1967
Suzuki SJ Gold Portfolio 1971-1997
Vitara, Sidekick & Geo Tracker Perf. Port. 1988-1997
Toyota Land Cruiser Gold Portfolio 1956-1987
Toyota Land Cruiser 1988-1997
Toyota Supra Performance Portfolio 1982-1998
Toyota MR2 Gold Portfolio 1984-1997
Toyota MR2 Takes On The Competition
Triumph TR2 & TR3 Gold Portfolio 1952-1961
Triumph TR4, TR5, TR250 1961-1968
Triumph TR6 Gold Portfolio 1969-1976
Triumph Herald 1959-1971
Triumph Vitesse 1962-1971
Triumph Spitfire Gold Portfolio 1962-1980
Triumph 2000, 2.5, 2500 1963-1977
Triumph GT6 Gold Portfolio 1966-1974
Triumph Stag Gold Portfolio 1970-1977
Triumph Dolomite Sprint Limited Edition
TVR Performance Portfolio 1986-1994
TVR Performance Portfolio 1995-2000
TVR Performance Portfolio 2000-2005
VW Beetle Gold Portfolio 1935-1967
VW Beetle Gold Portfolio 1968-1991
VW Bus, Camper, Van Perf. Portfolio 1954-1967
VW Bus, Camper, Van Perf. Portfolio 1968-1979
VW Bus, Camper, Van Perf. Portfolio 1979-1991
VW Karmann Ghia Gold Portfolio 1955-1974
VW Scirocco 1974-1981
VW Golf GTI Limited Edition Extra 1976-1991
VW Corrado Limited Edition 1989-1995
Volvo PV444 & PV544 Perf. Portfolio 1945-1965
Volvo 120 Amazon Ultimate Portfolio
Volvo 1800 Ultimate Portfolio 1960-1973
Volvo 140 & 160 Series Gold Portfolio 1966-1975
Forty Years of Selling Volvo
Westfield Performance Portfolio 1982-2004

RACING & THE LAND SPEED RECORD

The Land Speed Record 1898-1919
The Land Speed Record 1920-1929
The Land Speed Record 1930-1939
The Land Speed Record 1940-1962
The Land Speed Record 1963-1999
Can-Am Racing 1966-1969
Can-Am Racing 1970-1974
Can-Am Racing Cars 1966-1974
The Carrera Panamericana Mexico - 1950-1954
Le Mans - The Bentley & Alfa Years - 1923-1939
Le Mans - The Jaguar Years - 1949-1957
Le Mans - The Ferrari Years - 1958-1965
Le Mans - The Ford & Matra Years - 1966-1974
Le Mans - The Porsche Years - 1975-1982
Le Mans - The Porsche & Jaguar Years - 1983-91
Le Mans - The Porsche & Peugeot Years - 1992-99
Mille Miglia - The Alfa & Ferrari Years - 1927-1951
Mille Miglia - The Ferrari & Mercedes Years - 1952-57
Targa Florio - The Porsche & Ferrari Years - 1955-1964
Targa Florio - The Porsche Years - 1965-1973

RESTORATION & GUIDE SERIES

BMW 2002 - A Comprehensive Guide
BMW '02 Restoration Guide
BMW E30 - 3 Series Restoration Bible
Classic Camaro Restoration
Engine Swapping Tips & Techniques
Ferrari Life Buyer's Portfolio
Land Rover Restoration Portfolio
PC on Land Rover Series I Restoration
Lotus Elan Restoration Guide
MG 'T' Series Restoration Guide
MGA Restoration Guide
PC on Midget/Sprite Restoration
PC on MGB Restoration
Mustang Restoration Tips & Techniques
Practical Gas Flow
Restoring Sprites & Midgets an Enthusiast's Guide
SU Carburetters Tuning Tips & Techniques
PC on Sunbeam Rapier Restoration
The Great Classic Muscle Cars Compared

MILITARY VEHICLES

Complete WW2 Military Jeep Manual
Dodge WW2 Military Portfolio 1940-1945
German Military Equipment WW2
Hail To The Jeep
Combat Land Rover Portfolio No. 1
Land Rover Military Portfolio
Military & Civilian Amphibians 1940-1990
Off Road Jeeps Civilian & Military 1944-1971
US Military Vehicles 1941-1945
Standard Military Motor Vehicles-TM9-2800 (WW2)
VW Kubelwagen Military Portfolio 1940-1990
WW2 Allied Vehicles Military Portfolio 1939-1945
WW2 Jeep Military Portfolio 1941-1945

ROAD & TRACK SERIES

Road & Track on Aston Martin 1962-1990
Road & Track on Austin Healey 1953-1970
Road & Track on BMW Cars 1966-1974
Road & Track BMW M Series Portfolio 1979-2002
R & T BMW Z3, M Coupe & M Roadster Port. 96-02
R & T Camaro & Firebird Portfolio 1993-2002
R & T on Cobra, Shelby & Ford GT40 1962-1992
Road & Track on Corvette 1968-1982
Road & Track on Corvette 1982-1986
Road & Track on Corvette 1986-1990
Road & Track Corvette Portfolio 1997-2002
Road & Track Dodge Viper Portfolio 1992-2002
Road & Track on Ferrari 1975-1981
Road & Track on Ferrari 1984-1988
Road & Track Ferrari V-12 Portfolio 1992-2002
Road & Track Ferrari F355 360 F430 Portfolio 95-06
Road & Track on Fiat Sports Cars 1968-1987
Road & Track on Jaguar 1950-1960
Road & Track on Jaguar 1961-1968
Road & Track on Jaguar 1968-1974
Road & Track on Jaguar 1974-1982
Road & Track on Jaguar 1983-1989
R & T Jaguar XJ-S - XK8 - XKR Portfolio 1975-2003
Road & Track on Lamborghini 1964-1985
Road & Track MX-5 Miata Portfolio 1989-2002
Road & Track on Mercedes 1952-1962
Road & Track on Mercedes 1963-1970
Road & Track on Mercedes 1971-1979
R & T Mercedes SL - SLK - CLK Portfolio 1990-2003
Road & Track on MG Sports Cars 1949-1961
Road & Track on MG Sports Cars 1962-1980
Road & Track Mustang Portfolio 1994-2002
Road & Track Nissan 300ZX & 350Z Portfolio 1984-03
Road & Track on Porsche 1951-1967
Road & Track on Porsche 1968-1971
Road & Track on Porsche 1972-1975
Road & Track on Porsche 1975-1978
Road & Track on Porsche 1979-1982
Road & Track on Porsche 1985-1988
Road & Track Porsche 928 Portfolio 1977-1994
Road & Track Porsche 911 Portfolio 1990-1997
R & T on Rolls Royce & Bentley 1950-1965
R & T on Rolls Royce & Bentley 1966-1984
Road & Track on Saab 1972-1992
R & T on Toyota Sports & GT Cars 1966-1984
R & T on Triumph Sports Cars 1967-1974
R & T on Triumph Sports Cars 1974-1982
Road & Track on Volkswagen 1951-1968
Road & Track on Volkswagen 1968-1978
Road & Track on Volvo 1957-1974
Road & Track on Volvo 1977-1994
Road & Track - Best of PS
Road & Track - Peter Egan Side Glances 1983-92
Road & Track - Peter Egan Side Glances 1992-97
Road & Track - Peter Egan Side Glances 1998-02
Road & Track - Peter Egan Side Glances 2002-06

CAR AND DRIVER SERIES

Car and Driver on BMW 1957-1977
Car and Driver on Corvette 1978-1982
Car and Driver on Corvette 1983-1988
Car and Driver on Ferrari 1955-1962
Car and Driver on Ferrari 1963-1975
Car and Driver on Mustang 1964-1973
Car and Driver on Porsche 1955-1962
Car and Driver on Porsche 1963-1970
Car and Driver on Porsche 1970-1976
Car and Driver on Porsche 1977-1981
Car and Driver on Porsche 1982-1986

HOT ROD 'ENGINE' SERIES

Chevy 265 & 283
Chevy 302 & 327
Chevy 348 & 409
Chevy 396 & 427
Chevy 454 thru 512
Chrysler Hemi
Chrysler 273, 318, 340 & 360
Chrysler 361, 383, 400, 413, 426 & 440
Ford 289, 302, Boss 302 & 351W
Ford 351C & Boss 351
Ford Big Block

MOTORCYCLES

To see our range of over 70 titles visit www.brooklands-books.com

25/06Z7

Contents

Contents - Continued

Brooklands Books

Acknowledgements

Brooklands Books has been publishing '*road test*' books such as this on a wide range of makes and models for over 50 years. This is our fourth book on Maserati which covers the history of their road going models from 1957 to 2007. The purpose of our series is to let enthusiasts trace the development of the marque through contemporary magazine articles.

Our thanks go to the numerous authors and photographers who have generously allowed us to reproduce their road tests and other stories in this format. The series however would not have been possible without the help and understanding of the worlds leading motoring journals, who have supported us for many years. We are sure that Maserati owners will wish to join with us in thanking the managements of the following magazines: *Autocar, Autosport, Car, Car and Driver, Classic Car, EVO, Motor Australia, Motor Sport, Octane, Road & Track, Road & Track Specials, Sports Car International, Top Gear* and *Wheels*.

R.M. Clarke

Maserati is one of those deliciously Italian names that rolls phonetically off the tongue with a slight roll of the "r" sound and a short "i" at the end. Said properly it sounds beautiful, just like the famous cars to which it is attached. After some years in the doldrums Maserati is back with a vengeance.

The resurgence began with the 3200 GT coupe back in 1998 and, slowly-but-surely, there has been a re-emergence of one of the motoring world's most iconic makes that has a fabulous history. This includes World Championships in Formula One with Juan Manuel Fangio winning the driver's championship and the company winning the Constructor's Championship in 1957 after an amazing drive by Fangio on the tough Nürburgring against the Ferraris of Hawthorn and Collins. It was one of the epic drives.

Over the past decade the coupe (and the later convertible) have been upgraded with larger capacity engines and the Cambiocorsa semi-automatic paddle shift gearbox that has drawn its fair share of criticism from the media in particular.

Today's range is, for the performance connoisseur, nigh on perfect. If you want a beautifully styled coupe there is the delectable 4200 GT; if your heart desires a convertible then there is the drop-top version of the 4200 GT; and if you have family matters to contend with and need a high performance long distance limousine there is the gorgeous Quattroporte. The coupe and convertible were styled by Giorgetto Giugiaro at Italdesign and the big Quattroporte was the work of the Pininfarina studios. Many critics have said that it is the best looking high performance limousine ever made and they may well be right.

Technically all three models are bang up-to-date with light weight alloy quad cam V8 engines under their hoods driving to a rear-mounted transaxle-gearbox and differential combined in one unit - that helps to balance the weight distribution; the suspension systems are wishbone and coil springs at all four wheels and there are electronically controlled dampers plus huge ventilated brake disc rotors to cope with the enormous speed these cars can be driven at. And inside all passengers travel in sybaritic comfort on beautifully crafted leather seats and in a climate controlled environment listening to their favourite music on a top quality audio system plus all the electronic toys needed to keep in touch with the world while crossing the Continent. All will exceed 170 mph given the right conditions and will blast from rest to 60 mph in around 5.0 seconds and use fuel at a rate close to 15 mpg - if you can afford these cars filling the tank should be a minor concern.

For the extreme extroverts there was the MC12, a 630bhp 6.0 litre V12 engined powered race and street car of which only 50 were made and sold. Capable of over 200 mph and a storming 3.8 seconds 0-62 mph acceleration time, it was developed by Maserati's engineers from a Giugiaro idea with the idea that the trident would return to the international racing scene.

Few marques have put the word "Grand" into Grand Touring the way that Maserati has.

Gavin Farmer

Dave Smith, Administrator: Maserati Club,
2, Sunny Bank, Widmer End, Bucks. HP15 6PA, UK.
Phone & Fax: 01494 717701   E-mail: admin@maseraticlub.co.uk

HOLY
MAS

DRIVE `MASERATI 3200 GT` Our faith in Maserati's ability to produce fine GT cars has been restored with this handsome new coupe. Peter Robinson reports

So it's 3200 GT. Not Mistral, or Indy, or Sebring as mooted, but a revival of a number that goes back more than 40 years to Maserati's glorious past and the 3500 GT, the first modern Maserati road car. Now, as then, the number rounds out the engine capacity.

The rebirth is deliberate, of course. New owner Ferrari believes the Maserati Grand Turismo coupe bridges the philosophical gap between the '60s and '70s, when Maseratis were great, and a new generation of cars. It returns the Trident to its rightful place as one of the world's great marques, up there with Jaguar, Porsche and Aston Martin, if one rung below Ferrari – thus ignoring the disastrously unreliable and boxy cars from the de Tomaso era. Forget the much improved but still flawed Quattroporte Evo. Maserati's renewal truly begins with the 3200 GT.

Say the name in Italian. *Tre mille due cento*. It spills roundly, romantically, from the mouth. In English, "three thousand two hundred" sounds banal, prosaic (although Italians might think it sounds great in English). Fortunately, the new coupe looks pure *tre mille due cento*. This is Giorgetto Giugiaro's idea of how a Maserati GT should look. If there are obvious links in its classical proportions and details with other front-engined, rear-drive GTs like the DB7 and

XK8, then so be it; Maserati wanted a conservative design rather than something radical or extreme.

The 3200 GT is more masculine, more aggressive than the beautiful Aston Martin. In profile it looks taller and thicker than you expect, especially around the rear flanks. But from the front you see the strong taper, the understated flare of the front guards and the exquisitely crafted details of the grille with its prominent trident emblem.

The rear is also strongly tapered in both glasshouse and tail, where Fiat boss Paolo Cantarella's twin-boomerang LED tail-lights (claimed to be the first in the world) mean the Maserati is going to be instantly recognisable at night.

Some bits don't quite gel. The headlight fit into the all-steel body is inconsistent, for example, but Maserati is still playing with the details. The rear Maserati script is to be enlarged and a 3200 GT badge added to the C-pillar, if my already-released Bburago scale model is accurate. These are pre-series cars, destined to be sent to major distributors around the world as part of Maserati's incredibly thorough durability road testing programme, before production of left-hand-drive models begins in January.

By the time the 3200GT reaches the UK in March – at a price that's directly competitive with the £60,000 XKR – Maserati is convinced most of the details and dynamic flaws ◆

◆ will have been ironed out.

Colour? Choose from 14, including the aptly named Moss green (Stirling Moss drove a 250F with great distinction in the '50s), Indianapolis red (where Maserati won in 1940), Birdcage white (Alfieri's brilliant late '50s sports car), Villoresi red (the famous Italian driver) and the colour of the car shown here, Argentine blue (after Fangio's homeland).

The only element carried over from the current Quattroporte is the basic size of the twin-turbo V8 engine. Otherwise the 3200 GT is a new car from the ground up. It has new double wishbone suspension, mounted on separate subframes, a 10mm longer wheelbase than the four-door and a body that is exceptionally rigid. And it all shows in the way it drives.

Open the driver's door and the

STAN PAPIOR

Trident dominates understated grille

window drops a few millimetres to help the sealing. You're welcomed to a leather-dominated interior that is traditional in appearance, superbly finished, classy and rather more roomy than the competition from Jaguar and Porsche.

The driving position, superbly comfortable and much higher than you might expect from a GT car, reminds me of the Ferrari 550 Maranello, not least because they share the same Momo steering wheel, the only difference being the badge.

The firm and supportive electrically adjustable bucket seat grabs hard. The wheel moves up and down and through a ridiculously small range of reach, but no matter, for the location of seat, pedals, wheel and controls requires no compromises. Only the reach to fifth gear makes the driver stretch – a blemish which should become a virtue on right-hand-drive cars. Both the driver's door and windscreen seem close, which helps create the desirable impression that the

The only wood you'll find in cabin

Maserati is no bigger than it needs to be.

You'll notice the battery of instruments are visible through the top half of the wheel and that the dashboard is a simple affair, the top section in black and the predominant lower area in one of 15 different leathers. Apart from the Alcantara headlining, virtually every surface is finished in leather. Air conditioning controls, the sound system and two rows of small grey buttons are surrounded by the only wood you'll find in the 3200 GT.

Maserati stays rock steady on open road right up to 140mph

Virtually every surface of classy interior is leather

When Ferrari took over it completely redesigned the interior, replacing wood with leather on the steering wheel, hand brake, gear lever and dashboard, and improved the ergonomics, but it is still not finished. Changes will include the colour of the buttons, brighter lights for the ASR traction control and Sport damper settings, and the addition of the trident symbol to the head restraints. Even the boot – small at the moment – is to be enlarged by moving its outer walls closer to the body.

Is the 3200 GT a true four-seater? More so than a 911 or an XK8, but you'll still need to be under 1.8 metres tall and sitting behind a driver of the same size to fit comfortably. Maserati claims there's 40-50 per cent more space in the rear compartment than either rival and says it's designed to fit almost any human.

What's this: a Maserati turbo V8 that's refined and progressive? The seductive V8 burble at idle and smooth power delivery suggests so. But the gearchange is heavy and notchy until the gearbox oil warms up; then it's slick and fast. Ratio for ratio it's the same Getrag 226 six-speed box used in the BMW M3 and M5 – even the final drive – and not the Getrag 266 from the Quattroporte.

Lights part of classic Maserati look

Rear space trounces rivals like XK8

Straight away it's obvious that this is no on/off turbo engine like the Maserati saloon. Substituting a variable-flow IHI turbo for the old radial-flow blower and using 425mm-long induction pipes improves responses by 20 per cent. Roberto Corradi, the engineer who took over as project leader

after Ferrari bought Maserati in June 1997, says 90 per cent of the engine is new.

The figures are confirmed by its mostly civilised manners and wonderfully tractable character. Peak torque of 362lb ft is developed at 4500rpm, but between 2700 and 5500rpm at least 326lb ft is on tap. Peak power is 370bhp at 6500rpm, a considerable improvement over the Quattroporte's 336bhp and 332lb ft of torque at 4400rpm.

With a 25kg weight advantage over the 363bhp, automatic-only XKR, Maserati says it beats the Jaguar to 62mph by 0.4sec and matches the 170kg lighter but 70bhp less powerful 911's 5.2sec time. ◢

◆ It feels at least that quick, while its 174mph matches the Porsche and is 19mph quicker than the limited Jaguar.

The power delivery isn't completely linear. There's a progressive burst of energy from 3000 to 4500rpm, where the turbo's whistle and wastegate sigh during gearchanges all but drown out the V8 exhaust. But there isn't the lag which has made previous Maseratis difficult to drive smoothly.

From 4500rpm to the 6500rpm red line the engine's potency is never in question. It

Momo wheel same as Ferrari 550's

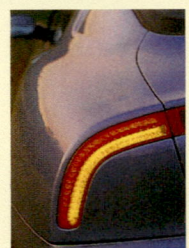

HOW GIUGIARO SHAPED THE 3200 GT

Giorgetto Giugiaro began work on the 3200 GT shortly after Fiat Auto took control of Maserati in 1993.

"The classic Maseratis of the late '60s were our inspiration," says the maestro. "We wanted to take the Maserati image a step further by emphasising its muscular quality. There were pauses between my sketches and the final model, and we made a series of changes in light of wind tunnel tests.

"The front caused the most trouble. In the end, it reflects all that is recognised in the Maserati tradition, with classic flared headlights.

"In side view, despite the hint of a tail-end, the 3200 looks like a hatchback. However, the overhead view with its tapered roof line reveals the two-and-a-half-box design. In three-quarter view the hint of a boot becomes an emphatic statement."

What Giugiaro doesn't admit is that his original proposal for oval-shaped tail-lights which wrapped around to the sides was rejected by Fiat boss Paolo Cantarella, who has a fetish for distinctive tail-lights. It was Cantarella who suggested the radical boomerang shape (pictured left) that is used in the production car.

flies, in any gear, at any speed.

Despite a drive-by-wire throttle, the behaviour of the engine when you first hit or lift off the accelerator isn't consistent, especially if the action is sudden. The resulting driveline snatch suggests there's room for further refinement of the engine management system,

for it spoils an otherwise very impressive drivetrain.

We're fast approaching 140mph on the autostrada and the 3200 GT sits rock steady, even hands-off. High-speed stability – the work of countless hours in the wind tunnel – is excellent, and here it feels better than its rivals. Not so good is

the steering; it feels fixed to the straight-ahead position. To move the wheel off centre you must overcome artificial resistance, so your input is greater than is really necessary. When it moves the car darts nervously as the steering becomes lighter. Only when you're constantly working the

Smooth twin-turbo 370bhp 3.2-litre V8 powerplant is virtually brand new

wheel through the twisty bits does the steering feel accurate and precise, though there's never any real feedback of information. There's nothing wrong with the gearing's 2.8 turns, though the turning circle is huge.

The 3200 GT picks up the 550 Maranello's ASR traction

Roof line is sharply tapered at rear

control system. It is integrated into the electronics that control the Sport dampers, with a 14-mode range of settings from near rigid to firm. The ASR delivers three levels of traction. In the normal default position, the ASR cuts power before there's even a chirp from the massive 18in Michelin rear tyres, and shuts down the engine even when the 3200 GT is driven only briskly through a corner.

Even with the dampers set to Sport, the driver's control of the throttle disappears the moment the car begins to move around, or when understeer intrudes. Safety in all conditions is the system's objective.

Turn the traction control off, however, and the contrast couldn't be more vivid. Suddenly, the 3200 GT turns into a power oversteerer that demands respect, but equally allows the enthusiastic driver

Electronic dampers have no fewer than 14 different settings

Brembo brakes nestle behind alloys

complete command and the option of selecting exactly how the car should behave. Which is impressively, with huge grip and a real adjustability. Still, for such a sporting car maybe the electronic intervention should be biased more towards allowing driver input at higher lateral speeds, especially in Sport mode.

At suburban speeds the ride is lumpy, and although it improves significantly the faster you go, expansion joints and potholes can catch the suspension out, which is to be expected in a car

Production car will get larger boot

with a 174mph top speed and 35-aspect tyres. The anti-dive, anti-squat specification can't completely eliminate longitudinal or lateral body movement. Nor do the brakes feel especially powerful; the pedal travel is too long and the action far too spongy for progressive modulation. A surprise from Brembo kit.

Maserati acknowledges many of these defects and is literally working seven days a week to correct any flaws in the car before production begins. The pre-series 3200 GT is so close to being a brilliant car that, with a little development in the areas of steering refinement, brakes and engine management, it will be a more than credible rival for the Jag and Porsche. And with the dedication of much the same team who developed the 550 Maranello, it will be a shock if they don't get it right. **◐**

Subtlety the key to exterior details

FACTFILE

MASERATI 3200 GT

HOW MUCH?	
Price	£59,990 (est)
On sale in UK	March

HOW FAST?	
0-62mph	5.1sec
Top speed	174mph

HOW THIRSTY?	
Urban	11.2mpg
Extra urban	17.0mpg
Combined	24.3mpg

HOW BIG?	
Length	4510mm
Width	1822mm
Height	1305mm
Wheelbase	2660mm
Weight	1590kg
Fuel tank	90 litres

ENGINE	
Layout	8 cyls in 90deg vee, 3217cc
Max power	370bhp at 6250rpm
Max torque	362lb ft at 4500rpm
Specific output	115bhp per litre
Power to weight	233bhp per tonne
Made of	Aluminium alloy heads and block
Bore/stroke	80/80mm
Compression ratio	8.0:1
Valve gear	4 valves per cylinder, dohc per bank
Ignition and fuel	Electronic fuel injection, IHI TTW twin turbochargers

GEARBOX	
Type	6-speed manual
Ratios/mph per 1000rpm	
1st 4.23/5.5 **2nd** 2.51/9.3 **3rd** 1.67/13.9 **4th** 1.23/23.3 **5th** 1.00/23.3 **6th** 0.83/28.1 **Final drive** 3.23	

SUSPENSION	
Front	Double wishbones, coil springs and adjustable dampers, anti-roll bar
Rear	Double wishbones, coil springs and adjustable dampers, anti-roll bar

STEERING	
Type	Rack and pinion, power assisted
Lock to lock	2.8

BRAKES	
Front	330mm ventilated discs
Rear	310mm ventilated discs
Anti-lock	Standard

WHEELS AND TYRES	
Size	n/a
Made of	Alloy
Tyres	235/40 ZR18 (f); 265/35 ZR18 (r)

All figures are manufacturer's claims

VERDICT

Potentially brilliant Italian DB7 at a Jaguar price. Simple, elegant interior and exterior, powerful performance, but still needs some dynamic refinement.

MASERATI 3200GT

THE COMEBACK KID

Will this new **Maserati coupe** bring back the **golden days**? Motor racing **success** in the '50s gave Maserati the **glamour** and **momentum** for some **sexy** road cars, but it all **dried up** after the '70s. With a little **help** from **Ferrari**, can they at last **return**?

Story: Kevin Blick Photography: Jim Forrest

If you've ever had an older brother who was always top of the class *and* good at sports *and* good with girls, then you'll know what it's like to be Maserati.

When your home town boasts Ferrari, and Lamborghini is just down the road, then anything you do risks being outdone by your elders. Pretty soon, chances are that your folks and your teachers will lecture you on the dangers of becoming a dropout and a waster. They just won't understand.

Then, big brother finally decides to take you under his wing and help you with the football, the homework – and the girls. Finally, things look up, in a manner of speaking. Which is exactly what has happened to Maserati. Adopted

by the Fiat family in 1993, responsibility for getting it back on the straight and narrow was given to glamorous big brother Ferrari just a year ago.

Some job. A company that hadn't made a profit for 15 years, with a tiny, elderly model range, hardly any dealers anywhere and a motor racing reputation that no-one under the age of 50 was likely to recall in any detail.

So, Ferrari put £150 million aside to sort it out, with the first £35 million going into gutting the archaic factory and developing an all-new car.

The result is the Maserati 3200GT, a 370 horsepower, £60,000 coupe intended to slot right into the gap between the Jaguar XKR and the Porsche 911. If you'll excuse the pun, the famous trident badge has a three-

13

pronged strategy for success – passion, performance and (very odd in an Italian car) practicality.

So, does it work? Well, let's dismiss the dullest p-word first. The practicality bit is certainly true. The Maserati was designed to carry grown-ups rather than simply squeeze protesting children in the rear seats and it can – just. Despite its compact proportions – it's only three inches longer than a 911 – it is remarkably space-efficient.

You wouldn't want to be stuck in the rear seat for the trip from Modena to Maidenhead but you could happily survive a run to a country pub and back, which is more than you'd want to do in either of its rivals. But coupe drivers are selfish swine, otherwise they'd be four-door owners. Looks and performance are what count with them.

And, despite being penned by the legendary Giorgetto Giugiaro, the Maserati doesn't have knock-you-flat good looks. It's handsome from certain angles, awkward from others. Some details like the grille and nose treatment look great, others, like the boomerang-shaped rear lights, too gimmicky. But all of us who drove it liked the interior – all leather, no plastic, as the Maserati spokesmen were at pains to point out – and its restrained, yet handsome layout.

Overall, though, maybe the Maserati is not quite individual enough. Too many elements of its styling seem too close to other cars. But that's only my opinion; others thought it looked fine – and someone even liked the rear lights. Performance, however, certainly doesn't let it down. It comes with a mouthwatering technical specification, from the V8 engine to the six-speed

What's this? A coupe in which a grown-up can actually sit comfortably in the back? Well, yes. And there's not a hint of plastic in sight, just the reassuringly luxurious pong of leather – and for £60,000 you wouldn't want anything less, would you. That engine is a proper-looking thing, too, even if it is covered with alloy baguettes

manual gearbox (a four-speed auto-box is optional) to the all-round double wishbone (cast-alloy, natch) suspension.

The latest incarnation of Maserati's 32-valve, twin-turbo V8 engine has 'mixed flow' turbo turbines for fast response, and electronic engine management including a 'drive-by-wire' throttle. The result is 370bhp, 362lb ft of torque and a power-to-weight ratio that betters the XKR and the 911.

It also translates into blistering acceleration, especially in the mid-range where turbo engines traditionally do so well. The 3200GT always seems to have potential acceleration on tap, and plenty of it. Even when you've dropped it into the sixth speed of the manual box to cruise down the autostrada it can reach for the skyline at a prod of the throttle

Ever since Italian designers discovered retro they've dreamed up loads of fab details, like the intake vent above and the faired-in 250GT-ish headlights. But those rear lights were obviously the result of eating far too much cheese for supper

and the claimed 174mph top speed doesn't seem quite the piece of Italian bravado one might have suspected. At speed, it's closer to the responsive, slightly nervous feel of a 911 than the swishingly fast solidity of a Jag. More a sports car than a grand tourer.

The engine's relatively lag-free, though it lacks the instant pick-up of a non-turbo, and it sounds nice as well, with a fruity idling-speed roar mellowing into a turbo-silenced, slightly spooky, background howl.

Away from the straights, the Maserati is more enigmatic. I must admit that at first I didn't like it much. The driving position is a touch old-fashioned, with the gearstick a tad too far away (unless one sits close to the wheel). The steering feels a little too soft and slow, the

brakes too springy underfoot and the ride awkwardly squirmy and uncertain at moderate speeds on indifferent surfaces, whether the electronic damping is switched to sports or standard setting.

But then as the roads improved, so seemingly did the car. Steering feel improved, and the combination of good grip and that surging mid-range reponse saw me blasting from bend to bend up a twisty mountain road with a grin as wide as the 3200's grille.

Keeping the traction control on does have the Maserati understeering and rolling a little more than an out-and-out sportscar like the 911 would; switching it off, on the other hand, is probably something best done by only the skilled or foolhardy, for there is ample power to tear the rear tyres loose

and blast the tail wide. Good fun, until you discover just how viciously quickly a turbo engine can deliver all its mid-range force. Overall the Maserati is impressive and enjoyable; more nimble, compact and chuckable than a big XKR but not as taut as the Porsche.

As Maserati say, there is a gap between the German and the Brit, and the Maserati fits in it, albeit closer to the Porsche than the XKR. But is that, and extra rear seat room, enough? Given Maserati's modest ambitions in Britain, probably. The company only aims to sell 350 cars here next year so it will be an exclusive and individualistic choice.

For sure, it will be a fun choice, too, but will it also be a wise one? The 3200GT comes stacked with all the gizmos expected in a £60,000 motor

plus a two-year warranty to answer the final question – will it hang together better than some Maseratis of old?

There were certainly a few quirks in our pre-production cars – poor air con, clunky drivelines, the odd poorly fitted panel – but all will be rectified by the time the cars go on sale early next year, insist the Maserati men. And with big brother Ferrari helping them out, you're inclined to believe them □

FACT FILE	
Model	luxury coupe
Engine	3,217cc V8, twin turbo, 370bhp
Performance	0-62 5.1 secs/174mph
On sale in the UK	April 1999
Price	£60,000 approx
Rivals	Jaguar XKR,
	Porsche 911, BMW 840Ci

Going for the
Jagular

This is the Maserati's first big test. Jaguar's XKR has rapidly established itself as the king of cool – everything the Italian coupe so desperately wants, and needs, to be...
Story by Mark Walton. Photography by Alex Puczyniec

SINCE I GOT BACK FROM Italy, everyone's asked me the same thing: so which wins, the Jaguar or the Maserati? And I reply, er, I don't know, because I know the XKR is a better car, but somehow I want the Maserati more. So you work it out.

In a town where glamorous supercars are run-of-the-mill, commonplace and (yawn) a little bit humdrum, a British Racing Green Jaguar XKR is a rolling street carnival of attention. Modena approves. Beautiful girls wave and beckon, men point and stare, and your humble writer's ego becomes supercharged like the Jag's V8. It's an experience that just adds to the magic of this exceptional Brit super-coupé.

The Maserati's first test, then, was just to be parked next to it. And in my eyes, the Maserati wins. Controversial yes, and difficult to explain because I'd readily admit that the XKR is smoother, more beautiful and, yes, proportionally easier on the eye than the 3200GT. The XKR also has more interesting headlights and better wheels. So what's left?

Well, there's something about the Jag that looks feminine – something delicate and feline in its long nose, slender hips, high tail and odd ground clearance. The Maserati's face does look ugly next to it, but ugly is masculine, ugly is aggressive, and its sweeping lines look lower and more in touch with the road.

These visual differences are reflected in the driving too. Get out of the Maserati and drive away in the Jag, and suddenly the 3200GT you just left behind feels like a raw sports car – the XKR feels so liquid in comparison, with its lighter steering, oozing power delivery and relaxing ride. It's almost impossible to make the Jaguar jerk, on or off the power (unlike the 'shunting' Italian), and the sound of its gradually rising Eaton supercharger and squashing acceleration are the harshest sensations you have to bear.

It's the same on the motorway. The Maserati has a sixth gear you can drop into for effortless cruising, and (out of Sport mode) the ride, the interior and the Becker stereo all make it a genuine luxury GT. But the Jaguar, with its smooth 4.0-litre engine, feels mechanically more relaxed at 100mph.

A sports coupé must have two sides to

SPECIFICATIONS
MASERATI 3200GT

Price
£60,000 approx

Engine
Twin-turbo V8
3217cc 32V 4ohc

Power and torque
370bhp at 6250rpm
362lb ft at 4500rpm

Transmission
Five-speed manual

Suspension, front
Double wishbones

Suspension, rear
Double wishbones

Weight
1588kg

Maximum speed
174mph

0-62mph
5.1sec

its personality: half luxury car, half driver's car. That's certainly the Jaguar's strength, the reason it won our big coupé test (*CAR*, June). But the Maserati runs it very close, gaining in driver appeal where it loses on refinement. The Maserati allows the driver more contact with the road than the Jaguar, through its more resistant steering and tauter ride; it allows you to feel more excited and more involved in your speed too. They have very similar power outputs (370bhp for the Maserati, 363 for the XK), but their delivery is so different you'd swear the Maserati is quicker. Rougher, but quicker.

In terms of handling they're similar – the Maserati has forged-aluminium double wishbones all round, the Jag is wishbones up front, wishbones and driveshaft upper links at the rear. On the road, they both belie their size and weight to feel surprisingly nimble when

'The Maserati will succeed because it's different, because it sets you apart from the XK set'

you push them. During the time I drove them back-to-back the Jaguar's more linear power delivery did allow you to feel more confident, to get a bit cheeky with it, but I suspect that once you got used to the Maserati's… let's say 'characterful' V8, it would ultimately be more rewarding. If the Jaguar gets out of shape, the steering tends to go a bit numb, as if its power assistance can't keep up with your rapid movements. The Maserati's steering felt absolutely faultless.

Another area where the Jaguar loses is space. Normally the Jaguar feels cosy inside, but if you're getting in after driving the Maserati, it just feels plain small. The tight dashboard-to-knee relationship, shoulder-to-door and head-to-roof, all make the Jaguar seem claustrophobic.

The Maserati feels more upright (even though they're exactly the same height)

SPECIFICATIONS JAGUAR XKR

Price
£60,005

Engine
Supercharged V8, 3996cc 32V 4ohc

Power and torque
363bhp at 6150rpm
372lb ft at 3600rpm

Transmission
Five-speed automatic

Suspension, front
Double wishbones
372lb ft at 3600rpm

Suspension, rear
Driveshaft acts as upper link, lower wishbones

Weight
1650kg

Maximum speed
155mph (limited)

0-60mph
5.3sec

with more space for elbows, knees and feet. In the back seats, there's no contest: I could go on a short to medium journey in the back of the 3200GT and I wouldn't need physiotherapy afterwards. I'd need surgery after a long journey in the back of the Jaguar.

The points are adding up on the Maserati's behalf.

There's more. The Maserati interior also looks more timeless. That now infamous plank of wood across the Jaguar is too deliberately retro, and a teeny bit naff compared with the black leather of our test Maserati. The switches are better in the British car, and the graphics on the XKR's dials are less ostentatious, but the plank is overwhelming.

Still, plank or no plank, most of this is irrelevant. Jaguar has one almighty advantage over its new Italian rival – it is established. The Jaguar is now on the

wish list of half the world's population, it has elevated Jaguar to a new level of desirability, and it is already being driven by the rich, the famous and the beautiful, from Beverly Hills to Brunei. The Maserati, in real showroom terms, can't compete with that, not least because this market plays right into the Jaguar's hands. This sector might be part-luxury, part-sports car, but it's the luxury bit that's most important to buyers, and that's where the Jaguar's silky, effortless progress wins. It's the Jaguar that remains today's archetypal luxury sports coupé.

Maserati will have an auto box soon, but it will still take a very particular type of customer to choose it over the Jaguar. Someone who would put up with its harsher engine, its more challenging drive and, let's face it, that Maserati reputation. They need somebody that resembles me, in fact. Only with a lot more money.

Maybe, just maybe, the Jaguar will be a victim of its own success. Maybe there are so many Jaguars around now (they've sold more than 28,000 XK8/XKRs since 1996), the Maserati will succeed because it's different, because it sets you apart from the XK set. Maybe the Maserati will succeed because, well, because *it's a Maserati*.

So, the 3200GT gets my vote, partly because it's a great car and partly because, after weighing up the technical information, the statistical analysis and the projected sales figures, so many people clearly think I'm wrong.

PREVIEW

Maserati 3200GT

A comeback kid for the coming millennium, available at your local Ferrari dealership.

BY PETER ROBINSON

Come late 2001, you'll be able to walk into your local Ferrari dealership and buy a Maserati 3200GT coupe or a short-wheelbase spider. And Jaguar and Porsche will suddenly have a serious new rival.

The rebirth of Maserati comes under new owner Ferrari, which believes the 3200GT is a proper successor to the great GTs of the '60s and '70s, when Maseratis were beautiful and highly regarded cars. It also returns the trident to its rightful place as one of the world's great marques, although understandably one rung below Ferrari. It is hoped we'll forget the disastrously unreliable and boxy Maseratis from the era of de Tomaso ownership.

This is Giorgetto Giugiaro's idea of how a Maserati GT should look. If there are obvious links in its classical proportions and details with other front-engine, rear-drive GT cars like the Aston Martin DB7 and Jaguar XK8, then so be it. Maserati wanted a conservative design rather than something radical or extreme. The 3200GT is more masculine, more aggressive than the beautiful DB7, and from the side it looks taller and thicker, especially around the rear flanks, than one would expect. The double-boomerang LED taillights are claimed to be a world first.

Color? Choose from 14, including the aptly named Green Moss (Stirling M. drove a 250F to great distinction in the '50s), Red Indianapolis (where a Maserati won in 1940), White Birdcage (Alfieri's brilliant late-'50s sports car), Red Villoresi (a famous Italian driver), and the color of the car we drove, Blue Argentine (Fangio's homeland).

Only the basic architecture of the twin-turbo V-8 is carried over from the old Maserati. Otherwise, the 3200GT is new from the ground up. New are the unequal-length control-arm front and rear suspensions (mounted on separate subframes), a wheelbase that is, surprisingly, longer than the Maserati Quattroporte sedan's, and a body that's exceptionally rigid.

Open the driver's door, and you're greeted by an all-leather interior that's traditional in appearance, superbly finished, and roomier than the cabins of the Jaguar and Porsche competition. The driving position—splendidly comfortable and much higher than you might expect from a GT car—reminds us of the Ferrari 550 Maranello's, not least because they share the same marvelous Momo steering wheel. The power driver's seat, firm and supportive, grabs hard. The location of the seat, the pedals, the wheel, and the controls requires no compromises. Only the reach to fifth gear demands a stretch. Is it a true four-seater? More so than a 911 or an XK8, but it's still tight in the rear seat for adults.

What's this, a Maserati twin-turbo V-8 that's refined and progressive? The seductive V-8 burble at idle and smooth takeup of power suggest so. The gearchange is heavy and notchy until the gearbox oil warms up; then it's slick, fast. Ratio for ratio, it's the same Getrag 226 six-speed box used in the European BMW M3. Immediately, it's obvious this is not an on/off turbo engine. Substituting variable-flow IHI TTW9 turbos for the old radial-flow blowers, and using 16.7-inch-long induction pipes, improve low-end response by 20 percent.

The figures are confirmed by mostly civilized manners. The peak torque of 362 pound-feet is developed at 4500 rpm, with at least 326 pound-feet on tap between 2700 and 5500 rpm. The DOHC four-valve-per-cylinder engine pumps out 365 hp at 6250 rpm. Maserati claims the 3200GT will hit 62 mph in 5.1 seconds. However, it nearly matches the (automatic only) Jag XKR's power and weighs about 250 pounds less, so that claim sounds conservative by several 10ths. (A 2000 XKR we tested achieved 60 mph in 4.9 seconds.)

Power delivery isn't linear. There's a progressive burst of energy from 3000 to 4500 rpm. From there to the 6500-rpm redline the engine's potency is never in question. It flies in any gear, at any speed. Despite a drive-by-wire throttle, tip-in and tip-out aren't consistent.

At 140 mph, the 3200GT is rock steady. High-speed stability—the work of countless hours in the wind tunnel—is excellent. Not so good is the steering. It feels fixed to the straight-ahead position. To move the wheel off-center demands overcoming artificial resistance, so you input more force than is necessary. When it moves, the 3200 darts aggressively, nervously. Only when you're constantly working the wheel through the twisty bits does the steering feel accurate and precise, the weighting consistent.

The 3200GT picks up the 550 Maranello's ASR traction-control system that's integrated into the electronics that control the adaptive dampers. The ASR delivers two levels of traction. In the "standard" position, ASR cuts power

before there's even a chirp from the massive 18-inch Michelins and shuts down the engine even when the Maser's driven halfway briskly through a corner. With the dampers set to "sport," the driver's control of the throttle disappears the moment oversteer intrudes. Turn it off, and the contrast couldn't be more vivid. Suddenly, the 3200GT turns into a power oversteerer that demands respect but, equally, allows the enthusiastic driver complete command in determining exactly how the car should behave. And it behaves impressively, with a huge amount of grip and real adjustability. At suburban speeds, the ride is lumpy, and although it improves significantly the faster you go, expansion joints and potholes can jar the suspension.

In three years, any dynamic flaws will likely have been sorted. Why do we think so? Because many of the same team members who developed the brilliant 550 Maranello have the responsibility for getting this Maserati right.   ●

MASERATI 3200GT
Vehicle type: front-engine, rear-wheel-drive, 2+2-passenger, 2-door coupe
Estimated base price: $75,000
Engine type: twin-turbocharged and intercooled DOHC 32-valve V-8, aluminum block and heads, Magneti Marelli engine-control system with port fuel injection

Displacement	196 cu in, 3217cc
Power (SAE net)	365 bhp @ 6250 rpm
Torque (SAE net)	362 lb-ft @ 4500 rpm
Transmission	6-speed manual
Wheelbase	104.7 in
Length	177.6 in
Width	71.7 in
Height	51.4 in
Curb weight	3500 lb

Manufacturer's performance ratings:

Zero to 62 mph	5.1 sec
Top speed (drag limited)	174 mph
Fuel economy, European combined cycle	15 mpg

The rebuilding of
MASERATI

In the year since Ferrari took control, it has turned Maserati around.
With a new factory, and great new cars, the future looks bright

STORY BY
RICHARD BREMNER
PHOTOGRAPHY BY
TIM ANDREW

WHEN I ASK ANTONIO Ghini what the Maserati factory was like when Ferrari took it over, he holds his head in his hands, smiles, and after a pause says, 'It was a mess.' Given that Ghini is communications director at Ferrari and Maserati and that, being a PR man, he is not one to issue negatives about those for whom he works, we can take it that we're dealing with a grade one mess here – a mess resulting from years of insufficient money, management effort and morale.

Since Ferrari came along in July last year (when Fiat group managing director Paolo Cantarella insisted that Ferrari take operating control of Maserati from Fiat Auto, which had run the company for the past four years) there's been a lot more of the first, plenty of the second and, as a consequence, an escalation of the third.

So, how big was the mess? Maserati's Modena factory was old, peeling, dark and dirty, and by all accounts equipped with a lot of kit that would have been new when your grandfather was a working man. Cars came out of the gates, but, as most of us know, they were not of your finest quality, even if they were always quick.

Fiat Group's contribution to the company's gradual regeneration has been to bankroll the exercise; more specifically, Fiat Auto, the car division, overhauled the Quattroporte for its third birthday last year, with an eye to improving quality and reliability. But these second-generation Quattroportes are going to be rare animals, because three months after Ferrari took over it decided to shut down production of the car altogether, in order to tear out the production line, install something modern and give the factory a lick of paint. More than a lick, actually – gallons must have been got through, coating everything from the exterior walls to the floor of the engine assembly room. There's a new blue 'Maserati' sign on the factory roof now, and an air of quiet purpose about the place that has been absent for years. Things are going on. Quattroporte production is slowly building – currently they're turning out two a day, but this will soon climb to 10 – and the new coupé, out later this year, was to be seen flitting about the plant, heavily disguised. It's said to be very pretty, and looked handily compact and muscular beneath its plastic cladding.

It will be built on the new production line together with the Quattroporte, the first examples of which are emerging now. That line is impressive (very impressive if you're a long-serving Maserati worker), mainly because it's shiny, new and appears well organised. More to the point, production is arranged along the

'It might have lost its trademark clock, but there's no doubt it's a better car'

same lines as the Ferrari factory at Maranello, where cars of very high, if not unimpeachable, quality emerge. So there's more than idle reason to expect Maserati to turn out cars of high quality too.

But what of the car itself? Well, it looks pretty much the same. Points of identification for the keen include reshaped door mirrors and, more explicitly, 'V8 Evoluzione' badges on the front wings. The super-keen might notice that, miracle of miracles, the body panels align very tidily, and that the paint has a mirror sheen unlikely to be found encasing an early Quattroporte. Yet beneath the surface, there are scores of changes – indeed, around 400 parts have been redesigned, and another 800 have been improved. New, for instance, are belt drives for the ancillaries, the cylinder heads of the V8, which have been redesigned for improved cooling, the alternator, power-steering pump and air-conditioning compressor, which are all upgraded, the engine management logic, which has been remapped for smoother power delivery, and the door seals, which have been redesigned (again) for quieter high-speed running, the quest for which is aided by the more tightly assembled body.

That's just a sample. Among the visible changes are new seats with more adjustment in them, new briarwood trim for the interior, new instruments with a built-in outside temperature

gauge, new pushbuttons for the minor controls, a new steering wheel and a new clock. Yes, the rather ornate Swiss chronometer that was the centrepiece of every Maserati, has gone. It was, says MD Paolo Marinsek, 'too much a symbol of the De Tomaso era'. Such an attitude seems a bit petty, and it's even sillier when you realise that the replacement is a tuppenny-ha'penny digital clock rendered unreadable by a combination of its location – down by the gearlever – and bright sunlight. What were they thinking of?

But don't be disheartened, because there's no doubt that this Quattroporte is a Better Car. You notice it immediately with the doors – 'They clunk, rather than kerbam shut,' said one Maserati employee – the smooth paint, and the wood, which looks like it was fashioned by someone possessed of more than rudimentary cabinet-making skills, in contrast to the previous QP. Sink into your leather chair and you'll discover that, provided you can insinuate a hand between door and electric controls (the gap is tight), it's possible to manoeuvre your body into a comfortable position relative to the pedals, although the wheel is still a stretch.

But, be in no doubt that you are in a luxury car – sumptuous and extravagant materials abound. Alcantara mock-suede dresses the ceiling, the facia, the instrument binnacle hood, parts of the doors and pretty much anything else that isn't faced in wood and leather.

FIRE THE V8, AND IT IDLES QUIETLY. But it doesn't take long to discover its potency, gentle pressure on the accelerator revealing a car that just wants to bound away. But first, we must leave the factory, and Modena, for the autostrada.

That journey's long enough to demonstrate that it's reasonably easy to master clutch and gearchange (this car is a six-speed manual – a four-speed auto is optional) for a smooth advance, and that it's not impossible, when sitting at the lights, to engage reverse, which is parallel to first, and give the guy behind you a fright, which I did. I'm pleased to say that a Maserati man confessed to a similar error, though he pointed out that it's one you're unlikely to make again with 335bhp beneath your right foot. Quite.

To the autostrada, the toll booth, and a chance to test... the electric windows. Yes, because in QPs of old, they never felt committed in their ascents and descents. The driver's door window seemed fine, though, gliding briskly, both down and up. I checked the others too, and they were as swift, though one sounded a bit grinding. Hmm.

And onto the dual carriageway itself. In Italy there's a 130km/h speed limit – that's 81mph – but ignoring it, with prudence, is possible and so it was that we were able to run the Quattroporte out to 150mph for the odd burst, at which speed it is impressively quiet, has more to come, and feels pretty stable, if not quite as well planted as some German 'bahn stormers. And it slowed down well too – necessary, with the odd lumbering truck. Curious then, that when we got off the straights and onto the twists, the brakes didn't feel anything like as responsive or progressive. Perhaps they need heat in them. Or perhaps we'd cooked them. One thing's certain though: that pedal feel is much improved.

The Maser's body control seems to have improved too, though no great claims are made in this direction. The 'normal' setting of the three-position dampers seemed satisfactory most of the time, allowing less heave over crests than in the last car I sampled.

There's a fair bit of roll in hard cornering with this setting, and if the 'sport' setting doesn't arrest this as much as you'd hope, it does batten things down usefully for a hard charge, at the expense of disturbed thumping over pot-holes. 'Soft', incidentally, is useful on bad urban roads, but that's about it.

The Maser handles pretty entertainingly for one quite large, its adjustability in bends helped by the sizeable slug of torque that the V8 can deliver. The steering is fairly precise (though the valving makes it feel a little sloppy), grip plentiful in the dry (watch it in the wet – there's no traction-control system beyond prudence) and

On the right line at last

MASERATIS WILL BE BUILT JUST LIKE FERRARIS

The life of a Quattroporte starts not at Maserati but at a company nearby called Goldencar, which manufactures the bodies, to a considerably higher standard than was previously the case. The shells are then trucked to Maranello, where they are painted in the same shop that sprays Ferrari's own cars, before being sent to the new assembly line at Modena. You can tell the line is new, because the bright yellow cradles that carry the shells are unmarked, there's a smell of newness in the air, and the floor is surfaced with (rather attractive) ceramic tiles.

The painted shell is suspended from a cradle, stripped of its doors and introduced to its electrics, sound-deadening, glass, facia and drivetrain as it passes through 13 separate work stations. Each car is accompanied, on its journey toward birth, by a rather finely fashioned multi-decked trolley upon which are carried all the components specific to it. This saves your Quattroporte V6 receiving the wiring loom of the V8, and is exactly the same

system as employed at Ferrari. Later this year, it will ease the task of building the coupé and the Quattroporte – very different cars – on the same assembly line.

Once it has passed the 13th station, the Quattroporte can roll on its own wheels, and travels in the opposite direction on a so-called rolling carpet, where its interior and a hundred other sundry parts are added, bringing it to life so that it can be passed to the vibration station, which is designed to settle the dampers, and chase out any squeaks and rattles before the car reaches the great outdoors.

The magnificent powertrains are built up on site in an adjacent block, each unit specific to a car. The V8 cylinder block and the lower part of the V6 come from a foundry near Brescia, the V6's upper block and the V8's heads come from Maranello's foundry, and the V6 heads come from British firm Zeus. Machining is done on site at Maserati – though eventually it will be done by Ferrari – the engines built up by

hand before being mated to their transmissions and exhausts.

The assembly process is modelled on the same lines as Ferrari's, and uses a multidisciplinary approach to problem-solving of the sort that the Maranello factory adopted in 1993. The aim is to solve problems swiftly, which in Maserati terms constitutes something of a modern approach.

Of course, proof that the Quattroporte is a sorted car will only come when several hundred take to the road and actually stay there. But take a trip round this factory, and you'd conclude there is more than a fighting chance.

Maser mind

THE MAN AT MASERATI'S HELM

Paolo Marinsek is the lucky man who is managing director of both Ferrari and Maserati. He reports directly to Luca Di Montezemolo, and has so far overseen the spending of more than £7 million on Maserati, with more planned as the new coupé comes on stream.

The object is to increase Maserati production more than fivefold, from the paltry 698 cars that were produced in 1997, to 1000 this year and some 6000 by the year 2000. Around 2000 of the 6000 will be accounted for by Quattroportes, Marinsek hopes (with some fervour, one suspects, because he reckons Maserati needs to build 'a minimum of 2000 units to justify a model'), the remaining 4000 being coupés and the forthcoming spider version of the coupé, which is two years away.

Despite the rising volumes, it will be some time before Maserati turns a profit, red ink disappearing by 2001. During that time the break-even point will fall from 4000 cars now, to 3000 by 2003. So it's easy to see that Ferrari is in for the long haul. Then again, there are going to be no quick fixes at Maserati, though Maranello must be delighted that the promising new coupé will appear less than 18 months after it took over the company.

Of course, it takes more than money and motors to make a company, and much of Ferrari's effort has been directed at training Maserati's management and reorganising the company along the same lines as the parent company, in which teamwork plays a key role. Commercially, there are plans for Maseratis to be on sale in 39 countries as opposed to today's 17, the most important of which is the USA, where Marinsek reckons on selling 2000 cars annually after the company re-enters in 2001 with the coupé and spider. The task will be eased considerably by the existence of an extensive Ferrari network – of the 115 Maserati dealers planned worldwide by autumn '98, some 82 will be joint Ferrari outlets. Personal service for the customer will be a major item on the agenda for these dealers, and that will include the chance for owners to participate in driving courses and historic races. Sounds good.

So, indeed, do Ferrari's plans for Maserati, which, while earth-shattering in terms of Maserati's recent history, are modest in global terms. After all, 6000 cars is nothing in the face of what Mercedes, BMW and Jaguar sell in similar market segments, and on the face of it, under-uses what Marinsek himself describes as 'the great and prestigious Maserati name'. But Marinsek is adamant that the company will remain an exclusive, small-scale producer, with designs on modest volumes. Now, imagine what might happen if Ferdinand Piech had got hold of it.

'The turbos spool up with astonishing ease, giving you the grunt of a field full of pigs'

the car pleasingly wieldy. In the final analysis – indeed, well before you get there – this car has not got the depth of competence that its British and German rivals have, but it's pretty good and, more important, there's a have-a-go bravado in its character that makes it more fun than any of its more sober rivals.

Contributing considerably to this is that belter of an engine. The twin-turbo V8 puts out 332lb ft of torque at 4400rpm, but more important is that the turbos spool up with astonishing ease, giving you the grunt of a field full of pigs at almost any speed, and in almost any gear. If you can afford not to think of the fuel you're burning, you'll love this motor. Especially if you give it full throttle in second, when its rapid, hard burble sounds like a NASCAR stocker's motor on a hard charge.

Still, the QP always had the engine on its side. What it has now is a far more convincing feel of solidity, and an awful lot of rough edges burnished off. Granted, the air-conditioning is still pretty feeble (and sounds like an electric hand-dryer on anything over the first speed), the instruments collect reflections like a fashion victim, the buttons in the centre console would disgrace a Skoda and the new outside temperature gauge is near impossible to read. Never mind. The list of downsides is now much shorter than it was before.

O F COURSE, IT'S STILL ENTIRELY illogical to buy a Maserati Quattroporte. You'd be much better off with a Mercedes, a Jaguar or a BMW, because they are better cars. They're more modern, more capable and equipped with state-of-the-art systems. Yet they are nowhere near as exclusive and, with the possible excep-

tion of the XJR, not half as much fun as the Italian car.

When you're about to spend £60,000, however, that is not enough. The crunch, even for those given to the odd irrationally indulgent flurry, will be residual values. And when it comes to Maseratis, the residue doesn't usually amount to much beyond a sinking feeling in the pit of the stomach.

The remedy, however, could be at hand, for Andrea Zappia, Maserati's sales director, says that the company is considering offering guaranteed buy-back prices to dull the sting come trade-in time. We have yet to hear how sizeable the offer will be, but if it matches a Mercedes', you can enjoy indulging a Maserati with near impunity. And in these days of samey, slightly soulless execu-mobiles, it's tempting to say what the hell – just do it.

SPECIFICATIONS

Price	£60,000 aprox
Engine	Longitudinal front-mounted 3217cc 32-valve dohc twin-turbo V8
Bore/stroke, mm	80/80
Compression ratio	7.3 to one
Power	355bhp at 6400rpm
Torque	325lb ft at 4400rpm
Transmission	Six-speed manual or four-speed automatic, rear-wheel drive
Front suspension	MacPherson strut, coil springs, electronic dampers, anti-roll bar
Rear suspension	Semi-trailing arms, coil springs, electronic dampers
Brakes front/rear	Ventilated discs, ABS
Tyres	Front: 225/5 ZR17 Rear: 245/40 ZR17
Weight	1647kg (1675kg auto)
PERFORMANCE	
0-62mph	5.8sec
Top speed	168mph (165mph auto)
Mpg (EC combined)	Na

Maserati 3200 GT

Bound for the U.S.: a car with 911 performance and Italian style

BY PAUL FRERE

FOR THE YOUNGER GENerations, the mention of Maserati may not recall any particular memories. Maserati's days of glory are too far back, and little has been done in the last 25 years or so to uphold the marque's reputation. After a succession of owners—Citroën and De Tomaso, to name two—Fiat stepped in to save the firm from extinction and, recently, has largely integrated Maserati into Ferrari.

As such, the two companies have a common president, Luca di Montezemolo, but separate engineering and development teams. Both make high-performance cars, but Maseratis are less expensive and more family-oriented than the Maranello-built cars. The two 1999 models from Maserati are the Quattroporte and the new 3200 GT, a 2+2 intended to compete with cars such as the Porsche 911 and Jaguar XKR.

True to the tradition of the Ghibli, Khamsin and Bora, the styling of the 3200 GT was entrusted to Giugiaro, who has managed to recapture the fascination of "real" Maseratis in the gracefully flowing lines of a modern 2+2 coupe.

The 3200 GT is based on an entirely new platform. Suspension is by coil springs, double wishbones and anti-roll bars front and rear, using rubber-mounted subframes. The differential is of the limited-slip type with a 25/45-percent locking factor for, respectively, drive and coast.

The all-aluminum, 3.2-liter, 4-cam, 32-valve V-8 engine, a development of the Quattroporte powerplant, employs twin turbochargers that provide high boost from low engine revolutions. Included as well are other modifications required to ensure reliability from an engine that produces 370 bhp at 6250 rpm and maximum torque of 362 lb.-ft. at 4500. Throttle control is now electronic for smoother operation, and for independent operation by the traction-control system, which can be switched off at will. The 6-speed Getrag gearbox, also a Quattroporte development, features 3-cone synchromesh in 1st and 2nd, reducing effort. A 4-speed automatic with converter lockup and an adaptive program is also offered.

With a better power-to-weight ratio than a Porsche 911, the Maserati is a very fast car. Claimed 0–62-mph acceleration is 5.1 seconds, with a top speed of 174 mph. And the engine has impressive flexibility, with plenty of torque from 2500 rpm onward. Driving the car over the old Mille Miglia route leading from Florence to Bologna over the Futa and Raticosa passes, I soon found that the use of 2nd gear for fairly slow bends brought no advantage compared with staying in 3rd and accelerating from around 3000 rpm. Turbo response is exceptionally good.

Even though they call it a GT, the Maserati coupe is really a sports car capable of carrying four people and a fair amount of luggage. Except for its overall shape, it has nothing in common with the magic-carpetlike Jaguar XKR that I had borrowed only a few days earlier. In the Maserati,

■ **The 3200 GT will appear in the U.S. sometime soon after the year 2000, allowing Maserati time to set up proper dealer and parts distribution networks. The car will be sold at Ferrari dealerships, though set apart from the cars from Maranello. The price of the 3200 GT is expected to be around $85,000, and Maserati expects to sell perhaps as many as 2000 each year in the U.S.**

you feel you live with a machine. You hear the powerful engine all the time, though it never becomes obtrusive, and the ultra-low-aspect-ratio tires (235/40ZR-18 in front, 265/35ZR-18 at the rear) leave you in no doubt about the road surface when driving at low speeds around town. But once you are out on the road, bump absorption is excellent and there is never any harshness. On the old Mille Miglia route, the car belied its 3500-lb. weight, displaying good agility and cornering in a very neutral attitude, easily adjusted with throttle position.

With well-controlled, hardly noticeable roll; almost negligible squat and brake dive; quick, well-weighted power-assisted steering; and first-class brakes, this is a car you simply long to drive fast. As far as dynamics are concerned, I would ask only for a little more feedback from the steering wheel.

Maserati's sales ambitions are modest, at least until the marque is reestablished on the market, with estimated European sales of around 2000 cars a year. And who will buy them? Porsche drivers are an obvious target, especially if they have children who are about to outgrow the 911's rear seats. Some Jaguar XK drivers might also be tempted if they find their mount too soft, in the broadest sense of the word. And could not some Ferrari drivers be tempted by a car offering real exclusivity and near-Ferrari performance at less than half the price?

Return to Splendour

THIS IS THE 3200GT, THE CAR CHARGED WITH RETURNING MASERATI TO ITS FORMER GLORIES. IT'S EASY TO FAULT, ARGUES ANDREW FRANKEL, BUT IT'S STILL THE MOST CAPABLE CAR TO WEAR THE TRIDENT FOR TWENTY YEARS

photography by Stan Papior

Buy a new Maserati 3200GT and, as you hand over your cheque for £59,925, you will be handed not only the keys but also a 42 page brochure. The car I shall come to in a minute, but much is to be learned about it and the way its makers wish you to feel about it from that glossy pamphlet in your hands.

Most striking is the fact that, despite 42 pages not being a lavish amount of space to describe an all new car tasked with the revival of one of the world's great marques, the first 30 are occupied by pictures and one line sentences to illustrate the single word

pages, a simple spread of black and white shots of the road and racing cars from Maserati's history. All the great racers are here from the 4CM past the 300S and 250F to the Birdcage and some of the less successful ones too like the V12 250F. The road car names trip off the tongue with similar ease: Mistral, Indy, Ghibli, Bora… and then you turn the page and, nothing. End of brochure. In all, five cars are included from Maserati's first 21 years as a road car constructor and not one from the last 21 years. Half of the marque's history in the only field in which it competed after the early 1960s has not been deemed worthy of inclusion, a fact all the more remarkable given that it is the most recent half.

I mention this now because it is important to

touring market and Ferrari the ultimate presence among supercar buyers. That is why, despite the fact that few people seem prepared to wax lyrical about it, the old Maserati Quattroporte Evoluzione remains in production.

Before we start, therefore, you need to know the one towering ramification of all of this: The 3200GT is not a sportscar, nor was it ever intended to be so. Approach it without this knowledge and I would not bet on your relationship getting off on the correct foot. It is an alternative to a Jaguar XKR, and most emphatically not a baby Ferrari.

I didn't like the shape at first. It seemed too curious and insufficiently classical for a car such as this, one which tried too hard to be quirky (I'm still not sure

"Before we start you need to know the one towering ramification of this: The 3200GT is not a sportscar, nor was it intended to be so"

Maserati has decided is the value by which the car must stand or fall. That word is 'emotion'. The emotion of Maserati, the emotion of a Maserati, the emotion of the chassis, the engine, the cabin… You get the idea. This is a car Maserati want located firmly under your skin.

The next ten pages are less attractive but more useful and contain the car's basic specification and an explanation of the challenge which faced Giorgetto Giugiaro's Italdesign team when charged with creating a safe, aerodynamically efficient, spacious and unforgettable shape for the new Maserati. But what really caught my eye was the final two

understand the context of the new car, just how big a break from the Maseratis of the all too recent past its new masters at Ferrari wish to make. Even so, it's not quite as clean cut as that. For a start, the 3200GT is not a Ferrari car, it is Maserati's, Maranello coming along too late to influence its fundamental design. Secondly, Maserati must now subscribe to the same Fiat-decreed strategy that has dictated the way things are at Ferrari for a generation. There is a hierarchy. There are the massed production marques, Fiat with its respectively luxury and sporting spin-offs, Lancia and Alfa-Romeo upon which stand the low volume, prestige marques, Maserati representing the grand

about those LED tail-lights) and not sufficiently hard to be pretty. But, having seen it on the move, my views have softened. Follow one for a few miles, see how the shape flows over the road, try to avoid comparing its backside to that of the Maserati-powered Citroen SM and you'll see the shape has more than a certain presence, it's actually rather attractive.

Better still is the interior, particularly if you avoid the expensive temptation of covering the centre console in wood or carbon fibre. The upholstery is magnificent, while the controls and instruments strike a near perfect note of classy clarity. The seats are big, supportive chairs, the steering wheel

Maserati is no joy to drive on the limit: Grip is good but the suspension is too soft allowing too much bodyroll while the turbo engine and auto 'box means there is precious little opportunity to neutralise the understeer with the throttle. Sadly, it's probably best to leave the traction control switched on

adjustable for all shapes of driver so a perfect driving position, not something you'd even look for in any previous Maserati, should be attainable. Except it's not. Having got the basics right, Maserati forgot about your left leg which, given that it is completely redundant in this automatic car, is a sizeable omission. Try putting it on the thin ledge that seems to have been provided and you'll likely as not hit the brake pedal unless you have either small feet or thin shoes. I have neither and ended up driving in my socks.

Even so, first impressions are broadly positive. The cabin is spacious (even if the boot is worryingly small) meaning two parents and two single-figure children should not find long-distances unduly irksome; the whole exudes an air more opulent

such great effect by both Alfa Romeo and Ferrari has been denied the Maserati.

The engine sounds superb at idling. A deep, woofling burble, full of class and purpose, promises great things to come and as you trickle out into the traffic for the first time, the sense of occasion is almost palpable. Road users react inquisitively, not with green eyed envy and at motorway velocity, you are struck by how calm is the ride and how muted is the wind noise around the frameless doors. So far so good. On a crowded M4, the 3200GT was proving itself a pleasantly capable cruising device.

Which is all very well as far as it goes but, frankly, if all you want is a car which sits quietly and comfortably on the motorway I could give you a

Disappointingly, the engine sounds less interesting with every passing revolution. It may seem a shame that such a powerful Italian V8 should sound best at idle but, considering the method of its forced induction, it's not a surprise. Throttle response is good (but not exceptional as Maserati would like you to believe) for a turbocharged unit but it is still a world away from a normally aspirated engine or, for that matter, the supercharged and identically powerful V8 under the bonnet of the Jaguar XKR. That said, there's no doubting the performance. It's strong rather than savage and I'd take a sizeable bet this automatic 3200GT would no more reach 60mph in the 5secs flat alluded to by its maker than it would jump over the moon. Still, you'll not find it sluggish. Overtaking

"The engine sounds superb at idling. A deep, woofling burble, full of class and purpose promises great things to come"

than extravagant which is exactly how it should be.

Better still is the engine, a reworked version of the twin-turbo V8 which first saw service in the quick but brutal Karif. It's a 3.2-litre, 32-valve quad-cam motor, producing 370bhp backed by a convincing 362lb ft of torque, almost all of which is available throughout the bulk of the rev-range. Two gearboxes are available, a six-speed manual is standard while a four-speed automatic can be chosen for another £2000, something Maserati thinks most customers will select. But while this latter transmission works undeniably well, it's puzzling to note that the semi-automatic transmission technology used to

list as long as you liked of alternatives available for under half the price. It was pleasing that the Maserati, unlike so many exotic Italians of years gone by, did not fall at the first by concentrating on the dream not the reality but this, really, was no kind of test at all. So we headed for the mountains.

Cut loose from the shackles of commuters and salesmen, over the border into Wales and on to the Brecon Beacons, it was time to extend the 3200GT. Not yet to drive it as fast as it would go but, more representatively, to dig a little further into the reserves of those abilities to see if the depth was there to accompany the breadth that I no longer doubted.

performance, if the transmission is left in its Sport setting, is flashing and while I am in no position to confirm or deny its claimed 174mph top speed, I can tell you it accelerates rapidly up to any speed a sane person could deem sensible on most public roads. By the time the paint on the rev-counter turns yellow at 6000rpm, there's little more than a muted and unappetising blare coming from beneath the bonnet and you need again to remind yourself again that this is not a sportscar to avoid disappointment.

The final proof of the 3200GT's role in life comes when you take it to traditional supercar territory and throw it across the scenery really very hard. ≫→

Maserati cabin is one of the car's triumphs. It's spacious and leather upholstery strikes exactly the right note. Steering wheel is adjustable for height and rake and Ferrari-sourced column stalks feel right and work well. Becker stereo is confusing but otherwise the ergonomics are unexpectedly impressive

Rear tail lights are two parallel strips of LED displays. Look quirky at first but grow on you after a while. No bulbs involved so should last forever

Elegant ten spoke alloy wheels look great and come covered with acres of Michelin rubber providing great grip in the dry, and safe progress when wet

It's been a long time since the famous Maserati Trident has adorned a car as good as this and, with Ferrari now in charge, it should get better still

V8 engine is quite familiar now but remains undeniably effective. Uses twin turbos to prise 370bhp from just 3.2-litres. Looks better than it sounds

SPECIFICATION

Maserati 3200GT

ENGINE

Type	90deg V8 dohc, 3217cc four valves per cylinder
Bore/stroke ...	80x80mm
Fuelling	Electronic injection, twin IHI turbochargers
Max power ...	370bhp at 6250rpm
Max torque ...	362bhp at 4500rpm
Transmission ...	Six speed manual/four speed automatic

CHASSIS

Steering	Powered rack and pinion
Brakes f/r	Ventilated drilled discs; (f) 330mm, (r) 310mm
Suspension f&r	Wishbones, coils, adaptive dampers, anti-roll bar
Wheels	Alloy, 8 x18in
Tyres	235/40 ZR18 (f), 265/35 ZR18 (r)

DIMENSIONS

Length/width ...	177.6in/71.7in
Height/wheelbase	51.4in/104.7in
Kerb weight ...	1590kg

CLAIMED PERFORMANCE

Max speed ...	174mph
0-60mph ...	5sec

At medium effort, the Maserati handles superbly. Grip from the 18in Michelin tyres is never an issue in the dry and even if its raining fast progress is usually interrupted only by a gently blinking light on the dash telling you the effective traction control is silently keeping watch, trimming the rough edges off your driving. The steering is direct and devoid of kickback, the brakes massively powerful.

Try harder however and the Maserati will slowly relinquish this admirable fluency. It never gets ragged or even uncomfortable but the time comes, sooner than some drivers will wish, when it's travelling as fast as it cares to. First, the steering refuses to weight up in fast turns, denying the driver the meaty helm

rides and steers a little better, comes with a five speed auto 'box and a longer list of standard equipment. People will argue which is better looking (I prefer the British car's appearance) and without having both side by side, I am not in a position to say which is more refined and spacious but there is little in it. I do know the Jaguar has the bigger boot and the Maserati massively better brakes. This, however, does not begin to make up for the shortfalls, particularly when you consider the fact that the Jaguar is, in real terms, cheaper too. In the end, the bottom line is the Jaguar is the better car, pure and simple.

Yet I do not feel ill-disposed towards the 3200GT and, on the contrary, welcome both it and what it

"In the end, the bottom line is that the Jaguar XKR is the better car, pure and simple"

response such corners command, then the body control starts to be undermined; it wallows a little too much in the dips and find one which also includes a curve and you will hear a gentle rubbing under the car, probably as tyre meets wheel arch. Ultimately the car is too soft, even with its dampers set to Sport, too heavy and insufficiently communicative to make a joy out of such conditions.

Given this, it would be both easy and legitimate to construct a case that said the 3200GT is a brave effort but ultimately one which fails to move the game on even to the point its rival from Jaguar reached some time ago. The Jaguar is at least as fast and has a considerably more charismatic engine; it handles,

represents. For while in no objective sense could you call it a great car it is equally apposite to observe that it's the best Maserati in the last 20 years and, as steps in the right direction go, they don't come much bigger than that. Moreover, while it lacks the on-paper and, many of the on-road credentials to beat the likes of the XKR, there's another quality, less tangible but still important which the 3200GT possesses by the bucketload. It's everywhere from the curve of the dashboard to the smell of the leather; from the artfully crafted Maserati-script on the bootlid to those beautiful ten-spoke alloy wheels; The people who built it call it 'emotion' and, after two days pondering, I now, finally, know what they mean. ◪

At speed over the Welsh mountains: Maserati offers fine and fast progress to those in a hurry, riding well, steering precisely and covering the ground with great efficiency. For those looking for a thrill, however, it is less convincing, failing to communicate either through the chassis or steering sufficiently well

MASERATI 3200 GT

MODEL TESTED Automatic
LIST PRICE £62,950 **TOP SPEED** 155mph
30-70MPH 5.2sec **0-60MPH** 6.2sec
60-0MPH 2.8sec **MPG**
FOR Looks, interior quality, steering, cabin size
AGAINST Harsh ride, dated auto 'box, thirst

YOU MIGHT call it a lengthy gestation period, or you could just say it's taken quite some time for Ferrari's influence at Maserati to come to fruition. Either way the new £62,950 3200 GT automatic you see here may look identical to the car we drove in June last year, but according to Maserati it is a very different animal indeed.

Despite all its performance and unmistakable Latin charm, last year's 3200 GT was badly let down by poor steering, horrid throttle response and an unyielding ride. Parent company Ferrari had only been in charge at Maserati for a short period and their engineering skills hadn't been allowed to flourish.

Not any longer. That the sheet metal hasn't changed at all is no great surprise. The 3200 GT is a great-looking car. But beneath the skin there are parts of the car that are almost unrecognisable compared with the original. Some of the front suspension geometry has been modified, as has the steering rack and there's an uprated ECU (electronic control unit) that is said to greatly improve the response from the drive-by-wire throttle.

But the basics remain the same. A classic front-engined, rear-drive layout with double-wishbone suspension all round has the job of controlling a 1565kg car that's powered by a storming 3217cc twin-turbocharged V8 engine. If that sounds impressive the actual outputs are better still: 370bhp at 6000rpm (250rpm lower than in the manual) and 362lb ft at

4500rpm. Considering it weighs significantly less than an Aston Martin DB7 or a Jaguar XKR and outguns them both on the dyno, it should be uncatchable on the road.

Yet on the track the 3200 GT failed to match either Maserati's claimed acceleration figures or those of its rivals, as verified by us. A damp track and an initially lethargic four-speed auto gearbox meant we couldn't better 6.2sec to 60mph (Maserati claims 5.7sec to 62mph). And it took a brisk but still slightly disappointing 14.7sec to 100mph. Whichever way you look at it a Jaguar XKR is significantly quicker, taking just 5.1sec and 12.4sec to cover the same increments. Flat out it managed 155mph, the same as the Jaguar but without a restrictor.

That said, the performance is massively more satisfying than before. Throttle response has been much improved thanks to the ECU retuning, and most of our complaints have been redressed concerning the auto 'box. There's no unnecessary hunting at a steady cruise and the engine responds smartly and smoothly to large and small throttle inputs alike, though there's still a fair amount of turbo lag.

On the road the 3200 GT never feels anything less than a very rapid car, despite being at least one gear ratio short of most rivals. By today's standards, particularly those of parents Fiat and Ferrari, the four-speed gearbox (made by Australian company BTR) is ◆

HISTORY

This marque has an illustrious past. Start during the good times: the '70s. Bora, Merak, Indy, Ghibli and Khasmin were all stunning mid or front-engined sports cars. Then owner Citroën went bust and De Tomaso took over. The 1976 Kylami was the first of the square cars that took Maserati through the next two decades with little to shout about. Awkward-looking Biturbo cars had little style and plenty of iron oxide. Last Ghibli was a fun if fragile tool. The Ferrari takeover in '98 brought more money – and a future.

PERFORMANCE AND SPECIFICATIONS

ENGINE

Layout 8 cyls in vee, 3217cc
Max power 370bhp at 6000rpm
Max torque 362lb ft at 4500rpm
Specific output 115bhp per litre
Power to weight 236bhp per tonne
Torque to weight 231lb ft per tonne
Installation Front, longitudinal, rear-wheel drive
Construction Alloy heads and block
Bore/stroke 80.0/80.0mm
Valve gear 4 valves per cylinder, dohc
Compression ratio 8.0:1
Ignition and fuel Electronic fuel injection, twin IHI turbochargers, two intercoolers

GEARBOX

Type 4-speed automatic by BTR
Ratios/mph per 1000rpm
1st 2.39/8.1 **2nd** 1.45/13.3
3rd 1.00/19.3 **4th** 0.68/28.3
Final drive 3.91

MAXIMUM SPEEDS

1st 49mph/6100rpm **2nd** 81/6100
3rd 117/6100 **4th** 155/5470

ACCELERATION FROM REST

SURFACE DRY

True mph	sec	speedo mph
30	2.8	32
40	3.7	42
50	4.8	53
60	6.2	63
70	7.9	73
80	9.6	84
90	11.2	95
100	14.7	105

Standing qtr mile 14.6sec/100mph
Standing km 25.9sec/122.6mph
30-70mph through gears 5.2sec

KICKDOWN

mph	
20-40	1.9
30-50	2.0
40-60	2.5
50-70	3.1
60-80	3.4
70-90	3.3
80-100	5.1

STEERING

Type Rack and pinion, power assisted
Turns lock to lock 2.7

CONTROLS IN DETAIL

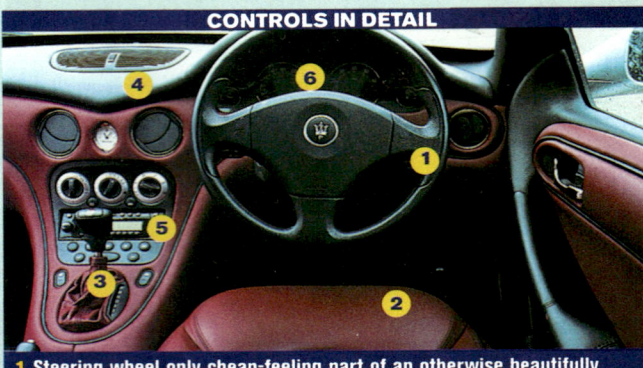

1 Steering wheel only cheap-feeling part of an otherwise beautifully built cabin 2 Seats are plain bad: short on comfort and support 3 Only four gears but surprisingly easy to shift manually 4 All-leather dash feels very expensive 5 Becker hi-fi easy to use but not powerful enough to sound good at speed 6 Odometer is an old-style analogue

SUSPENSION

Front Double wishbones, coil springs, anti-roll bar, adaptive damping
Rear Double wishbones, coil springs, anti-roll bar, adaptive damping

WHEELS & TYRES

Wheels 8Jx18in **Made of** Cast alloy
Tyres 235/40 ZR18 (f), 265/35 ZR18 (r) Michelin Pilot SX
Spare Full size

BRAKES

Front 330mm ventilated, cross-drilled discs
Rear 310mm ventilated, cross-drilled discs
Anti-lock Standard

BRAKES

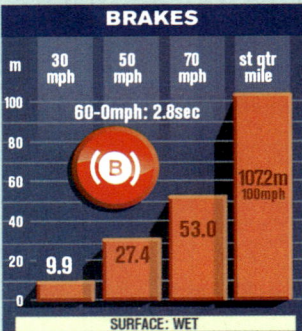

60-0mph: 2.8sec

m	30 mph	50 mph	70 mph	st qtr mile
	9.9	27.4	53.0	1072m 100mph

SURFACE: WET

GEARING

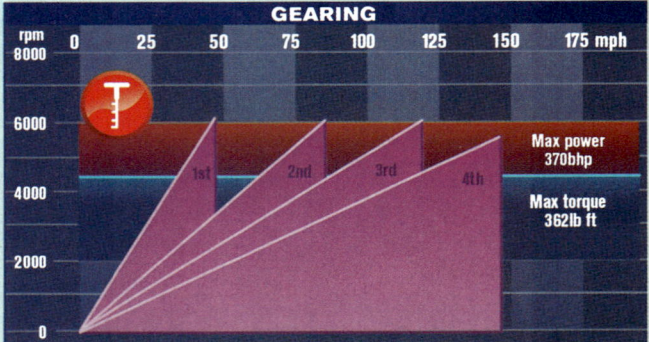

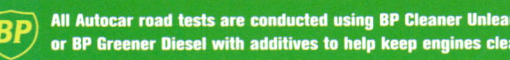

All Autocar road tests are conducted using BP Cleaner Unleaded Fuel or BP Greener Diesel with additives to help keep engines cleaner

FUEL CONSUMPTION

TEST RESULTS

mpg	Average	Touring	Best	Worst
	16.5	15.5	20.9	5.3

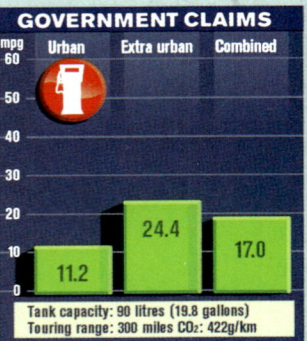

GOVERNMENT CLAIMS

mpg	Urban	Extra urban	Combined
	11.2	24.4	17.0

Tank capacity: 90 litres (19.8 gallons)
Touring range: 300 miles CO$_2$: 422g/km

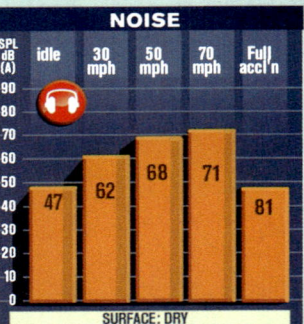

NOISE

SPL dB(A)	idle	30 mph	50 mph	70 mph	Full accl'n
	47	62	68	71	81

SURFACE: DRY

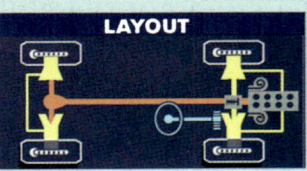

LAYOUT

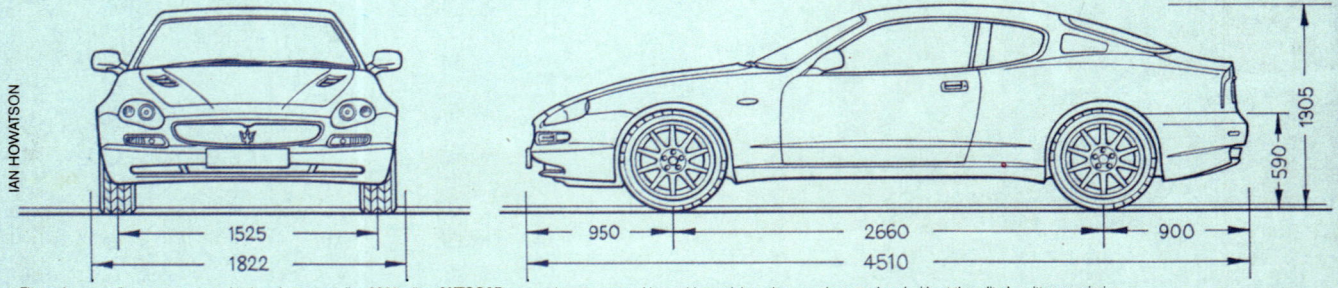

Body 2dr coupe hatchback **Cd** n/a **Front/rear tracks** 1513/1462mm **Turning circle** 10.8m **Min/max front leg room** 840/1060mm **Min/max rear leg room** 990/770mm **Min/max front head room** 870/900mm **Interior width front/rear** 1490/1435mm **Min/max boot width** 860/1200mm **Min boot length** 640mm **VDA boot volume** n/a **Kerb weight** 1565kg **Weight distribution front/rear (per cent)** 59/41 **Width (inc mirrors)** 1822mm

IAN HOWATSON

1525
1822

950 2660 900
4510

1305
590

New ECU improves throttle response

Steering slightly vague in corners but much improved; huge brakes superb

Suspension fails to soak up bumps

◆ far from cutting edge. It doesn't have a +/- mode, just a familiar PRND321 gate.

An inability to change gear in a semi-auto mode will frustrate some people, but truth be told it doesn't detract from the driving experience too much. In normal mode shifts happen at 6100rpm, but select the Sport mode, which also stiffens the adaptive dampers, and it'll go to 6500rpm before changing up. The real weakness involves the kickdown mode in which shifts are accompanied by an occasional thump from the back of the car.

Irritatingly the gearbox will also hold on to a low gear for too long even when you've backed off the throttle. Gears can be

manually selected using the lever and the electronics will allow you a small blip on the throttle to smooth out downchanges. But it's not one of the greatest auto transmissions.

The brakes are far from ordinary. Massive all-round cross-drilled discs do a fantastic job in the wet or dry and there's terrific pedal feel; a 60-0mph time of 2.8sec in the damp is exceptional.

Unlike the fuel economy. Even on our economy route it could manage no better than 16.5mpg and on average it recorded a dismal 15.5mpg. That means a real-world touring range of no more than 300 miles despite the vast 90-litre tank.

The raft of changes to the suspension and steering have released much more of the car's dynamic potential. But more interestingly they have helped to define the true identity of the 3200 GT. Forget the last two letters of the car's name: in reality, despite the four seats, gracious shape and automatic gearbox this is very much a sports car. One that focuses on driving enjoyment much more than it does cruising comfort.

The first message is the hard, almost unyielding ride. Bumps that wouldn't faze an XKR send mighty shudders through the frame and the tyre roar at anything above 60mph is quite intrusive. Switching between

Sport and Auto on the electronic dampers seems to make little difference to the situation.

But there's a huge pay-off in the form of exemplary body control at any speed and an uncanny ability to mask its size and weight on British roads. For a big car the 3200 GT is astonishingly nimble, changing direction with real precision and requiring only the deftest steering inputs to make it slice from apex to apex. More significantly, it never feels nervous at either end while doing so.

Much of the credit must go to the steering, which is unrecognisable from before. At 2.7 turns lock to lock it is sensibly geared and well weighted just off-centre. If it has a weakness it's in longer sweeping corners, where there's a slight vagueness and lack of resistance that can be disconcerting.

Grip levels are huge in the dry from the 235/40 front and 265/35 rear Michelin Pilots but switch the standard-fit traction control off in the wet and it can be quite a handful. A limited-slip differential mixed with a surge of boost can be a recipe for brutal oversteer.

Inside, the 3200 GT is something of a flawed diamond. Be stunned by the high equipment level, the beautiful fit and finish, the subtle smell of leather and the surprisingly good dashboard ergonomics. Like the exterior it looks and feels much more special than anything else at the price: you can sense the Ferrari genes.

But the driving position is close to unacceptable for anyone over 6ft tall and the seat itself is woefully flat across the shoulders and waist. Front head room is a real problem for taller types and the boot is borderline pathetic for a supposed GT car. And yet there's enough room in the back for two adults to stretch out in relative comfort.

Despite all this the 3200 GT auto still paints a far rosier picture of the way they do things at Maserati compared with the manual we drove last year. It's much more of a sports car than we imagined a 3200 GT could ever be, and although a Jaguar XKR or Aston DB7 may be more comfortable and easier to live with every day, neither can match it as a purist driving machine.

At last Maserati has built a car enthusiasts can relish.

WHAT IT COSTS

On-the-road price	£62,950
Price as tested	£62,950
Co²g/km	422

EQUIPMENT
(**bold** = options fitted to test car)

Anti-lock brakes	●
Front foglights	●
Airbag driver/passenger/side	●/●/–
Air conditioning	●
Metallic paint	●
Alloy wheels	●
Alarm/immobiliser	●/●
Leather trim	●
Navigation system & Hi-fi upgrade	**£2314**
Electrochromic rear-view mirror	**£199**
● standard – not available	

INSURANCE

Group	20
Typical quote	£1669

WARRANTY
36 months/60,000 miles,
12 years anti-corrosion

SERVICING
Minor 6250 miles **Major** 12,000miles

Sumptuous leather but little head room for tall drivers; seats woefully flat

Best Maserati in 20 years
★★★★

Maserati Quattroporte

Richard Meaden calls this Italian supersaloon the sensible choice. That's why we like him

An old Maserati? I'm joking, right? Well, no actually. Firstly it's not that old (barely two years and 25,000 miles), and secondly, well, alright, I'm probably not firing on all my cerebral cylinders, but if dodgy old Masers have been good enough for **evo** MD Harry Metcalfe in the past, then a two-year-old V8 Quattroporte evoluzione for around a third of its original asking price will do me very nicely, thank you.

It seems hard to believe you can get what was sixty grand's worth of 330bhp, twin-turbo luxury saloon for the price of a new Toyota Camry, but that's the beauty of unfashionable Italian exotica like the Quattroporte. Profiting from some poor sap's rash two-year-old purchasing decision seems evil, but it makes perfect sense when you're sat in the Quattroporte's snug, leather-lined cockpit, pushed firmly into the backrest by the torrent of eye-widening power and revelling in the understated, individual, mildly eccentric Maserati experience.

Don't be fooled by the looks. This is a four-seater saloon like no other. The engine is one of the most charismatic forced-induction engines ever made,

and when hooked up to a six-speed manual 'box (most were autos, sadly) and wrapped in a slim-hipped, Giugiaro-designed body, you've got a car that can stand toe-to-toe with an M5 in pure performance terms. With a top speed of 170mph there are few faster means of transporting four adults.

This particular example drives as well as I remember a factory-fresh press car. Which means plenty of wheelspin in anything but dry conditions, ride quality that varies from firm to jiggly depending on which of the three settings you've selected for the electronically adjustable dampers, a classically awful Italian driving position and a few squeaks and rattles from the interior. On the positive side, the steering is sharp, the performance truly awesome in any gear at any revs, and handling on the hairy side of entertaining.

I'm sure our resident prophet of doom, Roger Green, will find a myriad of good reasons not to buy the Quattroporte. Had I not driven this example I would probably share his scepticism, but compared with the trio of motley money-pits my esteemed colleagues have pinned their hopes on, I can't help thinking the youthful, low-mileage Maserati is the sensible choice. And no, I'm not joking.

Now *that's* cool. A speedo that goes all the way to 200mph makes this our sort of saloon. Below: twin-turbo V8 gives massive stonk, and fairly impressive bills, too, if it goes wrong

👁 Owner's view

Roger Bovingdon

'Until recently I was a very happy 405bhp R33 Skyline owner; that was until the police discovered that the car had been stolen in Tokyo along with quite a few others. I was left with nothing more than a bitter taste in my mouth and a resolve never to buy another grey import.

'Where do you go from a Skyline? It had to be fast and it had to be rare so I started looking at Ghiblis, but the ones I saw were either too expensive or too cheap. What I hadn't realised was that the Quattroporte fell neatly into my price range. It might not have the Skyline's handling, particularly in the wet, but it certainly has the speed and presence. The car I bought was one of the first in the UK and has now covered about 23,000 miles. It has had a new cambelt and as I don't intend to cover many miles in it (about 6000-8000 per year) the high running costs aren't the issue they might be.

'We have bought the car to keep for quite some time, so the practicality of the four doors and the huge boot will prove very useful. For me, it seems the Quattroporte is the perfect solution.'

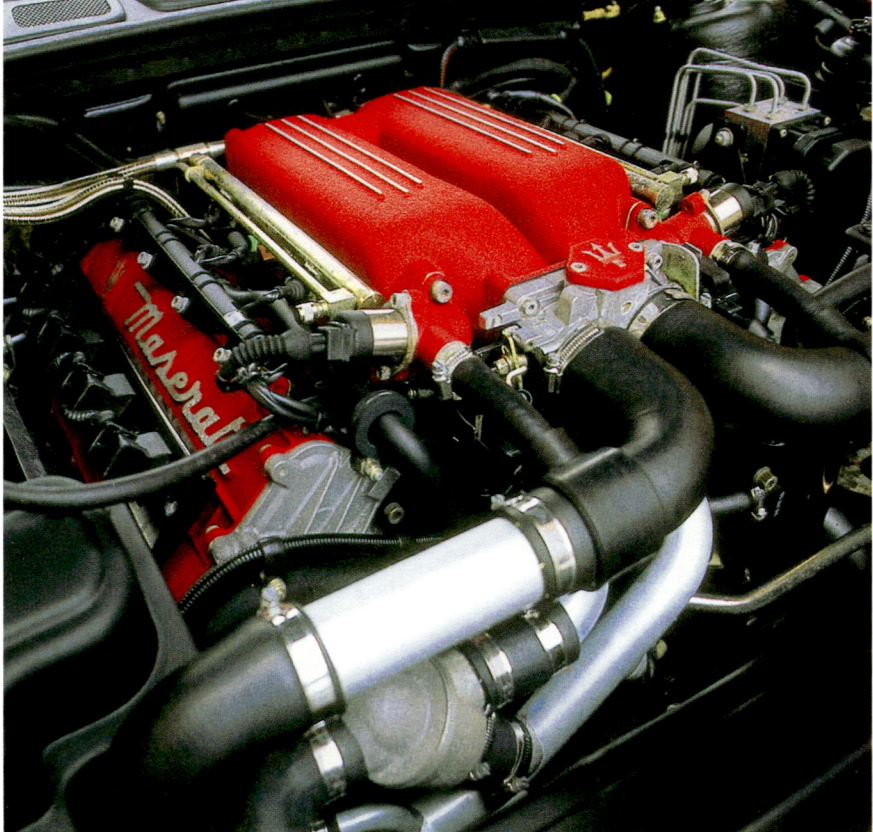

'Sixty grand's worth of 330bhp twin-turbo luxury saloon for the price of a new Camry'

⊕ The expert's view

On the face of it the Quattroporte represents a stonking deal; resale values have been in free-fall – and there are no signs that they're slowing down. Whereas Ghiblis have always been bought by enthusiasts who know the score and are prepared to put up with the odd rattle and hum, the Quattroporte was bought by people who wanted a Mercedes that looked a bit different. Those guys didn't keep the car for long.

These were also the last cars designed before Maserati was taken under Ferrari's wing and it seems that the new management was anxious to move them on and concentrate on the 3200GT; production of the Quattroporte ceased completely in December last year. It was never a fast seller, so prices were slashed to such an extent that these nearly-new machines easily come into our self-imposed price bracket.

Despite it being the newest car here by quite some margin, you need to pay attention to the service schedule and the costs involved. A quick glance at the parts table on page 128 highlights that the Quattroporte is going to cost more to run than

just about anything you can think of. This was another factor that reduced demand, pushing residuals ever lower, and it's also reflected in the insurance costs. So before you get too excited about the amount of stylish Italian metal available for so little cash, get the calculator out and start pushing the buttons.

Furthermore, it's worth checking exactly where you can get the work done, because both specialist garages and official outlets are few and far between.

There are two big services to worry about and it comes as no surprise to find that a lot of these cars are sold just before one of them is due. A new cambelt is required every 24,000 miles, and at

48,000 the timing chains have to be done as well. To replace the chains the engine has to be removed, which is why the cost is so high.

On the plus side, Quattroportes have a good reputation for reliability and most other problems that you may come across will be relatively minor. The switchgear is a little flimsy and the window motors can fail (new ones cost £200), but the electrics are generally good.

If the car you buy is less than two years old, it'll still have the remainder of the original unlimited-mileage Maserati warranty and it'll definitely still be well within the six-year anti-corrosion warranty, so in the mechanical sense this is the safest choice of our selection. **RG**

Maserati Quattroporte V8 evoluzione	
Engine	V8, 3217cc, 32v, twin turbo
Max power	331bhp @ 6400rpm
Max torque	331lb ft @ 4400rpm
Power to weight	204bhp/ton
0-60mph	5.5secs
Top speed	167mph
Price new	£58,795
Price now	£20,000 - £28,000

Unblown in the wind

No roof, no turbochargers and no trademark boomerang rear lights – but Maserati's latest effort is even better than the coupe

I'M ENJOYING ONE of my best ever drives. So far I've tackled the awesome Passo della Raticosa that wiggles past the hilltops of the Bolognesi countryside, I've lashed through 10 tunnels in a row with a glorious wall of sound chasing hard behind me each time, I've diced with a high-speed section of autostrada and I'm now preparing to strut my stuff in front of the Piaggio-riding 'slapperati' that cram Bologna's town centre.

I'm also in the midst of experiencing the daily commute of the incomprehensibly jammy boss of Ferrari and Maserati, Luca

Cordero di Montezemolo. For most of us the equivalent schlep to work is an arduous task, enlivened only by the opportunity to head-bang to a favourite CD or to have a good ferret about in your schnozzle. For Luca, though, the only inconvenience involves deciding which car in which to relish the drive.

Even he is said to view the likes of a 360 Modena as an extravagance better saved for weekend blasts. A diesel Fiat Multipla simply wouldn't do, while a big Alfa would be only marginally more appropriate for the occasion. Which is why, since Ferrari was handed the

considerable task of sorting out Maserati's problems in 1997, he has set about creating his ideal set of commuting wheels.

And here it is. The Maserati Spyder may look like just a soft-top conversion of the 3200GT coupe, but in many respects it's a radically different car. A radically improved one, too. The engine, gearbox and brakes are all new, the suspension has been heavily tweaked and the body, as well as losing its roof, has lost over 20cm of metalwork lengthways. As a result, the Spyder is more compact, better proportioned and arguably

WORDS
PETER GRUNERT

PHOTOGRAPHY
JIM FORREST

more visually aggressive than the coupe that came before it, only missing the original's distinctive 'boomerang' tail-lights. Maserati plans to head back into the US next year following a 12-year absence and market research has shown that potential customers over there weren't keen on them. A shame.

Even so, the Spyder looks pretty sensational, even with the hood up. Swiftly stow this away behind a solid, body-coloured cover, via the prod of a button and the whirring of electrohydraulic gubbins, and it looks better still. The drama is increased further by 18-inch, 15-spoke wheels, a pair of part leather-trimmed roll-hoop covers and a quartet of exhaust pipes. Pootling through Bologna's mediaeval backstreets, the latter emit the most fantastic burbling noise. This is a car that sounds as though it should be stupidly quick, even when it's scarcely moving.

In place of the standard car's six-speed manual 'box, I'm driving the Cambiocorsa version (it means 'racing gearshift') complete

with the latest development of the F1 paddle-shift transmission also available for the Ferrari 360 Modena and Spider. As with those cars, it's got a fully automatic function – now offering smooth rather than jerky shifts while toddling through the traffic.

Driving over countless cobbles and discarded espresso cups also exposes a smidge of body shake transmitted up through the steering wheel, the penalty for losing the bracing provided by the coupe's solid roof. Hence I'm keen to get back out onto northern Italy's best roads. At this point, Signore di Montezemolo would head north for Maserati's factory on the outskirts of Modena, currently being completely rebuilt and modernised. I'd rather retrace my steps and give the Spyder another caning south-wards along the route I've just tackled.

The autostrada beckons again and, right now, there's a long line of dusty, overloaded trucks wobbling along the inside lane with just a tiny gap in between them that I'm

focusing on. I flick the left-hand lever to instantly blip the gearbox down into the second of its six ratios and press the drive-by-wire throttle. The Spyder plummets alarmingly forward up the slip road, slotting easily into the gap. And my foot has only used up a quarter of the pedal's lengthy travel.

Such oomph is provided by a new light-weight, all-aluminium, naturally aspirated 4.2-litre V8, replacing the twin-turbo V8 of the 3200GT. It's due to be fitted to the coupe sometime next year, while rumour has it that elements of this powerplant will be developed for a future generation of Ferraris.

Soon the smart chrome-ringed instruments are indicating 200kph, very fast, yet with a 283kph (175mph) maximum still available. The engine feels so lively even at these speeds that it's undoubtedly got a huge amount more to come if asked for, but I prefer to cruise along steadily for now. Comfort levels are generally impressively high, wind buffeting being kept well suppressed by the optional

The Spyder loses a little rigidity without the metal roof, but the new engine has an extra litre of capacity in place of the older coupe's two turbos. The result is a car that spins out more power and in a more predictable manner too. An imminent US relaunch is blamed for the loss of those characterfully curved rear light clusters

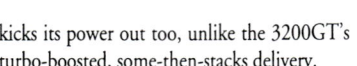

deflector strapped between the roll hoops on our test Spyder. Remember, it's a crime to ruffle the coiffure of the boss of an exotic Italian car company (or two).

The Spyder's fully adjustable driving position is a step up from the gibbon-like posture demanded by previous Maseratis I've sat in, while the leather-clad seats are suitably pliant. The dashboard is handsomely swoopy, the traditional rugby-ball shaped clock is still there (no longer in Ratners-style gold plate), while the switches on the centre console sadly remain as unremarkable as many Fiats'.

The hills are much closer now, providing a chance to put that fabulous engine back to work. I give the accelerator a hefty stamp and the V8 violently slings the car up the road, matched by an appropriately ferocious bark. It also proves instantly responsive on the couple of occasions I find myself caught out at low revs in a high gear, yet it still builds in its eagerness as the 7,600rpm red line approaches. It's predictable in the way it

kicks its power out too, unlike the 3200GT's turbo-boosted, some-then-stacks delivery.

A hike of 20bhp over its predecessor's already sizeable 370bhp output accounts only in part for the claim that the Spyder is the faster car – by more than five seconds – around Ferrari's Fiorano F1 test track. It also now handles better, although I am told that Michael Schumacher still reckons it's too soft. On the road, it certainly isn't. Our car came with the 'Skyhook' adaptive damping system (again an option) linked up to accelerometers on the body and wheels. This system has already helped keep the Spyder's ride quality respectably supple while I've been travelling sedately along and is now beefing itself up to maintain the car's poise as it senses a return to hilly hairpins.

The Spyder's steering is a little light, if very direct, the brakes offer plenty of feel and never show any tendency to fade, while the standard-issue traction control device is regularly called upon to keep things in order as I find myself

playing with the engine's full grunt. Through here the Spyder isn't quite so confidence-inspiringly settled as a 911 would be. Still, it's more agile than a Jaguar XKR.

On price and rooflessness alone, the Spyder will also be destined to stand comparison with the new Mercedes SL, but in truth it's a unique prospect. Maserati still builds just 1,800 cars in a year and exclusivity is further increased by the fact that each Spyder will be painted and trimmed to suit the customer's limits of budget and taste(lessness). Maserati also claims that quality levels have been improved to the extent that you can plan to rack up a big mileage in one without expecting to be bugged by continual glitches.

There is one major risk attached to Spyder ownership, however. Even if you don't live in the picturesque hills south of Bologna, the temptation to just skive off, and keep on going, will often prove too great to resist. ●

● **VERDICT** *Even quicker and more characterful than a Porsche 911 cabrio*

FACT FILE
● **MODEL**
Two-door cabriolet
● **ENGINE**
4244cc 32v V8, 390bhp
● **PERFORMANCE**
0-62mph in 5.0secs,
175mph max speed
● **COST**
£70,000 approx,
on sale by December
● **RIVALS**
Jaguar XKR, Mercedes-Benz
SL500, Porsche 911 cabrio

⊛ MASERATI 3200GT Assetto Corsa v Leo Nardo

Two variations on Maserati's storming coupe – which is the most convincing package?

Above: Assetto Corsa comes with cut-slick style Pirellis, which do it few favours. Steering feel is in short supply unless you're really pushing hard

Seeing any Maserati 3200GT on the road is a rare event. So you can imagine the quizzically admiring looks elicited by a pair of modified Masers as we charged through the Wiltshire countryside. I certainly doubt if Chippenham has ever throbbed to the beat of sixteen cylinders and more than 800bhp of Modenese muscle before.

Battle lines are drawn on the entertainingly swoopy A4, not far from Castle Combe. In the red corner we have Maserati UK's Assetto Corsa limited edition, in the blue corner Italian sports car specialist Caracalla's 450bhp Leo Nardo 3200GT. Each promises a richer, more focused drive. Which delivers most convincingly we're about to find out.

Let's start with the Assetto Corsa (it's Italian for 'racing spec'). Built in a limited run of 75 cars and costing £67,950, the UK-spec Assetto Corsa is available in red, black or silver, and in auto or manual form. Sadly the test car is an automatic, which is a shame as the Maser auto is a basic four-speeder, devoid of any fancy tiptronic-style shift mode. A bizarre choice for a supposed performance model, it has to be said.

On the plus side, it's shod with classy, graphite grey 18in alloys and Pirelli PZero Rosso Corsa tyres that resemble

those of a Lotus 340R. The suspension is also stiffer and 15mm lower and the brakes are bigger Brembo items.

With the rudely healthy, though now sadly endangered 370bhp, twin-turbo V8 snorting beneath the bonnet, the harder-edged Assetto Corsa should be a seriously quick, seriously suave alternative to a Jaguar XKR R Performance. It certainly has the looks to compete on equal terms, those long swooping curves and abruptly chopped tail containing more visual drama and fascination than a dozen XKRs. Somewhat disappointingly though, this particular Assetto Corsa rarely delivers the driver-focussed experience you rightly expect.

The gearbox is largely to blame. It blunts the V8's brutal power, slurring away the 3200GT's vibrant, horizon-yanking poke. In Sport mode the 'box punches down the cogs sharply but is then reluctant to shift up unless you gun it to the red line. Leave Sport deactivated though, and it becomes the transmission equivalent of Harry Enfield's teenager, grudgingly sulking its way into a lower gear. Consequently you find yourself fingering the Sport button in preparation for overtakes, then nudging it back into Kevin mode once safely passed the obstacle.

But what of the chassis upgrades?

Well, I'm a renowned sceptic of the 340R-style road-legal cut slicks, and the PZero Rosso Corsas do little to change my opinion of them. They drum up a load of road noise, while feel is almost non-existent until they've got some temperature in them. Power through the right corner in the right conditions and you'll find huge reserves of grip, but for 90 per cent of the time they are a complete waste of time. I'd take a set of standard PZero Rossos and a heap more wet road grip, ride comfort and steering feel along with them.

Like the tyres, the chassis only comes into its own when you're pushing really hard. The otherwise lumpy, unsettled ride smooths out, the direct but over-light steering gains feel, and the big Maser hefts itself into the tarmac. It's at moments like this, though, that you miss the added control and aggression of the six-speed manual, for the auto rarely allows you to get the chassis fully balanced on the power.

There's no such trouble with the Leo Nardo-modified Maser. Based on a standard, six-speed manual 3200GT, it is fitted with a raft of performance-enhancing hardware, developed in Germany with full TUV approval by specialist tuning company Dimex. Engine, chassis and cosmetics have all been tweaked to impressive effect.

Perhaps the most compelling aspect of the Leo Nardo conversion is the engine, which now develops 450bhp and 420lb ft, up from 370bhp and 362lb ft.

Liberated by the fitment of a more efficient intercooling system, free-flow inlet manifolds and stainless steel sports exhaust system, sports air filter and a reprogrammed management system, this 3200GT is amongst the most potent GT cars you can buy.

In an attempt to harness the prodigious power, the car sits on an exquisite set of 19in split-rim alloys, shod with Pirelli PZero Rossos (245/35 at the front, 275/30 at the rear). Shorter,

Photography: Andy Morgan

43

stiffer Eibach springs drop the car closer to the road by 35mm at the front and 20mm at the rear, giving the already muscular Maser an even tougher stance.

The moment you accelerate up the road in the Leo Nardo you know you're in a seriously quick car. Turbo lag isn't really an issue, you are simply swept forwards on an explosive shockwave of power. If it's dry, wheelspin is a possibility in the first three gears, while in the wet caution is needed well into the meaty bit of fourth gear. With the ASR system active, the almost constant flickering from the warning light is a graphic demonstration of how much power is hitting the tarmac. It's an animal and no mistake.

One major failing of the standard car is a hair-trigger throttle. Leo Nardo's management system tweaks are said to have addressed the problem, but any

softening of response seems to have been negated by the increased power and torque of the engine. Consequently the first few millimetres of throttle travel still unleash a torrent of acceleration and make smooth driving an object lesson in sensitivity and restraint.

Once up and running, though, it is utterly ballistic. There's more feel too, thanks to those less compromised tyres, and with the added control of the manual 'box you can really enjoy cornering, using the ample power to get the tail working. It's not perfect though. Unlike the Assetto Corsa, which feels best when working very hard, the Leo Nardo begins to lose composure when attacking bumpy, uneven tarmac. Wheel travel is at a premium, thanks to the more severely lowered suspension and 19in wheels, and although the tyres stay clear of the arches, big lumps and high

Above: Leo Nardo conversion includes lowered and stiffened suspension and a massive hike in power, from 370 to 450bhp

speeds give the bumpstops a work-out.

In keeping with the enhanced performance, the brakes have also been uprated, with steel braided hoses, high performance brake fluid and harder pads. As you'd expect, the result is improved stopping power in outright terms, with marginally better pedal firmness but a slight reduction in pedal feel until there's some heat in the pad material. There's certainly not much between the two cars in the stopping department.

Which would I choose? Well, it's not strictly a direct comparison as one is a new car, the other a conversion. That said, if the test Assetto Corsa came in manual form it would be a much closer run thing, but as it stands the auto 'box

hamstrings it from the start. It looks great and has undoubted exclusivity, but at around £7000 more than the standard manual 3200GT and no more powerful, it's hard to justify the added outlay.

The Leo Nardo conversion offers a huge hike in performance, looks even better than the Assetto and costs around £12,000 plus VAT. Not only can you apply the engine, suspension and cosmetic upgrades in stages, you are free to fit the kit to a used car and save yourself an absolute packet. With good used 3200GTs going for around £40K, a full-on Leo Nardo car could be yours for just over fifty grand. Not bad for an exotic, 180mph, four-seater GT.

Richard Meaden

For more information on Caracalla's Leo Nardo conversion, contact Simon Jordan on 0870 9090360 or e-mail sales@caracalla.co.uk

ASSETTO CORSA	
Engine	V8, 3217cc, 32v, twin-turbo
Max power	370bhp @ 6250rpm
Max torque	362 lb ft @ 4500rpm
Top speed	174mph (claimed)
0-60 mph	5.3sec
Price	£67,950
On sale	Now

evo RATING	★★★★1/2
➕ Gorgeous looks, image, charismatic V8	
➖ Muddled auto gearbox and chassis	

LEO NARDO	
Engine	V8, 3217cc, 32v, twin-turbo
Max power	450bhp @ 6500rpm
Max torque	420lb ft @ 4400rpm
Top speed	180mph-plus (est)
0-60 mph	4.9secs (est)
Price	£14,800 (conversion cost)
On sale	Now

evo RATING	★★★★
➕ Looks even better, goes even faster	
➖ Hairtrigger throttle, lacks on-limit composure	

'Imagine the looks as a pair of modified Masers charged through the Wiltshire countryside'

OVER-PAR FOR THE CORSA

**MASERATI 3200 GT
ASSETTO CORSA
PRICE £67,950
ON SALE Now**

THINK MY respect for the Maserati Assetto Corsa started to grow about five minutes after leaving the office. Pulling away from each junction on mildly damp roads, I found myself smirking happily as the rear of the car fought to break loose. And this was while feathering the throttle, barely waking the turbos.

Respect was duly given. The Assetto Corsa, or 'Performance Spec', is based on the existing 3200 GT and marks the swansong for the twin-turbo V8 engine, which will be replaced in the 3200 GT with a normally aspirated V8, already used in the current Spyder. This special edition also celebrates 75 years of Maserati and exactly that number will come to the UK, from a production run of 350. Heritage junkies will get another fix if they order the car in Rosso Mondiale (it also comes in grey and black): this was the racing colour that graced the works Formula One 250Fs of the 1950s.

So Maserati is stirring our emotions – but there's more to this car than cosmetics and a couple of badges adorning the interior. In an effort to distance the AC from the 3200 GT, Maserati has lowered the suspension by 15mm and fitted stiffer springs and dampers, and a beefier front anti-roll bar. We've said before that the standard car's ride was more than firm enough, so it seems a strange move.

The wheel and tyre sizes are unchanged from the standard 3200 GT's, but sexy new 15-spoke alloys and softer-compound Pirelli P-Zero Corsa tyres are there to improve grip while also adding glamour to a shape that can look awkward from some angles.

There's no change in power, as if the Assetto Corsa actually needs it: 370bhp at 6000rpm and 362lb ft of torque at 4500rpm are the headline figures.

We've talked a lot about how the 3200 GT has come of age in the past year – it has enjoyed significant improvements in steering and throttle response. So the Assetto Corsa should move the game further still. In reality, there's still not enough feedback just off the straight ahead to inspire supercar levels of feedback. And despite the fettling, fast A- and B-road work still exposes the rack's shortcomings: it's just not communicative enough and doesn't inspire confidence.

What you get is grip – and plenty of it. Most of the 400 test miles we drove was on wet and sometimes icy secondary roads where the AC produced levels of adhesion you'd normally experience in the dry. Enter a bend too fast, and – as long as you're off the throttle – mild understeer is as bad as it'll get.

Here's the problem, though: a combination of relatively stiff rear suspension and nigh-on 400 horses flooding from the rear wheels can be a fearsome thing. Once those 265/35 rears get a whiff of twin-turbo power in a bend, they'll snap from under you with hilarious ease – and

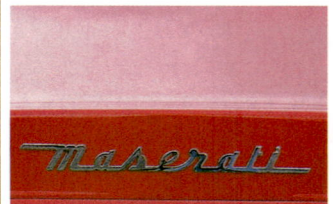   

Rosso Mondiale one of three colour options; grip superb, especially in the wet; 18in alloys wear Pirelli rubber; last stand for 3.2-litre V8

PHILIP RUSSELL

Factfile

Maserati build quality now up to German levels; seats as confortable as they look, even for rear adults

there's no stability programme to help you out, just a basic and surprisingly ineffective traction control arrangement. You'd better hope the rubber's warm, as well. These are Cup tyres, which fall somewhere between a road and competition compound, and need a sound thrashing before they get sticky.

Dynamically, the rest is a mixed bag. Body composure over a variety of surfaces is excellent, and stability at 60 or 150mph is peerless. But the ride is stiff, verging on harsh, whatever the road. Drive this Maser fast enough and you'll find that it cannot cope with cats-eyes or small ruts – it simply skates over them, banging and crashing as it goes. This, combined with the tyre's tendency to seek out cambers and white lines, can call for a great deal of concentration at speed.

And the speed is profligate. Maserati quotes 5.7sec for the 0-60mph sprint and when we tested the standard car last year we managed a top speed of 155mph (not governed) and 14.7sec to 100mph. The 0-100mph figure actually feels pessimistic, such is the generosity of thrust you get at 5000rpm right up to the 6500rpm redline.

Throttle response is instantaneous, and there's almost no play at the top of the pedal's travel. This is fine for fast road work, but annoying through towns where the merest brush with your right foot has the thing surging learner-style. In contrast, the brake pedal feels mushy, though the brakes themselves have harder-compound pads than standard and are nothing short of awesome, wet or dry.

When we drove the six-speed manual

"Snap it up if you want more raw than bore"

version of the Assetto Corsa earlier this year we complained of drive-line shunt at low speeds. This may be the reason that the UK importer opted to bring in the four-speed auto instead, made by Australian firm BTR. It's reasonably smooth on up-changes and – in Sport mode – complements enthusiastic driving by changing down abnormally early

before bends. But many will be frustrated that there's no semi-automatic mode and, at a time when BMW has just launched its own six-speed auto, four ratios are no longer enough.

Nonetheless, an auto does suit the engine's demeanour. Sit inside and you can quite happily imagine taking on a transcontinental mission. Swathes of black leather and red piping mix with carbonfibre trim to create a traditional Italian supercar interior, albeit one with decent ergonomics and Germanic build quality. There are two nicely upholstered bucket seats in the back, and unlike many other cars of this ilk, they are actually comfortable for adults.

Decision time. At £67,950, Maserati is asking £7k more than it does for the 3200 GT – or £2k less if you pick the manual car. For just over £56,000, however, you could have either the Jaguar XKR coupé or a Porsche 911 Carrera, both of which would leave your spine intact and blend nicely into the British roadscape. But if you want a budget Ferrari that is more raw than bore, then plunge in and snap up the Assetto Corsa. Few cars feel so special for the money. Or require so much driver input.
Simon Hucknall

MASERATI 3200 GT ASSETTO CORSA

How much?	£67950
On sale in UK	Now
How fast?	
0-60mph	5.7sec
Top speed	155mph
How thirsty?	
Urban	11.2mpg (est)
Extra urban	24.4mpg (est)
Combined	17.0mpg (est)
CO_2	422g/km
How big?	
Length	4510mm
Width	1822mm
Height	1305mm
Wheelbase	2660mm
Weight	1580kg
Fuel tank	90 litres

Engine
Layout 8 cyls in vee, 3217cc
Max power 370bhp at 6000rpm
Max torque 362lb ft at 4500rpm
Installation Front, longitudinal, rear wheel drive
Bore/stroke 80.0/80.0mm
Made of Alloy heads and block
Compression ratio 8.0:1
Valve gear 4 per cylinder, dohc
Ignition & fuel Electronic fuel injection, twin IHI turbochargers

Gearbox
Type 4-speed automatic by BTR
Ratios/mph per 1000rpm
1st 2.39/8.1 **2nd** 1.45/13.3
3rd 1.00/19.3 **4th** 0.68/28.3
Final drive 3.91

Suspension
Front Double wishbones, coil springs, anti-roll bar, adaptive damping
Rear Double wishbones, coil springs, anti-roll bar, adaptive damping

Steering
Type Rack and pinion, power assisted
Lock to lock 2.7 turns

Brakes
Front 300mm ventilated, cross-drilled discs
Rear 310mm cross-drilled discs
Anti-lock Standard

Wheels and tyres
Size 8Jx18in (f), 9.5Jx18in (r)
Made of Alloy
Tyres 235/40 ZR18 (f), 265/35 ZR18 (r) Pirelli P Zero Corsa
All figures are manufacturer's claims

THE AUTOCAR VERDICT

Hard-edged special edition of the 3200 GT delivers thrills and exclusivity in equal amounts. But harsh ride needs refining

Assetto Corsa sits 15mm lower than standard GT; looks as fearsome standing still as it does on the move

MODENA, Italy—Old rivals, hardened from decades of battle on the racetrack and in the marketplace, laid down their swords when Ferrari purchased Maserati in September of 1997. This March, the storied marque with the trident logo makes its return to U.S. with the 2-seat Spyder after an 11-year absence.

The new Maserati profits heavily from synergies with Ferrari on engineering, production and distribution fronts, though Ferrari chairman Luca di Montezemolo was quick to point out the differences: "If you want an extreme car—extreme in terms of drive, performance, design—you have to buy a Ferrari. If you want a sports-car attitude, GT, more comfortable, not extreme but sport, you have to buy a Maserati." At which point he urges the waiters at Il Cavallino, the famous *trattoria* on Ferrari's Maranello grounds, to speed up delivery of pasta and truffles. "I'm talking about a sports car, and we have to show that even in the kitchen we have a sports car!"

Built in a thoroughly modern factory—inside the original brick structure that was Maserati's Modena home after its move from Bologna in 1939—the Spyder is a serious performance car that uses the 3200 GT as a jump-off point. From that base, much has been changed, starting with an all-new 4.2-liter 90-degree V-8 that's 1.2 in. shorter and 44 lb. lighter than the 3200 GT's engine, despite an additional *liter* of displacement. Lubrication of the aluminum/silicon engine is via dry sump, and the Formula 1 experience shows with three scavenge pumps and one pressure pump, packaged with the water pump, in a neat bundle on the side of the engine. Roller chains drive four camshafts, the intakes under the control of a variable timing system, actuating four valves per cylinder via bucket tappets with built-in lash adjusters. Output is an impressive 390 bhp at 7000 rpm, with peak torque of 333 lb.-ft. at 4500 rpm.

Drive is taken through a small-diameter twin-disc clutch, and then through a driveshaft running in a torque tube that rigidly connects the bellhousing to the rear-mounted 6-speed transaxle. And that's where Cambiocorsa (Italian for "race change") comes into play. Developed by Magneti-Marelli and fine-tuned by Maserati, the system uses twin paddles behind the steering wheel for hydraulically actuated shifts in 0.25 second (the actual gearchange, without the clutching and de-clutching, takes place in a scant 80 milliseconds). A conventional 6-speed transaxle will also be available in the Spyder GT.

A tour of the assembly line allowed us to view the entire drivetrain before it was mated to the chassis, complete with steel subframes to which elegant aluminum links and forged aluminum hub carriers attach. A large Brembo brake disc and 4-piston fixed caliper caps off each double-wishbone corner. There are a suspiciously large number of electrical leads coming off each front hub—the usual ABS wheel-speed sensor, perhaps one for brake pad wear—but the third lead is for an accelerometer for the Skyhook adjustable damping system. With a total

Maserati
SPYDER
CAMBIOCORSA

A great marque restored

BY DOUGLAS KOTT

■ A new 4.2-liter 390-bhp V-8 uses dry-sump oiling, pulls like a freight train, and incorporates lessons learned from Formula 1; immaculately stitched interior conveys emotion of Italian motoring.

PHOTOS BY THE AUTHOR

of six accelerometers—on the body, each front hub and the right rear strut—the system's computer can compare the motions of both chassis and suspension and quickly adjust the damping accordingly. A console-mounted switch gives the options of Normal and Sport baselines, settings that also affect shifting aggressiveness.

The suspension proved quite capable as we tackled the narrow roads that took us over the Futa and Raticosa passes south of Bologna, part of the original Mille Miglia route. Roughly the size of a Porsche Boxster but significantly heavier (curb weight is a stout 3815 lb.), the Spyder has a sense of heft but also of agility, heightened by steering effort lighter than that of any Ferrari.

Helped by a 53/47 front/rear weight balance, the Spyder takes a cornering set with mild understeer and can be pushed quite hard before there are squeals of protest from the ample tires (either

Pirelli P Zero or Michelin Pilot Sport, 235/40ZR-18 front, 265/35ZR-18 rear). The only real hindrance comes from the really stout A-pillars that block the view considerably entering tight-radius corners. Overall, this is an easy, secure car to drive quickly; the learning curve to approach its limits is quickly climbed.

The interior is quite roomy in most directions, though the long-legged may wish for more rearward seat travel. The dash is an expressive double arch, done in two colors of leather of your choice (10 choices) with contrasting piping separating the two. Logical rotary knobs with silver backgrounds control the ventilation functions, a scheme mirrored in the black-in-silver gauge faces, with a big red pie-wedge marking on the tach denoting the 7500-rpm redline. The ubiquitous display screen occupies a good piece of the center dash, offering navigation system functions and illustrating the ventilation

control settings. Of course, the traditional Maserati oval clock takes center stage.

Actuation of the convertible top couldn't be simpler, with a single button controlling the entire operation, including the final, automatic cinching to the windshield header. When stowed, it's concealed with a hard cover that fits flush to the Giugiaro-styled body. Top down, airflow is managed quite nicely, with normal conversation possible at 80; briefly touching about 150 mph, my baseball cap stayed on! Of course, the muted metallic rasp of the engine is best heard in the top-down mode.

As a package, the Maserati Spyder (roughly $89,000 for the conventional 6-speed, and $93,000 for the Cambiocorsa) is an extremely well executed car, and an appealing alternative to the Porsche 911, Mercedes-Benz SL or Jaguar XKR. It should equal or better those cars in performance; I've no reason to doubt claims of 4.9 seconds to 60 mph, or a 175-mph top speed. And judging from the ultramodern factory, the assembly fit of our test cars and Maserati's chutzpah of offering a 4-year, 50,000-mile warranty in the U.S., these should easily be the most reliable Maseratis ever. 🔱

Heart of the Maser

Maserati's Coupe has had some mild cosmetic surgery, but it's the new 4.2-litre normally aspirated V8 that makes the 4200GT special ➲

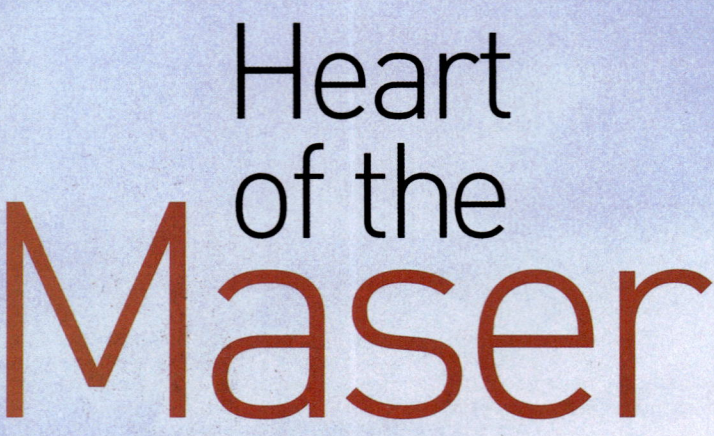

In these days of systematic, cost-controlled, safety-conscious, customer-cosseting car design, the specification is God. In 90 per cent of cases, how a car drives and sounds by the time the first prototype actually turns a wheel has been predicted a thousand times by a couple of million lines of computer code. It's true of some of the most revered **evo**-cars whose on-paper performance is dazzling, even if the smile they leave on your face is sometimes not. In the search for textbook ride, handling and performance, even the best occasionally miss the point.

Spend a few hours with the people from Maserati, now well into the swing of Ferrari ownership since the takeover from De Tomaso in 1997, and you get the distinct feeling that when it came to designing the replacement for the 3200GT, no computer was going to stand in the way of upholding traditional Italian values. Maserati people will politely go through the motions of presentations and diligently tell you all the regulation stuff. That torsional stiffness of the steel bodyshell has been improved by 15 per cent compared with the old car, that changes have been made to comply with European and US safety regulations and that the Skyhook electronic damping system is controlled by six lateral and vertical sensors.

But although their heads may be wrapped up in the task of operating an overhead projector, their hearts are still half way around Ferrari's Fiorano test track posting another quick lap.

That morning, we'd pointed the Maser's nose north west from Rome on a mixture of indifferently surfaced motorways and rural back-roads. First impressions were that the four-seat coupe felt less agile than the Spyder whose wheelbase is shorter by a full 220mm. On the launch of the Spyder last year, retracing part of the Mille Miglia route from Bologna, charging deep into corners, while flicking down through the Cambiocorsa gearbox and steering with the throttle on the way out, proved a cinch. Even better were the tight rhythmic sequences of bends where the Spyder's polite oversteer on the limit leaves you lusting for the next opportunity.

Under the skin, the Coupe has exactly the same suspension as the Spyder, with double wishbones and forged alloy arms and hubs. The 18in alloys (8J front and 9.5J rear) are clad with 235/40 and 265/35 ZR Michelin Pilot Sports. Braking is by Brembo (who else?). Monster discs, 330mm at the front and 310mm at the rear, are equipped with lightweight four-pot callipers and Ferodo HP1000 pads for ferocious

Deep, richly upholstered seats comfortable and supportive, even during hard cornering. Steering wheel reach / rake adjustable

Left: 4200GT can be hustled around corners with vigour, this car fitted with the optional Skyhook adaptive damping. Switches for Cambiocorsa semi-manual gearbox selector (above) sit below air-con controls and new, integrated 'info centre' stereo and (optional) sat-nav screen. Glorious 4.2-litre naturally aspirated V8 (right) has plenty of power and a spine-tingling soundtrack. Maserati claims its design is based on 'experience gained from the Ferrari F1 engine'. Hmmm

stopping power and a great pedal feel.

There are two choices of suspension systems, either conventional springs and dampers or the Mannesman-Sachs-developed Skyhook electronic variable damping. The Skyhook system uses accelerometers to compare wheel and body movements before adjusting in a nanosecond to an appropriate setting, and all test cars, both Spyder and Coupe, have so far been fitted with it. It has sport or comfort settings linked to the Cambiocorsa gearbox and traction control so that they too can change their spots according to your mood.

In sport mode, the worst surfaces we encountered set wheels pattering and even prompted the odd wiggle and squirm of the tail now and then. On the twisty stuff, which on the day had assumed a lethal-looking sheen thanks to a Spring shower, the 4200GT proved willing enough to swipe its tail out if hustled, the merest sniff at the throttle feeding a mountain of torque to the rear wheels. That liveliness is partly to do with the fact that traction control is backed-off in sport mode. The steering is satisfyingly beefy, loading up nicely as you get away from the straight ahead.

The ride is hardly blancmange-like, even with the sport button switched out, and if anything the chassis feels a tad over-sprung and under-damped. Indeed, the engineers say damping has been wound back compared with the Spyder to improve traction and that may be why that feeling of total commitment, which the Spyder invites, seems elusive at first.

But then this is a thoroughbred and, in equestrian circles at least, conventional wisdom has it that a little temperament goes hand in

hand with ballistic performance. And, yes, the performance is ballistic.

The Ferrari-built 4.2-litre, 90-degree V8 is simply a masterpiece. It has been designed, says powertrain engineer Mauro Rioli, 'drawing on experience gained from the Ferrari F1 engine'. The engine is dry-sumped, allowing the crankcase – made from tempered aluminium – to be 90mm shallower than that of the old engine. There's a tempered forged-steel crank and at the top end four cams with variable timing on the inlets, four valves per cylinder, and a drive-by-wire throttle. Maximum power of 390bhp is at 7000rpm but the short-stroke

V8 will happily wail all the way to 7500rpm and beyond. Nuff said.

At the rear sits the new six-speed transaxle gearbox which, like the engine, is shared with the Spyder and will eventually come with a manual shift as well as the Cambiocorsa system. Both engine and gearbox are next generation technologies, effectively one step ahead of anything at Ferrari, and it shows. Like all automated manuals, this one has proved controversial even though it is one of the most advanced in the world. So let's set the record straight – it is fast. Manufacturers often say a 'box like this will shift as fast as a human but

From this angle the new coupe is pretty much identical to the old 3200GT. It's still a handsome-looking car, especially at the front

don't take into account that since the human isn't doing anything (like working the clutch and gearlever) their senses perceive the robot shift to be slow. But in sport mode, the Cambiocorsa is positively brutal. With right foot buried in the carpet and neck muscles screaming submission, flicking the right paddle summons an almost instantaneous shift.

When it happens the clunk is violent enough to squeeze tears from the eyes of anyone with an ounce of mechanical sympathy. Want it smoother? Then learn the art of subtle throttle control between shifts just as you would with a manual. You won't get it overnight anymore than you'd beat Schumacher's lap time on a PlayStation 2, because it takes practice and

more kilometres than we were allowed. But if it's sheer shifting speed you want, you've got it. Benefits? It's fun for one thing and the sound of the V8 at full tilt catching its breath as the electronic throttle snaps shut for a millisecond, needs to be heard. Another is the way you can pile deep into a corner grabbing a late shift exactly when you want it, left foot jammed against the footrest and both hands on the wheel keeping steering inputs nice and smooth. When you hit the traffic, fully automatic mode can be had at the press of a button.

The driving position is great. Deep, electrically adjustable seats combine with a wheel that moves for rake and reach, and tucked away in the binnacle are a classic-looking set of instruments complete with Jaeger logos. Rear seats will just about take a couple of adults too – one of the things that attracts buyers most,

according to Maserati UK. All in, it's a damn fine office in which to go to work. It isn't claustrophobic and there's enough support to stop you rattling around as the Maser explodes out of corners, hitting 62mph in 4.9 seconds and rampaging over the quarter mile in 13

If the Maser's engine was running it'd sound sweet, even at rest. Sadly, this being a magazine, you couldn't hear it even if it was. Sorry

seconds. There's none of that namby-pamby rev limiter business either – keep your foot in and you can expect to see 177mph at 7750rpm.

And the looks? Well, those odd-looking eyebrow rear lights which some people liked but which others – including the majority of Americans quizzed at research clinics and a number of senior people at the factory – didn't, have been ditched in favour of the more conventional units debuted on the Spyder. Finish is lustrous, shut lines well up to scratch and the interior lusciously finished in soft leather. If you find the lighter shades a little too Sunset Boulevard there are deeper colours including a dark red which, when matched with a gunmetal exterior, conjures up images of a latter-day E-type Jaguar.

The outgoing 3200GT manual costs £60,950 and this one, on sale in the UK on May 24, will cost between £62,000 and £65,000, with the Cambiocorsa shift costing another £3000 on top. Maserati expects to pinch customers from the Mercedes SL, Porsche 911 and Jaguar XKR, their decision helped in part by the useable rear seats. Should they defect, they'll find the new Coupe surprising, not least because it's such a complex beast. It has a character whose depths will not be plumbed at the first meeting, unlike some from whom you can walk away after just a few hours, confident that you've learnt everything there is to know.

It's a proper sports car too, not a gentleman's coupe, and oozes heritage. It has a lot in common with some of the greats. Not because it's flawless, but because to drive it quickly demands concentration. And most of all, because the technology never masks the raw appeal of that sensational engine. ∎

'With right foot buried in the carpet and neck muscles screaming submission, flicking the right paddle summons an almost instantaneous shift'

Wheel-mounted paddle shifters (opposite, top) take some acclimatisation, especially in slightly brutal 'sport' mode. Or you can have a full manual and save around £3000. New tail lights (above), first seen on Spyder, replace 3200GT's unusual 'boomerang' lamps. Americans didn't like them, apparently

Specification

MASERATI 4200GT Cambiocorsa

○ Engine	V8, 90deg V
○ Location	Front, longitudinal
○ Displacement	4244cc
○ Bore x stroke	92mm x 80mm
○ Compression ratio	11.1:1
○ Cylinder block	Aluminium alloy
○ Cylinder head	Aluminium alloy, dohc per bank, four valves per cylinder
○ Fuel and ignition	Bosch ME7.3.2 electronic ignition and multipoint fuel injection
○ Max power	390bhp @ 7000rpm
○ Max torque	333lb ft @ 4500rpm
○ Transmission	Transaxle with rear-mounted longitudinal gearbox, semi-manual
○ Suspension	Front and rear: double wishbones and coil springs with Skyhook variable damping (optional)
○ Steering	Rack and pinion, power-assisted
○ Brakes	Brembo ventilated discs. 330mm front, 310mm rear, four-pot callipers, Bosch 5.3 four-channel ABS
○ Wheels	8x18in front, 9.5x18in rear, al alloy
○ Tyres	235/40 ZR18 front, 265/35 ZR18 rear
○ Fuel tank capacity	88 litres/19.4gal
○ Weight (kerb)	1680kg
○ Power-to-weight	236bhp/ton
○ 0-62mph	4.9sec (claimed)
○ Max speed	177mph (claimed)
○ Fuel cons (EC combined)	17.6mpg
○ Insurance group	20
○ Basic price	£62-65,000 (est)
○ On sale (UK)	May 24

evo RATING ★★★★

MASERATI

With a 4.2-liter 390-hp V8 engine providing
active suspension providing the poise, the

FOR MANY DECADES, Maserati and Ferrari locked horns on the
world's racetracks, streets and new car show circuit. When Ferrari
became Maserati's parent in 1997, the equation changed completely.
The question became: Could these two former adversaries exist in a
manner that was beneficial to both?

Spend several days with Maserati's just-launched Spyder, talk with
executives and historic personnel from both companies, and the
answer seems to be a resounding "*Si*!" This fact makes it all the more
ironic that the key to Maserati's success doesn't reside in Italy, but
with Ferrari's dealer network in the all-important American market.

Back on Track

by WINSTON GOODFELLOW
photography by THE AUTHOR

the performance and a sophisticated semi-Spyder shows great promise for Maserati.

From Orsi to Ferrari

As the Spyder is the first Maserati born under Ferrari's tutelage, one wonders whether it is merely an extension of Maranello's philosophy or a true Maserati, a machine that follows in the footsteps of the company's great cars of the 1950s, '60s and '70s?

During those heydays three decades ago, three cars helped define the classic Maserati spyder: the 3500, Mistral and Ghibli. All had a manual transmission as standard equipment, and the latter two had optional automatics. Elegant looks, a robust chassis, power steering, power windows and luxurious interiors rounded out the package.

That could easily describe some Ferraris, so the best way to understand what makes a Maserati a Maserati is to speak with engineer Giulio Alfieri (*SCI #142*). Now in his late 70s, Alfieri joined the company in the early 1950s when he was hired by Maserati padrone Adolfo Orsi. Alfieri became chief engineer in the mid-1950s, a position he held until 1975, when Alejandro De Tomaso purchased the firm from then-owner Citroen.

At the heart of every Alfieri Maserati was a charismatic engine, a fact undoubtedly linked to the way he views them. "The engine is not something that is static, a simple block of steel or aluminum," he says. "It's…something that needs thermodynamic modification…."

But Ferrari and Lamborghini also had alluring powerplants, so what truly differentiated Maserati from its competition? The first word that comes to mind is refinement—Maserati stressed occupant comfort as much as performance.

"(That) was my personal philosophy," Alfieri reflects. "When a man gets in a car, he speaks to it, and the car responds. You must make it so the car replies in relation to the man's wishes, for the man is the guest of the car and I liked the car to be a good host…. The driver must be the king of the car and not vice versa."

After Alfieri left in the mid-1970s, the company's car recipe got altered, a fact that can be traced directly to Maserati's multiple owners and struggle to survive. When the company introduced the Biturbo in the early 1980s, former key employee Giordano Casarini says its specifications and large production numbers were largely dictated by the firm's largest creditor, the Italian government. There was a lot of pressure to make a car that was more affordable. The conservatively styled, twin-turbo solution then served as the basis for most every Maserati well into the early 1990s.

Fiat bought the firm in 1993 then passed control to Ferrari in 1997. Maserati was already returning to its exclusive, performance-oriented roots, but the 3200 GT then under development was not up to Maranello's build quality and engineering standards. The model's launch was delayed a year but since then it has been nothing but good news. Outside the Biturbo and its derivatives, the 3200 is Maserati's best-selling model by a substantial margin.

Still, if the 170-mph coupe had a short-coming that held it back from joining the pantheon of Maserati greats, it was driving refinement. With its woolly twin-turbo V8's 370 horses coupled to a six-speed manual, smooth, effortless driving was a near impossibility. Its instantaneous power-on/power-off delivery would have made Alfieri wince, for the 3200 was king, not the driver—exhilarating to drive but a real handful, particularly in the wet.

Ingredients for Success

That, then, brings us to the current Spyder. To get an idea of how seriously Ferrari is taking this new car and the company's future, look no further than Maserati's historic works. In the same location in downtown Modena since 1939, the facilities are undergoing a massive expansion. An eight-story building is being erected near the front entrance, and the factory and production lines were completely gutted and retooled.

Inside those historic brick walls is an operation former Maserati owner Adolfo Orsi would have a difficult time recognizing. While there is still much hand assembly, the U-shaped production line is a combination of new and traditional techniques. On the line's first stages the cars move via a sophisticated overhead trolley, while the last stations use a conveyer.

Quality is closely monitored throughout the work process rather than only at the end, as was traditional Modenese practice. When a car is completed, it is taken to a final inspection area in another building. Each car is then subjected to a vibration bench test, as well as a 50-70 mile test drive.

Seventy workers man the 26 assembly stations sprinkled along the 200 meter-long production line. Everywhere you look the factory is spotless, airy and well lit. Current plant capacity is ten cars a day. During my visit in mid-November, the line was dominated by the Spyder but had a sprinkling of the new coupe, as well. Over the next three years the production facilities will expand and another assembly line will be added, bringing plant capacity to 10,000 cars per year.

Like the original 3200 GT on which it is based, the Spyder's styling is the work of Italdesign-Giugiaro, with Giorgetto Giugiaro and son Fabrizio overseeing the car's actual design.

"The Spyder is somewhat unusual in that we mostly worked with a full-scale model," Fabrizio says. "The first sketches were done with a photo rendering, and that revealed the coupe was much too long to transform into a spyder. After talking with (Ferrari/Maserati CEO Luca Cordero di) Montezemolo and others in Maserati's management, the decision was made to shorten the car. That changed everything."

The design and engineering team made the most of the opportunity. The wheelbase was reduced 8.7 inches to 96 inches, and the front end was subtly altered; it now has two small cut lines between the hood and grille, giving the front a more muscular and chiseled, but cleaner, appearance. The grille and valence pan were also smartly and carefully massaged, and a proper Maserati badge now resides on the nose (the 3200 GT had none).

The rear wheel arches and the shoulders,above them were also altered and the rear taillights were changed from the 3200's distinctive boomerang shape to a more traditional cluster. Fixed-hoop roll bars reside behind the seats, and offer rollover protection.

The top follows the 360 Spider's lead in being completely automated. Like the Ferrari, a switch in the interior causes the top to uncouple from the windshield frame and completely disappear into a compartment behind the passengers. The solution is more elegant and much simpler to use than the hood found on Aston's more expensive Volante.

The chassis is a stress-bearing steel platform that has a tubular superstructure integrated into the front. Not only were the engineers concerned with maximizing torsional and flexional stiffness, but front and lateral crash and rollover protection as well.

The front and rear suspensions use double wishbones made of aluminum, coil-over springs and anti-roll bars. Both have anti-dive and anti-squat geometry.

Optional (and heavily promoted by Maserati) is its Skyhook suspension system. Designed and engineered in conjunction with Mannesmann-Sachs, Skyhook is able to instantly optimize each shock's stiffness. The driver can choose normal or sport characteristics by actuating controls in the driver's compartment. To ensure maximum safety, Skyhook works in conjunction with the car's ABS, ASR (electronic traction control) and engine management systems. ASR also has normal and sport modes, and can be switched off by the driver.

Below, left to right: Spyder's interior is luxurious and all-day comfortable, yet sporty; restyled front end is more muscular and cleaner than the 3200 GT's; Cambiocorsa paddles are covered in pseudo-suede.

And like the Maseratis of the Golden Years, at the heart of the Spyder is a normally aspirated V8. The block and heads on this all-new 4,244-cc engine are made of aluminum and silicon alloy; the crankshaft is forged, refined steel. The double-overhead cams actuate four valves per cylinder and, in a break with most every modern engine, are driven by chains rather than belts. The engine produces 390 horsepower at 7,000 rpm.

Two transmissions are available: a six-speed manual and an F1-style paddle-shift Maserati calls Cambiocorsa. The longitudinally mounted gearbox is placed at the rear for optimal weight distribution.

Alfieri Should Be Pleased

The instant you slip behind the wheel it is clear Maserati has resuscitated the recipe that made it Modena's best-selling marque through much of the 1960s. The leather-dominated interior is sporty and luxurious, intimate and friendly. The electronically adjustable seats are tall and though there is minimal bolstering, they comfortably hold you in place. Legroom is just a little short for those large of frame, but most everyone should be able to get comfy.

The handsome dash is clearly legible, and is dominated by a 320-km/h speedometer and a tachometer that reads to 8,000; the redline is at 7,500. The traditional Maserati clock resides in the center of the dash, above the supplemental controls and between two air vents.

Our bright yellow test car had the Cambiocorsa transmission. Just behind the wheel are two paddles. The one on the right is for upshifts; the left for downshifts. The back of each is covered with a deliciously soft Alcantara-type material.

Reverse is actuated by a small black tee handle in the center console.

The engine fires quickly and even at idle makes a lovely, soothing symphony that is both intricate and involving. Alfieri would undoubtedly like this car, for the tractable V8 has gobs of torque down low. Refined and smooth, it will happily potter along at 1,500 rpm (or lower) then seamlessly provide warp-drive thrust the instant you dab the throttle. The higher the tach twists the better it feels, the energy and pulling power seem to increase exponentially with every 1,000 rpm.

Maserati claims 0-60 takes less than five seconds, and the quarter mile is covered in 13.3. Top speed is listed at 176 mph, making the massive ventilated Brembo discs a necessity.

And while the acceleration the engine provides is undoubtedly exhilarating, the V8's coupe de grace is the way it sounds.

Unlike Ferrari's V8-powered 360, the motor in the Spyder dominates the car's soundtrack. In this day of muted engines in which the exhaust is all you basically hear, the Spyder's orchestra of whirring cams, valves and, most importantly, metal chains is an absolute auditory delight. The only current production car that sounds this good is Lamborghini's Murciélago.

In normal mode, our Spyder's Cambiocorsa system seemed a bit lazy when shifting—smooth, but slow. As you'd expect, switching to sport mode sped up the shifts at the cost of smoothness. More troublesome was the smell of a burning clutch in stop-and-go driving that led us to question the system's longevity. Fortunately, Maserati is confidently offering U.S. buyers a 4-year/50,000-mile warranty. Still, I would order the standard six-speed manual, for shifting yourself is much more fun and involving than flicking a paddle.

The steering's directness and the rigid chassis feel make the Spyder an agile performer. While body lean is noticeable in normal mode, it is minimized in sport. Push this Maserati into corners and the central ECU works its magic. The suspension automatically tightens up, reacting seamlessly to a more aggressive driving style. While it reduces body roll as anticipated, it also does a lovely job of dishing out an excellent compromise between stiffness and comfort.

At 100+ mph this Maserati is truly in its element. Flick the left paddle twice and it quickly drops into fourth, plant the pedal on the metal and the Spyder unrelentingly lunges forward. At 130 it is just as stable and comfortable as it is at 80, and nowhere as frenetic as its 3200 GT predecessor.

Shortly after four memorable days with the Spyder, I spent time with three other Giugiaro-designed Maseratis: a Ghibli coupe and Spyder, and a mid-engine Bora. Using those yardsticks, there is no question Maserati's newest has effectively dipped into its deep gene pool. Comfortable and easy to drive, invigorating when you want it to be, the Spyder could be used every day.

And though that fabulous charismatic engine is undoubtedly the model's centerpiece, the car's manners are relaxed and assured, not frenetic and edgy like a Ferrari's. It is a fun, fast machine that the driver can easily control—the good host Alfieri always targeted.

The Crux of the Matter

Maserati has successfully combined civility with the right amount of brio to make an attractive and distinctive marketplace alternative. The Spyder also has the exclusivity and a corporate pedigree most every other manufacturer would kill for. Ferrari's seriousness about the whole effort is very reassuring, seeing how many times since 1973 Maserati promised then failed to deliver under its previous, pre-Fiat owners.

But everything Maserati has accomplished to date will go for naught if the sales organization on this side of the Atlantic doesn't perform. Though I have never bought a new Ferrari, I know numerous people who have and can't name one that holds their dealer up as the paragon of excellence in sales and customer service. This point is key, because most every Maserati will be bought at a Ferrari dealership.

Maserati stands on the brink of a massive expansion. The new Spyder and Coupe could herald the beginning of a new Golden Era, one that could easily rival and outlast the memorable Orsi/Alfieri years. Or it could be the beginning of a disaster, one that would make the quality and reliability issues that caused Maserati to leave America ten-plus years ago seem like child's play.

The difference this time around is there is no second chance—Maserati either sinks or swims. For the first time since the early 1970s, the product and factory have clearly done their part, and they should be rewarded for their efforts with marketplace success. That makes it all the more ironic that the firm's fate rests not in Italy but squarely in the hands of its dealers and sales personnel several thousand miles away. ●

SPECIFICATIONS

2002 Maserati Spyder

GENERAL

VEHICLE TYPE	Front-engine, RWD 2-door convertible
STRUCTURE	Steel unibody
MARKET AS TESTED	Europe
MSRP	$89,315

ENGINE

TYPE	V8 with aluminum block and head
DISPLACEMENT (cc)	4244
COMPRESSION RATIO	11.1:1
POWER (bhp)	390 @ 7000 rpm
TORQUE (lb/ft)	326 @ 4500 rpm
INTAKE SYSTEM	EFI
VALVETRAIN	DOHC, 32 valves

TRANSMISSION

TYPE	6-speed manual or Cambiocorsa
FINAL DRIVE	3.73:1

DIMENSIONS

CURB WEIGHT (lbs.)	3814
WHEELBASE (in.)	96
TRACK, F/R (in.)	60.0/60.5
LENGTH (in.)	169.4
WIDTH (in.)	71.7
HEIGHT (in.)	51.4

SUSPENSION, BRAKES, STEERING

SUSPENSION, FRONT	Double wishbones, coil springs, gas shocks with Skyhook variable damping, anti-roll bar
SUSPENSION, REAR	Double wishbones, coil springs, gas shocks with Skyhook variable damping, anti-roll bar
STEERING TYPE	Rack and pinion
WHEELS, F&R	7x18, 9x18 alloy
TIRES, F&R	235/40ZR18, 265/35ZR18
BRAKES, F&R	13.0-inch, 12.2-inch vented discs
ABS	Standard

PERFORMANCE

0-62 MPH (sec.)	5.0
TOP SPEED (mph)	176

CONTACT	www.maserati.it

STORY **Ged Bulmer** PHOTOS **Guido Napporo**

TRIDENT
TRUE

Maserati is back, and how. A sensational engine, revised
dynamics and a tougher look point to $200,000 well spent

Antonia Ferreira de Almeida waves in our direction as he turns the gun-metal coupe into the narrow piazza. It's lunchtime in Tuscanina and nothing disturbs the peace of the small village, apart from the murmur of conversation and the clink of coffee cups.

Then Almeida guns it.

Eight throttle bodies crack wide open and 451 Nm screws urgently rearwards. The noise from the Ferrari-built V8 rises in intensity, from a muscular rumble to an angry, barking salute. The Maser fishtails, right, then left, then straightens as the fat Michelins finally grip the shiny cobbles. Then it's gone, leaving the V8's symphony reverberating off the village walls walls long after it has disappeared out of sight.

You've got to love the Italians, with their lust for life and their healthy disregard for authority. It's something many Aussies readily identify with. It was once described to me by a German colleague thus: "The Italians trade in rules for feeling."

De Almeida, a flamboyant Portugese national is Maserati's head of public relations. He loves the job and the Maserarti brand with a Mediterranean passion, and his impromptu burnout was just his way of saying, "I'm excited!". And he did it with a good deal more style and flair than our own Big Kev could muster.

Over lunch, he explained that, "It's hard to respect the limits when you have a Maserati on your hands."

I knew this because my German co-pilot and I had spent the morning strafing the sinuous back-roads that criss-cross the hills and valleys around Tuscanina,

which is just outside Rome. We'd already had a chance to savour the delicious note from the Maserati Coupe's new 4.2-litre V8. It's a glorious piece of work, which we'll see here shortly for the first time in the just released Maserati Spyder (convertible).

But while the Spyder is an all-new model, the Coupe is an update of the existing 3200 GT. It's a pretty significant update, mind you, comprising a new suspension system, trick new F1-inspired gearbox, and superior weight distribution in addition to the new engine.

About the only thing that's not significantly altered is the styling. The original Italdesign-Giugiaro-penned form is still very much intact, the most obvious change being to the rear tail-lights, which have morphed into a more conventional triangular shape. But look closer and you'll see the bonnet is also new; all the better to house that stonking new V8.

The two model lineup will be known as the Coupe GT, (the conventional six-speed manual variant) and the Maserati Coupe Cambiocorsa ('racechange'), which is equipped with a Ferrari-developed, clutchless manual gearbox, complete with paddle shift operation.

The Coupe GT and the Coupe Cambiocorsa will be priced at $205,000 and $218,000 when they go on sale here in October. Maserati expects some 60 per cent of the 3500 Spyders and Coupes it will build in 2002 will be equipped with the new gearbox.

Cambiocorsa basically gives a driver the choice between driving the Coupe as a sporty manual gearbox, sans clutch, or as a fully automatic unit. In both cases the clutch is engaged and disengaged automatically, but if you choose to do the work yourself, gears are selected via paddles mounted behind the steeering wheel. There's a range of different settings for the gearbox, including Normal, Sport, Full Auto and Low Grip.

The shifts in Sport mode are lightening fast but also reasonably harsh, unless you make the effort to lift at the point where you're upshifting, just as you would in a conventional manual.

Like most of these systems we've experienced, the gearbox is at its best when being driven purposefully. Around town

It does a lap of the Fiorano test track
six seconds quicker than the old jigger

Quad pipes are
familiar, double
decker taillights
are not

it's quite acceptable, but the selector mechanism does clunk and carry on a bit when downshifting through several ratios in auto mode.

The real beauty of the paddle shift is that you can grab a gear up or down the 'box whenever you like, without ever taking your hand off the wheel. While it may not be the preferred driving style of purists, who would say you should be in the right gear *before* you commit to the corner, with Cambiocorsa if you muff a shift, you just right the wrong and and get on the noise again.

Once you've taken in some of the niceties this particular piece of Italian exotica has to offer, the mind, eye and ear wanders to what lies beneath the re-sculptured bonnet. It's a 90 degree, 4.2-litre V8, built at Ferrari's Modena plant. Despite displacing a larger capacity than the superseded V8 in the 3200 GT, the new engine is three centimetres shorter and 20 kg lighter, so weight distribution is better. All-alloy construction, chain-driven twin overhead camshafts per bank and four valves per cylinder are all de rigeur for a modern V8, but there's also plenty of trick bits, including a five-bearing crank, dry sump lubrication, and variable valve timing on the intake side of the cylinder head.

Net result? A thoroughly respectable 287 kW at 7000 rpm and 451 Nm at 4500 rpm, working on a kerb weight of 1570 kg. Claimed performance is 0-100 km/h in 4.9 seconds, 0-1000 metres in 23.5 seconds, top speed of 285 km/h, and a hot lap of Fiorano a full six seconds quicker than the old jigger.

Tickle the thin pedal and there's the sort of instantaneous, cracking throttle response available that wasn't in evidence with the laggy, twin turbocharged 3200 GT. Put that down to a low-inertia flywheel that weighs just a quarter of the old engine's flywheel,

and some good old Ferrari engine know-how.

The power delivery is smoother and far more progressive, too, without the awkward peaks and troughs that characterise the blown engine. The tacho needle gallops around the dial as the engine exhibits a clean-revving willingness all the way to its 7500 rpm cut-out, laying down a deliciously aggressive soundtrack en route.

At 160 km/h in sixth gear the engine is sitting bang on 4000 rpm; at 200 km/h it's a smidge under 5000 rpm, right in the meat of its torque curve and eager to go on with the job. Put the foot down at this speed and the Maser leaps forward, eager to kiss the redline.

The steering is quick and accurate, with excellent weighting. There's no shortage of grip from the Michelin rubber while Brembo cross-drilled discs clamped by four-piston calipers provide reassuring stopping power.

The handling is overwhelmingly predictable, thanks to two per cent better mass distribution over the rear axle, which endows the Coupe with close to perfect 50/50 weight distribution. The lighter engine plays a part, but

Suspension revisions work in harmony with stiffer bodyshell

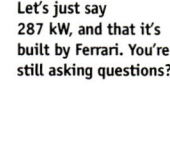

Let's just say 287 kW, and that it's built by Ferrari. You're still asking questions?

Bulmer's inability to separate darks and lights resulted in one mess of pink shirts

It's a package that should have Jaguar and Porsche worried

FAST FACTS

body	two-door coupe
drive	rear-wheel
engine	front-mounted 4.2-litre, 32-valve, DOHC V8
power	287 kW @ 7000 rpm
torque	451 Nm @ 4500 rpm
compression ratio	11.1:1
bore x stroke	92.0 mm x 80.0 mm
weight	1580 kg
weight/power	5.51 kg/kW
specific power	68.3 kW/litre
transmission	six-speed manual
final drive	3.73:1
suspension	double wishbones, coil springs, anti-roll bar (f); double wishbones, coil springs, anti-roll bar (r)
length/width/height	4523/1822/1305 mm
wheelbase	2660 mm
track	1525 mm (f); 1538 mm (r)
brakes	330 mm ventilated discs, four-piston calipers (f); 310 mm ventilated discs, four-piston calipers (r), ABS
wheels	18 x 8-inch (f); 18 x 9.5-inch (r), alloy
tyres	Michelin Pilot Sport, 235/40 ZR18 (f); 265/35 ZR18 (r)
fuel	88 litres, PULP
price	$215,000 (approx.)

there's also a totally new transaxle layout which features a newly-designed longitudinal gearbox at the rear of the car, and an integral self-locking differential.

It's overstating the bleedin' obvious that the Coupe will oversteer at the limits, but those limits are quite high unless you deliberately prode the tiger through the bars. For the most part it's a fairly gentle and predictable understeerer, but just in case you are inclined to provoke things and aren't totally confident in your abilities to bring it back, switchable electronic traction control (ASR) is integrated into the auto gearshift setup.

Underneath a 15 per cent stiffer body is an all-independent suspension that sports revised front and rear anti-roll bar rates, and anti-dive and anti-squat geometry.

All up the new Coupe Cambiocorsa is a pretty impressive package, one that has Maserati and its Ferrari masters brimming with confidence, and should have Porsche and Jaguar a little worried. It's a car that delivers on the emotional front as much as the old car did, but it feels far more convincing from a technical perspective.

Both the Spyder and the Coupe Cambiocorsa herald a remarkable return to form by Maserati. The historic Italian brand is once again building powerful, passionate cars that you can not only get enthused by, but have few qualms recommending. Buyers with a lazy $200k in their pocket would be foolish to write it off. ◪

Many bovines died bringing you this sumptuous interior

"We weel geev Senor Bulmer exactlee wan more meenute to reeturn ze carr. Or I weel keel heem"

Five reasons to find the dough for a Maser

1. The engine note
2. Awesome gearbox
3. The engine note
4. It's cheaper than a Fazza 360
5. The engine note

Bonnet bulge inspired by Falcon AU. Not

MASERATI
Coupe

A modern-day blueprint of the Italian GT

BY SAM MITANI

ALTHOUGH THE SPYDER officially marked the return of Maserati into the U.S. market, the Coupe, arriving in Ferrari/Maserati dealer showrooms in May, is the car I was waiting to drive. Why? Well, aside from the fact that I'm one of the few people in Southern California who prefer fixed-roofed cars over top-down ones, the Coupe boasts better performance than its convertible counterpart, thanks to a lower curb weight of 3675 lb. and a more rigid body structure. And, at $77,175, it is less expensive than the Spyder, at $83,175.

The Coupe, like the Spyder, is powered by a 4.2-liter 90-degree V-8 that produces 390 bhp at 7000 rpm and 330 lb.-ft. of torque at 4500. This 32-valve powerplant is compact in nature and extremely lightweight, mainly because it is constructed of aluminum and silicon alloy. It features variable valve timing on the intake cams, with valve actuation taking less than 0.15 second. This engine supplies gobs of torque all the way from about 1000 rpm to redline. In fact it's so flexible that it'll pull away in 6th gear from about 30 mph. It comes mated to either a 6-speed manual or 6-speed Cambiocorsa (the Formula 1-style paddle-shift system) rear-mounted transaxle.

The car I drove in Italy was equipped with the Cambiocorsa F1 paddle shifter, a $4000 option. And we were given a half-day to put the car through its paces on country roads north of Rome. The first thing you notice about the new Italian coupe is the sound of the engine. It has that distinct Ferrari wail that instinctively forces you to turn the radio down and put your hand over your passenger's mouth.

First gear is engaged by a blip on the right-side paddle. Step on the accelerator pedal and the Coupe leaves the line like a true Italian exotic, with the rear 265/35ZR-18 tires leaving long black streaks on the pavement. As you near redline, another blip on the paddle grabs 2nd gear, and you're treated to a robust forward burst that doesn't let up until you reach the 7600-rpm redline. Maserati claims that the Coupe will run from zero to 60 mph in 4.8 seconds, and to the quarter mile in roughly 13.0.

The Coupe is just as capable on the twisty stuff. The car's suspension system—upper and lower A-arms both front and rear—does a commendable job of providing optimal handling balance with minimal body roll. Of note here is the adaptive damping and acceleration sensors dubbed "Skyhook" that adjust the suspension in response to cornering loads and driving style.

The Maserati drives like a pure-blooded Italian exotic, but you'll be surprised to know that it's a genuine 4-seater. There's enough room in the rear seats for two adults, and the trunk holds a pair of small golf bags. Ride quality is excellent, and the car's cabin remains relatively quiet, with wind noise creeping in at speeds above 75 mph. The interior is plush and comfortable, with leather upholstery on the seats, dash and doors.

The exterior styling is both elegant and sporty. The front features a distinctive grille, with the famed "trident" emblem, and large oval headlights. The rear is highlighted by muscular quarter panels and triangular taillights.

But the best thing about the new Maserati is that it's a true grand tourer—a car that has the performance of a sports car, while being civil enough for everyday commuting. The Italians introduced us to the *Gran Turismo* genre more than 40 years ago, and today they seem to have perfected it in the form of the Maserati Coupe.

■ **A balcony view of the Maserati Coupe reveals its muscular haunches and a roofline generous enough to allow decent rear-seat space.**

AUTOCAR ROAD TEST

MASERATI COUPÉ

Number 4557

Maserati has always been a lesser mortal than its exalted sibling, Ferrari, and lost its way in the Grand Touring class over the past 20 years. Not any more, though

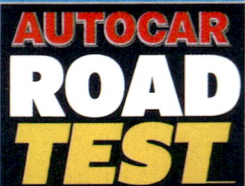

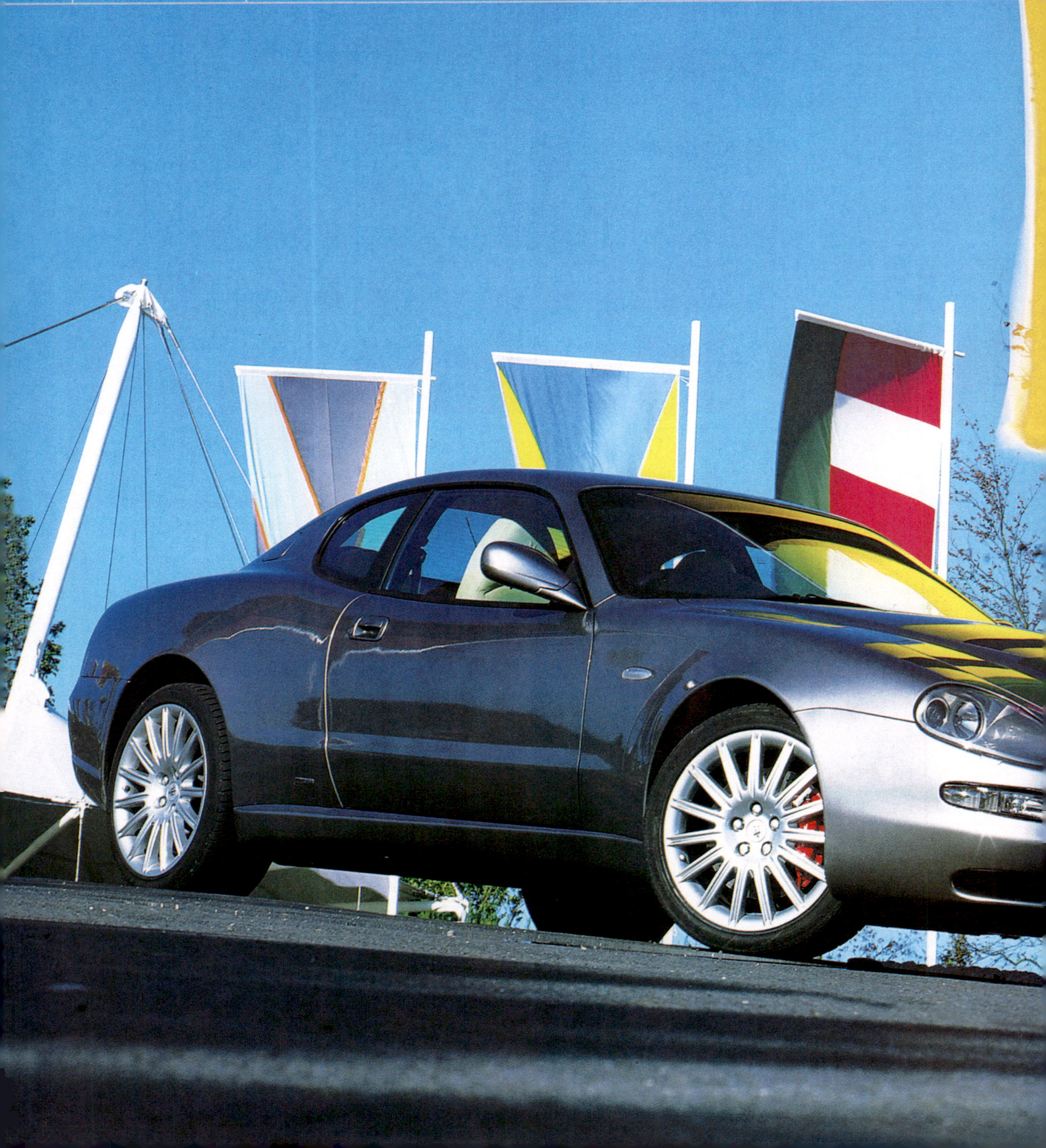

"THE MASERATI COUPÉ MUST PROVE THAT YOU CAN LOOK FURTHER AFIELD THAN STUTTGART FOR A £60K COUPÉ"

If sales volume alone is a fair measure of success, then the outgoing Maserati 3200 GT was pretty much a triumph in the UK: Brits bought 1653 in the three years it was on sale here.

Yet it wasn't an especially polished product, being constantly subject to spec changes, poorly finished and saddled with undeniably exciting but unruly dynamics. The bottom line was simple: the 3200 GT suffered from an identity crisis. It didn't know whether it wanted to be a sports car or plush GT. In the end, it was found wanting in both areas.

The new £59,950 Coupé, however, is much more focused. It wants to be an honest continent crosser in the traditional *Gran Turismo* sense, without sacrificing too much of the excitement associated with the world's best-sounding car name. It also needs to justify Ferrari's substantial financial commitment in resurrecting the Maserati brand, and to prove, at last, that you can look further afield than Stuttgart if there's a £60k Coupé on your shopping list.

DESIGN & ENGINEERING

★★★★★★☆☆☆☆

SAME STYLING HIDES VASTLY IMPROVED UNDERPINNINGS

The underpinnings of the Coupé have been so comprehensively modified that there's a strong argument which says they deserved a fresh set of clothes. Still, the outgoing car never looked stylistically shortchanged.

So apart from the slightly raised bonnet line, the sad demise of the narrow LED rear-light strip, and a heavenly set of new 18in alloys, the car looks little different.

Out goes the turbocharged V8 to be

HISTORY Not one of Maserati's weak points. The '70s were the best – Bora, Merak, Indy, Ghibli and Khasmin were all amazing mid- or front-engined sports cars. De Tomaso took over ownership from bust Citroën and things took a turn for the worse. The Biturbo cars suffered from rust problems and pretty dodgy styling, the last Ghibli was fun but fragile. Ferrari came to the rescue in 1998. More funds arrived, as well as this test car's predecessor, the 3200 GT. At the second attempt, the car was much improved but the ride and auto 'box were still weak points.

replaced by a unit of identical configuration but larger capacity and, this time, it's naturally aspirated. Closely related to Ferrari's own V8 but with a 90deg crank, the new 4244cc unit produces a sizeable 385bhp at 7000rpm and 333lb ft of torque at just 3300rpm. Very big numbers indeed when you consider that a 911 brings only 320bhp to the party.

Space constraints and the quest for perfect weight distribution have pushed the gearbox back next to the rear axle. The transmission itself is an all-new six-speeder offering the choice of manual or hydraulically actuated operation (although the photo car was a paddle shifter called Cambiocorsa). Given the longer set of legs Maserati has given this car, it seems odd that a conventional automatic 'box isn't also available. The test car came with a conventional manual shift.

Braking comes courtesy of the same 330mm front and 310mm rear ventilated discs, but this time they're cross-drilled as well. Uprated pads and larger calliper pistons should improve both deceleration strength and pedal feel.

Comprehensive modifications to the chassis include aluminium componentry, new spring and damper rates and the introduction of a new adaptive damper control – a £990 option called Skyhook – which was fitted to the test car. It has two settings, Sport and Normal, which Maserati hopes will satisfy the comfort and sporting aspirations of all drivers.

The steering rack, arguably the 3200 GT's weakest ingredient, has also been thoroughly revised to ensure a more linear response across the locks. It's slightly slower, too, at 3.0 turns lock-to-lock, which should pacify some of the 3200 GT's high-speed nervousness.

PERFORMANCE & BRAKES

★★★★★★★★☆☆

STUNNING ENGINE MATED TO A POOR GEARBOX

You don't need a bland expanse of test track to appreciate fully what Maserati has achieved with this car. You can forget the numbers, ignore the technical data and just drink in what is one of the finest engines currently in production. This car needed to offer an exceptional blend of performance, tractability and refinement if it was to make a serious impression on the opposition, and in many ways this powerplant actually tops that brief.

Suggestively muscular, even at idle, it will happily pull from 2000rpm in any gear, when you'll be rewarded with a genuinely new Maserati experience: ►

◆ consistent, predictable shove from low revs to limiter. It's an authentically exotic lump, too; the rev counter needle sweeps through its arc as myriad induction and exhaust noises swirl through the cabin, hitting their final crescendo at the 7500rpm red line. Even then, mechanical refinement remains superb.

And what of those numbers? Suffice to say, this car is staggeringly fast; it will blast to 60mph in 4.9sec and 100mph in a scant 11.3sec. It needs every last ounce of that straight-line speed, however, because the competition at this level is startlingly brisk: today's basic Carrera will hit the magic ton in just 10.1sec. But the Maser feels every bit as fast on the road, simply because it enjoys greater flexibility and a set of gear ratios that suit UK roads perfectly – second runs to over 70mph.

The in-gear times are a tribute to the coupé's wonderfully torquey motor. So happy is it to chug along at crank speeds barely above idle that you always find yourself running in one, even two gears higher than you might in a 911. For the record 30-50mph in fourth takes just 3.6sec while the benchmark 50-70mph in sixth is a curt 6.1sec jab of your right foot – even though it's gearing is short by GT standards: just 23.8mph per 1000rpm.

But the drivetrain is denied the stamp of perfection by its unresolved manual transmission. It's odd to come across a modern car whose gearbox needs 10 minutes to warm up every morning. Even when the oil has reached operating temperature the shift remains too obstructive and the clutch action too abrupt. There's plenty of driveline shunt, too.

All of which would be fine if a properly sorted automatic was available. We managed to spend time in a Cambiocorsa car as well during our test period, and despite righting some of the manual car's wrongs, a genuine self-shifter would complement this engine perfectly, and until one is offered the Coupé is missing a trick.

Braking performance was excellent, a solid pedal and very little fade combining to produce a 70-0mph distance of 51m.

HANDLING & RIDE

★★★★★★★☆☆☆

GENUINE GT OFFERS COMFORT – AND IT'S STILL ENTERTAINING

There is one simple way to ensure that your new Skyhook adaptive-damping-equipped Maserati Coupé remains a pleasant device on the road: identify the Sport button (just in front of the gearlever) find some gaffer tape, then once you're certain Sport mode *isn't* selected, use it to make sure the button is rendered inoperable. Permanently.

On its stiffest setting this car reawakens all that was wrong with Maseratis of yesteryear: an unyielding ride, non-existent low-speed compliance, and general inability to smother that particularly obnoxious brand of scarred blacktop that characterises most British roads.

To switch it off is to be released from poor-ride purgatory. Suddenly wheel travel seems to increase, and rather than

Out go boomerang-style rear lights, in come more conservative items to appease American market

Decent room for rear passengers

Cabin fit and finish much improved, driver now sits an inch lower; boot space not up to the job though

Coupé's new-found cruising ability makes cross-country blasts more enjoyable, but stick to the A-roads

skipping over bumps the car soaks them up and makes a pretty good fist of isolating the cabin. There's a price to pay in roll stiffness and outright body control, but the sacrifice is minute in real terms because the Coupé feels so much better planted that it actually gives you the confidence to carry much more speed.

Traction is fine in the dry, even with the ASR switched off, and full-power second gear exits will have the rears just pushing outwards, but the overall handling balance is reassuringly neutral. We always knew there was a fine-handling car lurking in there somewhere and it's frankly amazing how much of an effect the new engine has had. Where once you waited for the boost to appear and then just try to cope with whatever under- or oversteer arrived, now you can tailor the car's attitude with your right foot. One caveat, though: in the wet, with the ASR switched off, this is a very lively vehicle indeed. The limited slip differential locks easily and even small jabs of throttle will have you looking down the road out of the side window.

The steering isn't reference point stuff, certainly not in the same league as a 911's, but it's a happy compromise between feedback, clipping-point accuracy and motorway sneeze-factor imperviousness. Only a grumbling power-steering pump at low speeds spoils the party.

It's a car of singular character, the Coupé. Not quite the precise B-road tool a 911 is, but still capable of raising pulses in all the right ways. But the real result is its cruising ability: always controlled but never harsh, it's a genuinely comfortable car in which to pound out the motorway miles.

COMFORT SAFETY & EQUIPMENT

★★★★★★★☆☆☆

IF ONLY STANDARD KIT WAS AS GENEROUS AS CABIN SPACE

Even after allowing for its fantastic new engine, perhaps the most extraordinary thing about this car is, and always has been, it's ability to carry four adults in reasonable comfort. So spacious is the cabin rear that this genuine 2+2 Coupé offers a brand of sociable motoring that nothing else in the class comes close to matching. If only the boot was capable of swallowing four people's luggage.

The interior design has largely been left alone, although it now includes a new TV and sat-nav unit in the centre console and some redesigned buttons. The best news is that the driving position has been improved by dropping the seat 25mm. Even so, it still reminds us of how shabby the 3200 GT set-up was: the posture remains very much old-school Italian with the wheel set too far away, even though it has generous rake and reach adjustment. Still, the seats themselves are both grippy and comfortable. Poorly placed pedals don't help, either: learn to heel 'n' toe in this car and you'll manage it in anything.

Nor is Maserati especially generous on the standard equipment front. Our car ◆

PERFORMANCE AND SPECIFICATIONS

Engine
Layout 8 cyls in vee 4244cc
Max power 385bhp at 7000rpm
Max torque 333lb at 4500rpm
Specific output 91bhp per litre
Power to weight 229bhp per tonne
Torque to weight 198lb ft per tonne
Installation Front, longitudinal, rear-wheel drive
Construction Aluminium head and block
Bore/stroke 92/80mm
Valve gear 4 per cyl, dohc
Compression ratio 11.1:1
Ignition and fuel Bosch ME7 3.21 engine management system

Gearbox
Type 6-speed manual
Ratios/mph per 1000rpm
1st 3.29/6.1 **2nd** 2.16/9.3
3rd 1.61/12.5 **4th** 1.27/15.9
5th 1.03/19.6 **6th** 0.85/23.8
Final drive 3.73

Maximum speeds
6th 177mph/7500rpm **5th** 146/7500
4th 119/7500 **3rd** 94/7500
2nd 70/7500 **1st** 46/7500

Acceleration from rest
Surface dry

True mph	sec	speedo mph
30	2.2	32
40	2.6	44
50	3.9	54
60	4.9	65
70	6.4	76
80	7.7	87
90	9.1	97
100	11.3	108

Standing qtr mile 13.4sec/109mph
Standing km 24.7/132mph
30-70mph through gears 4.2sec

Acceleration in kickdown

mph	6th	5th	4th	3rd	2nd
20-40	-	-	-	3.0	2.1
30-50	11.8	4.8	3.6	2.7	2.1
40-60	6.1	4.5	3.4	2.6	2.0
50-70	6.1	4.3	3.2	2.7	-
60-80	6.0	4.2	3.3	2.8	-
70-90	5.9	4.7	3.7	2.9	-
80-100	6.0	5.12	4.4	-	-

Steering
Type Rack and pinion, power assisted
Turns lock to lock 3.0

Suspension
Front/Rear Double wishbones, coil springs, anti-roll bar, adaptive dampers

Wheels & tyres
Wheels 8Jx18in (f), 9.5Jx18in (r)
Made of Alloy
Tyres 235/40 Z18(f), 265/35 Z18(r) Michelin Pilot Sport

Brakes
Front 330mm ventilated drilled discs
Rear 310mm ventilated drilled discs
Anti-lock Standard

Govt fuel consumption claims

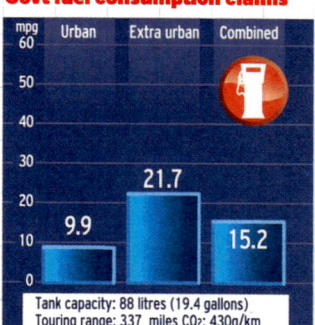

Tank capacity: 88 litres (19.4 gallons)
Touring range: 337 miles CO2: 430g/km

Fuel consumption test results

Layout

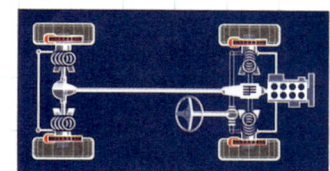

Brakes

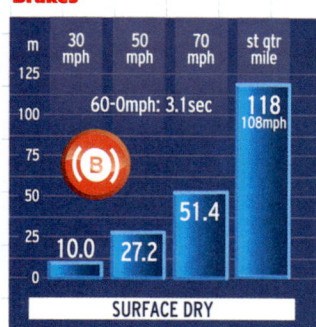

60-0mph: 3.1sec

SURFACE DRY

Noise

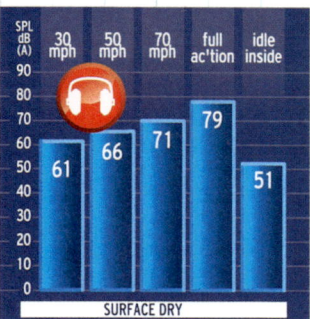

SURFACE DRY

AUTOCAR ROAD TESTS
...are the most exhaustive published in the UK. Each car is measured in detail, then performance tested on a neutral proving ground using the latest Racelogic VBOX equipment. We also cover at least 500 miles on all types of road, and measure economy in all conditions.

All Autocar road tests are conducted using BP Cleaner Unleaded Fuel or BP Cleaner Diesel with additives to help keep engines cleaner

Body 2-door coupe **Cd** 0.34 **Front/rear tracks** 1525/1538mm **Turning circle** 12m **Min/max front leg room** 840/1075mm **Min/max rear leg room** 755/1005mm **Max front head room** 875mm **Interior width** 1490mm **Boot width** 1200mm **VDA boot volume** 315 litres/dm³ **Kerb weight** 1680kg **Weight distribution front/rear** 59/41 **Width (inc mirrors)** 1871mm

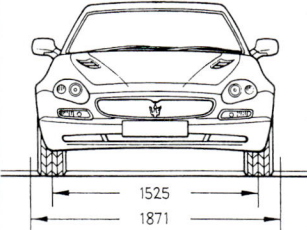

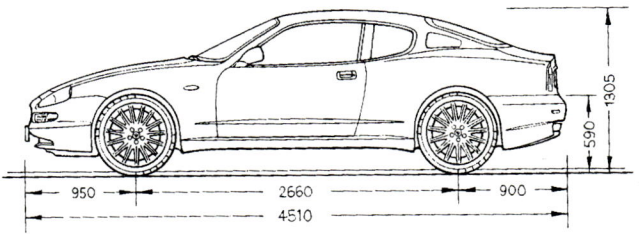

IAN HOWATSON

◀ came with superb xenon lights capable of floodlighting a football pitch, but then so they should for £920, and seeing both cruise control (£325) and sat-nav (£1640) on the options list was rather too Scrooge-like for our taste.

But interior build quality is out of the top drawer, and there are no rattles or squeaks to speak of, so at least the money is being spent where it matters. Four front airbags and a bodyshell that is 15 per cent stiffer than before encourage peace of mind, but the Coupé lags behind its rivals in offering only traction control and not a full-house stability control system.

ECONOMY

★★★☆☆☆☆☆☆☆

PAIN OF HUGE THIRST OFFSET SLIGHTLY BY LARGE TANK

Likes a drink does the Maser: we struggled to coax much more than 300 miles at a time from the 88-litre tank, and average consumption for our time with the car was 16.3mpg. Dip into the power, though, and that figure will fall dramatically, but probably not to the laughable (or perhaps terrifying) 8.6mpg we recorded at the track. Still, the large tank does give it that genuine 300-mile range.

MARKET & FINANCE

★★★☆☆☆☆☆☆☆

REMAINS THE RISKY CHOICE IN THIS PRICE RANGE

A sore subject with many existing 3200 GT owners who have experienced choking depreciation. The new car looks set to redress that balance somewhat, but oversupply and discounting coupled to a badge that still awakens bad memories, will stop it troubling Porsche for the time being. Worse still, the 430g/km CO_2 rating is a cruel joke next to the 911's 269g/km, although business users of both cars will be taxed at the same rate.

What it costs

On-the-road price	£59,950
Total as tested	£65,045
CO₂	430g/km
Cost per mile	na
Contract hire per month	na
Equipment	
(**bold** = options fitted to test car)	
Climate control	●
Xenon lights	**£920**
Metallic paint	●
Cruise control	**£325**
Skyhook electronic suspension	**£990**
Alarm/immobiliser	**£410**/●
RDS stereo/CD player	●
Sat-nav	**£1640**
● standard	
Insurance group	20
Typical quote	£2252.43
Warranty	
3yrs/unlimited miles, 3yrs anti-perforation, 4yrs Maserati Roadside Assistance	
Servicing First 6250miles, thereafter every 12,500miles	

New TV and sat-nav system are options

Four front airbags but no stability control system

Comfortable seats though pedals still poorly placed

4.2-litre V8 magnificent, and endlessly flexible

18in alloys harbour ventilated, cross-drilled discs

Set suspension to Normal for best ride quality yet

Maser's once-quirky oval clock lives on in Coupé

Cornering ability vastly improved – lack of turbocharger means 385bhp can be more delicately controlled

THE CLASS

Maserati Coupé £59,950 ★★★★★★★☆☆☆

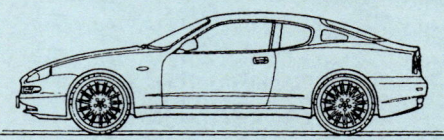

Capacity 4244cc
Power 385bhp
Torque 333lb ft
Max speed 177mph
0-60mph 4.9sec
CO_2 430g/km

The engine alone's enough to make you lust after it, but the Coupé's much improved ride and spacious cabin make it a fine everyday proposition, even if it still lacks the last pinch of greatness it needs to de-throne the 911.

TVR Tuscan R £75,000 ★★★★★☆☆☆☆

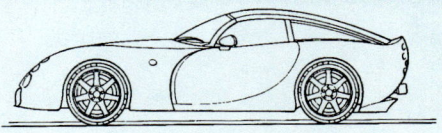

Capacity 3996cc
Power 440bhp
Torque 350lb ft
Max speed 195mph
0-60mph 3.8sec
CO_2 na

Seventy-five grand may sound like a lot of money for a TVR, but this is no ordinary Blackpool pleasure ride. Top speed is knocking on 200mph, acceleration is simply staggering, but ownership won't be Porsche-painless.

Porsche 911 Carrera £62,260 ★★★★★★★★☆☆

OUR CHOICE

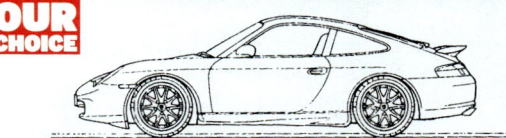

Capacity 3596cc
Power 320bhp
Torque 273lb ft
Max speed 177mph
0-60mph 4.6sec
CO_2 269g/km

Sports cars, GT cars, whatever the competition, the 911 will be at or near the top of our list. There's a little too much understeer for our taste but little else to detract from what remains the best car in the business.

Jaguar XKR £56,700 ★★★★★★☆☆☆

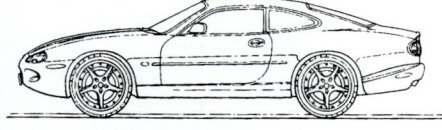

Capacity 4196cc
Power 400bhp
Torque 408lb ft
Max speed 155mph
0-60mph 5.2sec
CO_2 304g/km

Now complete with uprated 400bhp engine and superb six-speed automatic gearbox, the five-year-old Jag is still a compelling car. But it's more cruiser than sports car and can't match the Maser's overall appeal.

BMW M3 £39,730 ★★★★★★★★☆☆

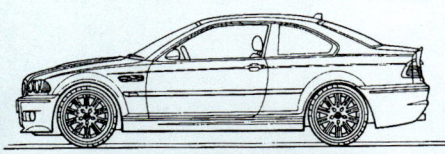

Capacity 3245cc
Power 343bhp
Torque 269lb ft
Max speed 160mph
0-60mph 4.8sec
CO_2 287g/km

The Bavarian may look a little out of its depth in this company but don't you believe a word. It matches the 911 for pace and the original M3 for fun. You'll try hard to find a better home for your £40k.

Mercedes-Benz SL500 £67,790 ★★★★★★★☆☆

Capacity 4996cc
Power 310bhp
Torque 339lb ft
Max speed 155mph
0-60mph 5.8sec
CO_2 300g/km

Merc has done it again. The latest SL is not only technologically impressive, but fantastic to drive as well, while no rival can touch it for residual strength. Only problem will be surviving the wait for a new one.

THE AUTOCAR VERDICT

STAN PAPIOR

THERE ARE, as there always will be with cars of irrepressible character, any number of objective reasons to strike the Coupé off your shopping list. The first, and most damning, is the spiteful manual gearchange. It's a 'box that tries hard to spoil a great engine, and simply doesn't sit harmoniously in such an otherwise improved car.

Even so, the Coupé does offer something currently missing in the market: a genuine alternative to the perennial Porsche. It has the pace, ride comfort and cabin space to slip into the GT role perfectly, and does so with all the charisma you look for in a Maserati. What it would be like with an automatic gearbox, we can only dream about, but as it stands the Coupé is a devilishly desirable piece of kit.

TESTERS' NOTES

When is leather not leather? When it's covering the Coupé's front seats it seems; the stuff in our test car felt, smelt and looked rather like vinyl to me. Great build, though **Ben Oliver**

Saw the Maser's engine line at Maranello last month. It's a reassuringly expensive and exclusive genesis being built just inches from the Ferarri 575's mighty V12 **Chris Harris**

Why can't they fit an external boot release, or put one on the remote key? Mosey back from the shops and you have to drop your gear to get the key in **Steve Sutcliffe**

Best Maser in decades ★★★★★★★☆☆☆ 7/10

Maz
Appeal

We slammed Maserati's
4.2-litre Coupe and
Spyder first time around.
Can the new, revised
versions win us over?
David Vivian reports ➔

'The list of changes is short but focused; it looks like a wish list answered'

Whenever possible, **evo** likes to cut to the chase. A good strop on a challenging road with the competition along for company tells you more about a new car than the carefully chosen scenic route and a long lunch with its maker's chairman.

So when, at the launch of the new Maserati 4200 Spyder Cambiocorsa back in autumn 2001, we decided to the give it the opportunity to prove its mettle on roads selected more for their bumps than beauty – and with a Jag XKR, BMW M3 convertible and new Merc SL in tow to set the bar – we knew we were doing the right thing.

And that it would probably land us in trouble.

To cram in all the driving and photography, not only did I miss the lunchtime pep-talk with Luca di Montezemolo, I nearly missed the plane home. My last-minute arrival at the airport was met with dark looks as the PR personnel put two and two together. There were muffled mumblings of sanctions, even ex-communication.

When the group test hit the shelves in October, (issue 037) we knew it would be worse than that. With the exception of its beautifully crafted cabin and utterly magnificent Ferrari V8, the paddle-shift Spyder Cambiocorsa turned out to be something of a shed, its numerous shortcomings swiftly identified and graded by the imported talent, and perhaps most

embarrassingly by the SL, which really did possess the advanced suspension the Maser claimed to have. We'd done the test, delivered the verdict.

Needless to say, Maserati/Ferrari went spare. How could we have been so nasty to the Spyder when everyone else on the launch was so nice? But the mood slowly altered as others emulated our comparison back in Blighty and came to much the same conclusion. The identically-engined, longer-wheelbase 4200 Coupe that followed in 2002 was a better car but still comfortably thrashed by the Jaguar XKR-R and Porsche 911 C4S in another **evo** group test (049). Richard Meaden concluded that despite fleeting moments of brilliance, he was too frequently

The Coupe we drove had the six-speed manual 'box (above); the Spyder we tried (right) had the Cambiocorsa paddle-shift, which has attracted flak in the past, now much improved

reminded of what an ill-sorted, unhappy car the Maserati Coupe was. Hard to interpret that as any kind of kiss-and-make-up gesture.

Which is why I wouldn't have put money on being back at Maserati's Viale Ciro Menotti factory in the centre of Modena on a bright and warm March morning just 18 months later. More disconcerting still, the Maserati welcoming posse is smiling broadly and shaking hands with gusto. All forgotten, then? Not quite, but potentially a distinct possibility. Seems that once the initial hubbub died down, Maserati elected to take the accumulated press criticism on the chin and do something about it. In a sense, we're back to give the '2003 evolution' improvements the thumbs-up. Or… and I almost hesitate to write it… not.

Our problems with the '01 Spyder Cambiocorsa were these: the generally crude and uncouth behaviour of the six-speed Cambiocorsa transmission; borderline scuttle-shake and a shuddery steering column when the front wheels encountered any type of bump or dip; steering that was both feel-less and very direct (an uneasy coalition); and adaptive damping that completely failed to live up to the 'seriously advanced' boast – acutely so in the Merc SL sense of the term.

Maserati's list of significant changes for the '03 Spyder and Coupe is short but focused. It includes new software for the Cambiocorsa transmission that prioritises engine torque rather than revs as a parameter, new software and dampers for the adaptive damping system, an all-new stability program called MSP, a new steering box with more direct gearing, larger anti-roll bars, grippier tyres and a bodyshell 20 per cent stiffer in torsion for the Spyder.

Out of this, only the even more direct steering (hard to imagine how it could be) is curious; the rest looks like a wish list answered. There's subtle cosmetic polishing, too. Most obvious are the optional alloys and new V8 badges on the front panels. More practical are the heated glass (rather than plastic) rear screen for the Spyder's powered hood and the easier-to-use functions and simplified screen displays of the optional navigation system. The previously dour black centre console in which it's set has been spiced up with a choice of grey or 'dark Bordeaux' finishes which are duplicated on the transmission tunnel and door-trims.

After a brief tour of the production lines, we bag a Bird's custard yellow Coupe GT with a conventional six-speed gearbox and an Ultra Brite white Spyder Cambiocorsa, successor to the

model that folded under pressure in 2001.

It's tempting to take both back to the roads that unravelled the original Spyder's case, but there isn't really the time and, besides, the showdown with rivals will take place on UK roads in a matter of weeks. The only condition I set for this excursion on the largely fast, flowing and smoothly-surfaced roads chosen by Maserati is that I enjoy the drive. Basically, that means being able to savour the fabulous 390bhp 4.2-litre 32-valve V8 without the foibles of the gearbox and chassis getting in the way – something the original Spyder would never have allowed.

But as snapper Shepherd and I head out of the factory towards the hills in the Coupe GT, we're puzzled. If the manual shift's this poor, no wonder 80 per cent of owners opt for the Cambiocorsa. But the Cambiocorsa, as remembered, is terrible. Who would you bet on if George Bush and

Michael Jackson's chimpanzee went head-to-head on Countdown? Similar dilemma.

But as the oil of the transaxle gearbox warms, the shift quality improves immeasurably. It's still necessary to push the medium-weight clutch all the way down and slot the stubby lever with deliberation but, after about five miles, the initial graunch and clunk gives way to a reasonably fluid and consistent action. It's fine, and something of a relief to be able to say so.

So too, we decide, is the cosy 2+2 cabin with its sexy yet ergonomically sussed architecture and swathes of tastefully crafted leather. As before, though, and even at these crawl-and-squirt speeds on the outskirts of Modena, it's the engine – essentially a slightly simpler, detuned but yet more sonorously tonsilled edition of the dry-sumped, quad-cam V8 in the Ferrari 360 – that dominates every second of the experience. The

ROAR APPEAL

David Vivian tackles the bellowing Maserati Trofeo one-make race car

Half-way across the covered bridge that spans the main straight of the Carano de Melegari circuit at Vareno, near Parma, I start to walk more slowly. It isn't that I can't maintain a constant pace and chew gum at the same time, just something that's suddenly dawned on me and dumped a few kilos of lead in each leg. It's this. The devastating Doppler shriek that's pitch-shifting beneath my feet doesn't belong to some savagely endowed single-seater in the hands of the next Brazilian wonderbrat on a hot lap, but the car I'm about to drive: a more or less standard Maserati 4200 Coupe Cambiocorsa.

Frankly, it doesn't compute. But then I suppose, up to this point, I hadn't really considered the 'more or less' too closely. Hadn't, for instance, tried to imagine what the normally mellifluous Maser might sound like *sans* silencers. Or pondered the effect easing up the

power to 413bhp could have on the alacrity with which the big V8 would hit its 7500rpm red line in the first four of its six gears. By the time I reach the paddock, this loud, hard, spiteful sound is vectoring through the circuit's cradling hillscape at a genuinely impressive lick. But it figures. Lop 250kg from the Coupe's kerb weight and you're down to a lean 1370kg delivering a 911 Turbo thumping power-to-weight ratio of 301bhp/ton. Mix in Pirelli PO slicks on 9J and 10Jx18in rims, massively stiffer springs and dampers, enormous uprated ventilated discs all-round and a bloody great wing on the boot and you've got, well, Maserati's official return to the world of motorsport.

Trofeo (Trophy) is both the car and a new one-make racing championship co-sponsored by Vodafone and Pirelli. The deal is that 26 drivers from Italy, France, Germany, Great Britain and Switzerland will compete in seven

races over the season. The series kicks off on April 6 at Barcelona at a round of the FIA GT championship. The final round is on October 19 at Mugello in Italy as part of the Ferrari-Maserati finals. All the Trofeo racers will be prepared and run directly by Maserati to ensure identical performance.

If the Trofeo is essentially a pseudo-racer, it's a remarkably convincing one. It has enough outright pace to thrill but never feels as intimidating inside as it looks from the outside.

All the dynamic cues feel authentic, from the meaty, nadgety feedback of the super-direct steering to the rock-hard ride to the sharp, jittery traction-scavenging antics of the limited-slip diff and ultra-grippy slicks. But it's not the fight you'd expect. Keep the traction aids on (I did because circuit coach Gabriele Tarquini told me to) and it's almost impossible to go wrong. Trouble is, you lose seconds a lap as the electronics smother drive out of Varano's tight bends. Later, riding with one of the circuit's regular pros, the advantage conferred by pure grunt and slicks is obvious. Resist the temptation to showboat and the Trofeo is faithful and forgiving.

Another ten laps would have been interesting. A road-going Trofeo would be better still.

Big wing, stripped-out cabin and over 300bhp per ton; Trofeo means business

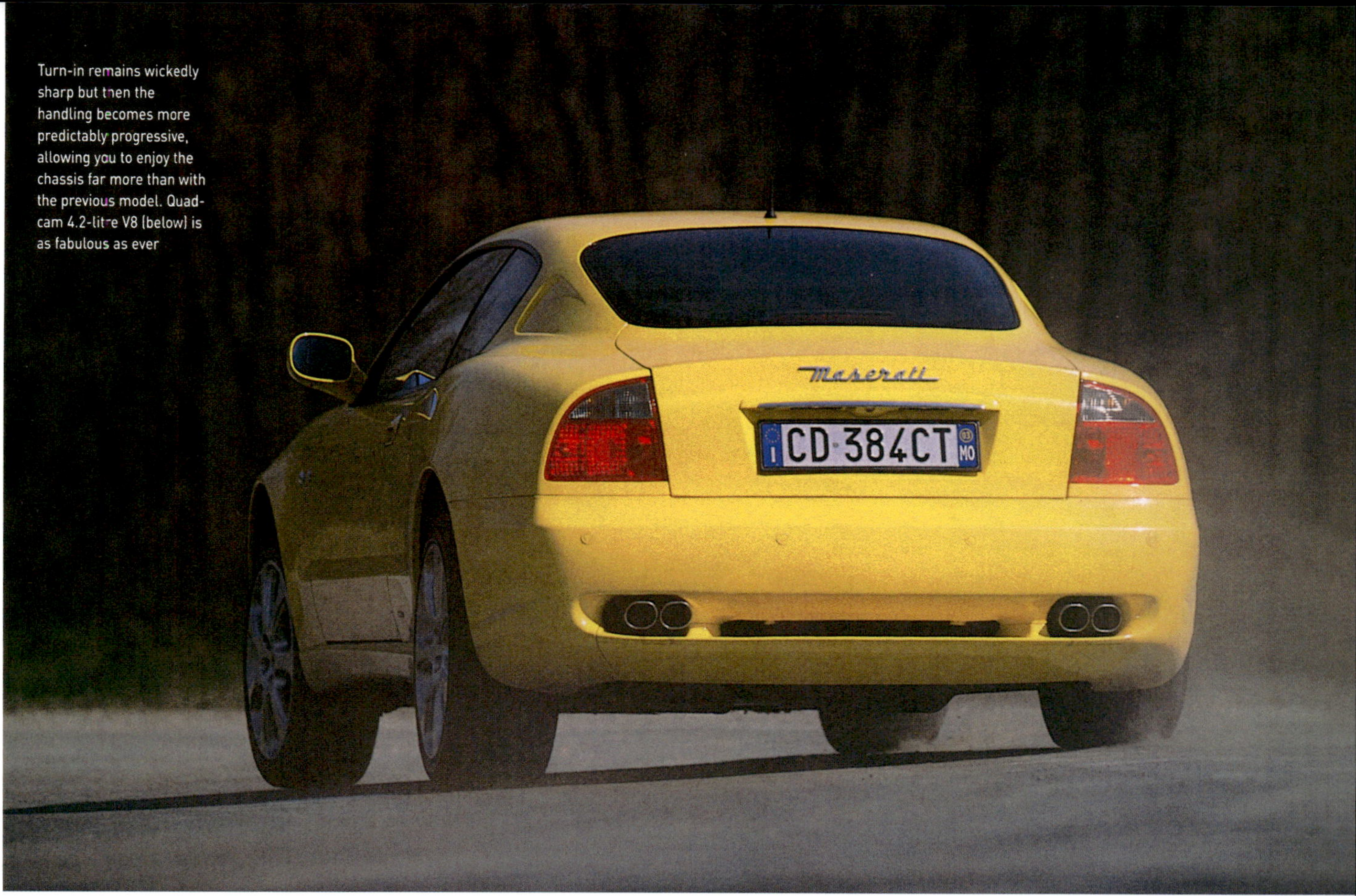

Turn-in remains wickedly sharp but then the handling becomes more predictably progressive, allowing you to enjoy the chassis far more than with the previous model. Quad-cam 4.2-litre V8 (below) is as fabulous as ever

delicious sensuality of the sonics, the electric throttle response and the lust for revs are all deeply engaging. But it's the raw, animalistic power of the thing that leaves the deepest impression. Just blatting past lorries and dawdling morning commuters, you don't have to refer to the performance stats to know that the Maser would simply chew up and spit out an M3. Hell, even an SL55 would have to watch its back.

Specification

MASERATI 4200

○ **Engine**	V8, longitudinally front-mounted
○ **Displacement**	4244cc
○ **Cylinder block**	Aluminium alloy
○ **Cylinder head**	Aluminium alloy, dohc per bank, 32v
○ **Fuel and ignition**	Bosch ME7.3.2 electronic ignition and multipoint fuel injection
○ **Max power**	390bhp @ 7000rpm
○ **Max torque**	333lb ft @ 4500rpm
○ **Transmission**	Six-speed manual or optional six-speed semi-manual 'Cambiocorsa', rear drive
○ **Weight**	1680kg
○ **Power-to-weight**	236bhp/ton
○ **0-62mph**	4.9sec (claimed)
○ **Max speed**	177mph (claimed)
○ **Wheels**	8Jx18in front, 9.5Jx18in rear
○ **Tyres**	235/40 ZR18 front, 265/35 ZR18 rear, Michelins or Dunlops
○ **Basic price**	£61,000 (Coupe), £66,800 (Spyder)
evo RATING	★★★★

The winding hillside tarmac is a more telling arena, though, and it's on these roads that Maserati has sought to make the crucial improvements. Certainly, there seem to be fewer dynamic distractions. The already very direct helm doesn't seem any more direct but it does feel meatier and easier to trust. Turn-in is wickedly sharp but the follow-through more predictable and controlled than before, although still accompanied by a surprising degree of body roll and mild power on/off pitching. Potent levels of grip are well balanced front-to-rear, if a little squealy on the new 235/40 ZR18 front, 265/35 ZR18 rear rubber, and braking power and feel is terrific. The Maserati Stability Program – which acts on the brakes and engine to curb over-exuberance – is subjectively quite subtle and can be switched off if you want to indulge in a spot of user-friendly tail-sliding. But the adaptive damping still seems susceptible to the shock of severe transverse ridges and sharp single-wheel inputs which send a shudder through the cabin.

Confounding expectations, the problem diminishes when we decamp to the Spyder. Despite its 220mm shorter wheelbase, it actually seems to ride more smoothly than the Coupe, though its chassis doesn't feel quite as crisp or responsive and the steering column shudder, while reduced, hasn't gone away. Maybe the slightly softer character is no bad thing. It seems to suit the Spyder well.

And here's the best news of all. The new software has completely transformed Cambiocorsa, which now allows the 4200 to pull cleanly and smoothly away from rest and swaps cogs on light to medium throttle with a delicacy I simply wouldn't have believed possible back in 2001. Full-throttle upshifts are swift whereas before they were merely savage and, although the show-off factor has been tuned out of the downshift blip, overall levels of smoothness and refinement are little short of revelatory.

If this was the only improvement Maserati had made it would have been enough to make the 4200 duo vastly more likeable and competitive. As it is, Maserati seems to have worked a little magic on the chassis, too. I enjoyed my drive. And I'm looking forward to the group test. ■

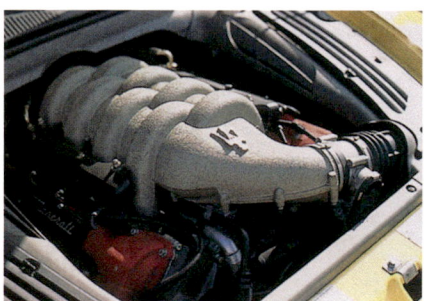

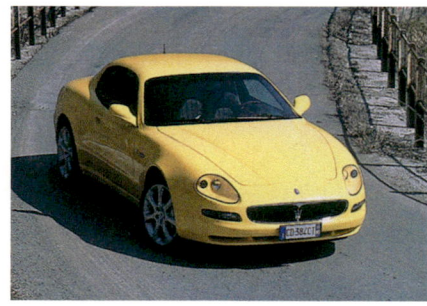

Maserati **Coupe**

Clutch and suspension changes make MY03 Maserati Coupe Cambiocorsa an even sharper tool

So we're trickling out of Maserati's driveway and, already, the hurried upgrade is doing its job. No more driveline slap, no more clutch drag noise, no more vibrations. Still bunny hops a bit, but it does it more politely than it did before, surging more than leaping.

That's the Cambiocorsa gearbox's weak link. Essentially the standard issue Ferrari family F1 paddle shift 'box, it hates to trickle. Which is odd, given that it's the 'box you get if you think

it's irksome to fiddle three pedals and a lever. The 'box is capable of being left in auto mode, leaving you to flick the paddles only when you're interested.

Yet so concerned was Maserati that it rushed through a mid-model upgrade to its storming V8 to halt the radiation of warrantied clutches from Modena. The issue has been that the Cambiocorsa is, essentially, a hybrid. It's a manual six speeder with a brain attached to take care of the clutch, gear selection, throttle positioning

etc. Except it didn't work as well as it might have, because where Ferraris are relative weekenders, Maseratis are practical enough for everyday operation – and that means heavy traffic, which means there's less definitive in-or-out clutch activity than the thing liked.

So it's fixed. Now, the computer on the gearbox determines what torque the clutch can handle, then asks the engine to send it that precise amount. It limits clutch slip, it's quieter and it's smoother. That's not to say it

won't still bang through high rev shifts with a jolt.

But Maserati also took the opportunity to tighten up a couple of other areas. The badging's subtly different, but the front end is demonstrably sharper. There's no body roll to speak of, never has been, but its turn-in bite has been lifted tremendously.

When you're up in the rarefied atmosphere in which Maseratis dwell, suspension hardware upgrades can sometimes be lost in the depths of the original

Fabulous interior is unchanged for MY03 Coupe

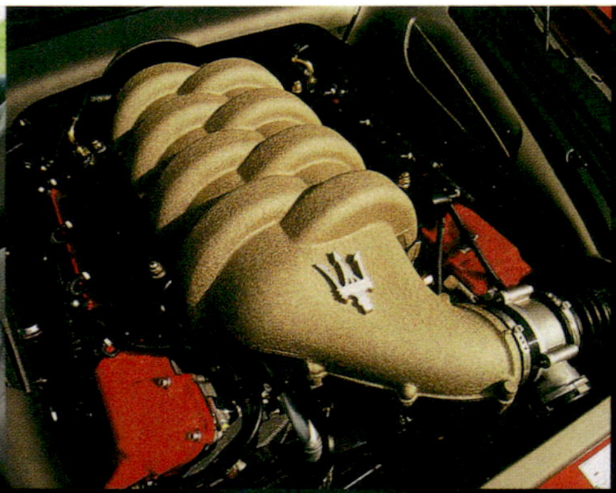

STORY Michael Taylor PHOTOS Mark Bean

Already grippy chassis has even more bite thanks to front end mods

performance levels. Not so here. The upgrade is as apparent as the unbelievable engine note.

The first time you really try to carry any of its startling straight-line speed into a corner it grips so hard it almost takes the bitumen with it. There's no question the Maser rides firmly but it does have suspension compliance mid-corner, when you need it, over ruts and bumps and refuses to unsettle those enormous rear boots,

The interior is seductively crafted and surprisingly practical for four people, but it's the engine note that will keep them coming back for more. There is simply no other car that comes close to approaching the Maserati's concert of hard, mongrel edge and cultured sophistication. How they tune the thing is a mystery of the arts, but it's brilliant. It just washes through you in a way that leaves nobody in its wake untouched. That it's accompanied by low-13 second 0-400m pace is a bonus.

But quarter mile runs do it no justice whatsoever. In reality, at the 180-odd km/h it's carrying at the end of the strip, it's just hitting its stride. The next 50 km/h disappear at an undiminished rate as well.

Wasn't that long ago Maserati was a fringe-dweller. A memory of what was. This wholesale reaction to a problem is both comprehensive and a reassuring sign of a company that wants to get it right. It's still not perfect, the Cambiocorsa, but it's way better than it was.

At 180 km/h at the end of the 0-400 m strip, it's just hitting its stride

Maserati Coupe Cambiocorsa		

FAST FACTS

engine
4.2-litre DOHC 32-valve V8
power/weight
287 kW/1680 kg
drive
rear-wheel
on sale
now
price
$220,500

GRAN TURISMO
FOR REAL

Who needs a PlayStation 2? Simply insert 120,000 euros in the relevant slot and join Maserati's pay as you race, Trofeo Challenge. Gentleman racers and novices welcome

STORY TOM FORD **PHOTOGRAPHY** BARRY HAYDEN

TWENTY MINUTES BEFORE the picture opposite was taken, Frank Mountain (seated) and Rob Wilson were in the midst of a 24-car race that made F1 look like a bunch of courteous OAPs wrestling in glue. Four-hundred horsepower, 177mph Maseratis were bouncing off each other with the kind of gay abandon that makes anyone with any mechanical sympathy wince until they get permanent creases. Italian racing drivers were having punch-ups in parc-fermé about incidents in the fourth lap, and our lads got busted for speeding in the pitlane. Politics, bribes, shouting and seriously knives-out

racing were the order of the day. Gentleman racers are certainly not what I imagined them to be. Yet it took just 15 minutes for the gelid calm to return to our protagonists' faces. Their small island of intellectual calm makes you proud to be British.

Incredibly, one of these two men has hardly set foot in a racing car and collected his first motorsport licence in February. Last week he took part in his third ever race – the Nürburgring 24hr – competing on the Nordschleife until his car grenaded in the company of co-driver Rob. This weekend he has driven to East Germany to race Maseratis

A race apart:
Englishmen Frank
Mountain (seated) and
Rob Wilson retain stiff
upper lips in the face
of overwhelming
Latin race-craftiness

Frank realises that Rob can levitate

'Yours is the red and white one.' Why single-make series have race numbers

Drivers' briefing: time to wake up now, boys

'Italian racing drivers were having punch-ups in parc-fermé about incidents in the fourth lap'

in a championship in which they are the only British entry. This year he will contend the Miami street race, Daytona mini race, the Trofeo championship (the Maseratis) and the legendary Bathurst. Next year he hopes to compete in the Porsche GT3 Cup with the ultimate aim of taking on Le Mans. He hasn't even raced for a full year. Meet Frank Mountain, gentleman racer.

The Maserati Trofeo challenge seems like the ideal entry into sports car racing. Okay, so you have to shell out a hundred-and-twenty-odd thousand Euros, but the idea is that you just turn up and race, with the cars being 'managed' by the Italian crews to ensure fairness. It's also a place where non-professional racers have the chance to compete in proper sports cars without committing to a career. It's serious, but supposed to be enjoyed for the sport itself; what they used to call a 'Gentleman's race series'. Which is why it appealed to our man Frank. Accompanied by his adopted racing mentor Rob, Frank decided that the best way to get some race miles under his belt was to compete in a championship just like this, racing on as many circuits as possible in cars that needed respect. In at the deep end certainly, but a place where you learn very quickly or learn to like being lapped. Also,

admit it, it's a bloody cool thing to be doing every other weekend; PlayStation for real.

And that's how Frank Mountain comes to be doing 165mph on a German autobahn telling me about his wife of eighteen years, Sally and his three kids (Harriet, fourteen; Charlotte, twelve and son Jack, who's eight). First impressions: he's average-to-tall, strawberry blond running to ginger, lots of freckles shading to tan, with a quick smile and a confident shake. For some reason I was expecting an overweight, cigar-smoking, greased-back Lex Luthor figure dripping with Jacob and Co and Asprey's sparkle because that's what I think of when you say 'property developer'. But that's not Frank. True, I do clock a nice-but-subtle Rolex and the kind of polish that comes from well-cut clothes, but there's nothing here to suggest that Mr Mountain might suddenly try to take over the world without so much as a by-your-leave. Evil henchmen (Rob excluded), are conspicuous only by their absence.

He recounts animatedly the story of how he went to pick his daughter up from school in his F40. He speaks about being in love with his wife, loving his kids, building his new house and the sheer down-to-earthness of the guy means that it's easy to warm to him. He

works incessantly – and seems the kind of individual that finds it hard to delegate in business, but there's an intense energy in Frank. When he sets his mind on something – be it motor racing or getting a cup of coffee – you better be ready for the onslaught. God help the MSA. On the drive down he buys a Ferrari 360 Spider *over the phone*. He's not being flash, but I can't help being just a little impressed and quite spectacularly jealous. In retaliation I order some pencils. But they're really nice pencils.

Twenty hours later we arrive in Cottbus in east Germany with four hours sleep to snatch before qualifying starts. Frank still has lots of bouncy, shiny energy; I have replaced my blood with Red Bull and my brain with straw.

QUALIFYING ITSELF IS A FRAUGHT affair which consists of standing about in the Maserati hospitality tent trying not to sweat on people. Its rainforest hot, with the added pressure of really good-looking people (who have their sweat glands surgically removed at birth) being casually attractive at every turn. The cars are all lined up in a tent behind us and the atmosphere of anticipation is rife with Italian cursing. Rob and Frank sit quietly discussing tactics. Rob uses cliché as an artful

Yellow strip on lamp identifies 'our' car. Not derogatory

Car 27. Karma in action

Ever seen a Mountain move this quickly?

A reassuringly expensive pressured spin by car 25

'Tear silk through Metallica's amplification stack while drinking Shell Optimax and strike a match'

form of expression: 'let someone else give you the place', 'to finish first, first you have to finish', 'keep it on the island'. Here Frank becomes quieter, more contemplative. A drivers' briefing is held; the Italians moan that they're not allowed to overtake on a safety car lap, that they're not allowed to leave the pits early from the compulsory minute and a half driver change. Sorry chaps, but they're what's known in polite circles as 'rules'.

Rob and Frank clear up a couple of points and head off to change, while I can't help noticing that one of the Italian drivers looks like Keith Harris' Orville – but with black hair. He may be rich, but he ain't pretty. An hour later and the Trofeo cars fire up and head for the pits; the noise is way past describing. Oh, okay, I'll attempt to do it justice: try tearing silk through Metallica's amplification stack while drinking Shell Optimax and striking a match. And then do it 24 times.

Qualifying goes well; out of twenty four runners our boys in car 26 have gone ninth. Frank was balked on his fast lap by a huge, sweating bull of a man called Rota in the number 27 car and is steaming, let's-have-a-word angry. Rob calms him down with a few choice football-coach phrases and a glass of water. But after all the build up, as we sit

checking sector times, it seems that the boys have got a duff car. On the straights, where less skill is involved, most of the other cars are outdragging number 26, while on the corners the lads are making up precious time.

Rob is not unfamiliar with the situation, explaining that if the engineers run an operational window of five percent, some of the cars can be 30bhp down on others. It just seems that the British entry always seems to get the bottom-end of the percentile. A proper chat with the engineers and some presidential campaigning by Rob and it is agreed that they can have another car for the race, a car they have not driven, a car they do not know. It's a serious gamble. But anything is better than the car they ran today.

Race day dawns bright and clear. Rob, in his motivational speech, describes the need to become one with the car. Then he begins to describe becoming at one with the surface of the track and Frank and I get a little confused. He obviously means 'drive really fast until the car breaks or you hit something hard'. I have become so caught up I'm convinced I'm driving. Or at least a fondly-regarded mascot.

Ninth, on the left-hand side of the grid, Frank starts the race with the noise of 24 unsilenced Maserati V8s rending the air. On

Of steering and stringbacks...

The stats are pretty impressive for the Trofeo race cars; the 4.2-litre V8 uses revised electronics and breathing tweaks to jump power six per cent (to 407bhp), but the most impressive bit is the fact that by removing the Coupé's air-con and generous sound-deadening, the portly Maser has lost 208kg over the standard car despite the FIA rollcage and other safety kit like fire extinguishers and cut-outs.

Obviously negating the power-to-weight ratio by merely stepping into the car earlier this year at Verano, I was surprised by the amount of road car still present in the Coupé. It's all recognisable and,

...but then the track is empty

Ford powers into the lead...

apart from clambering elephant-like over the rollcage, quite easy to get comfy in. Start the car and there's the aural assault to deal with. But if you like engines, it'll just make you weep with desire. Clomp first with the right-hand paddle, and clutch take-up seems better – a symptom of less weight.

After that it's how you might expect. Even on slicks the Maser understeers in the first portion of a tight corner, but injudicious – read clumsy – prodding of the throttle when the tyres are cold still brings the tail round. The suspension is much stiffer, making turn-in a delight and removing entirely the

diagonal nod of the road car. But it is a fairly safe car to drive fast, flagging up limits early and in glorious technicolour. Whether it's an easy car to race is entirely another matter and one on which I'm not qualified to answer. I prefer my track barren, not clogged with 23 other racers...

SPECIFICATIONS

MASERATI 4200 TROFEO

Price: EUR 120,000 (includes race series, but sadly you don't get the car)
Engine: 4244cc V8 32v, 407bhp at 7000rpm, 340lb/ft
Performance: sub-4.0 seconds 0-62mph, 177mph, sub-10mpg
Transmission: Six-speed paddle shift

'Where to next?' Le Mans

the pit wall, Rob and I flinch as those same Maseratis pinch and squeal their way into the first left-hander and wait puckered to see how it all shakes out. Frank is OK and spends a couple of laps getting the feel, settling down.

On his third lap he sets a time two seconds faster than qualifying, meaning the car must be better today and that the gamble has paid off. On his fourth he takes another car and pressurises the next into a spin (prompting more foreign swear-words and gesticulation from the tall bloke two sections down the pitwall); we're up to seventh. As he comes into the pits for the driver change, things are looking good; Frank has had a phenomenal race, being careful, taking it easy but setting Rob up for decent pursuit. He said on the way down that if he was way off the pace he'd give up; he isn't. Rob folds himself into the car and blasts away, we're all cheering and the testosterone sloshes around our ankles, baptising my shoes with adrenalin.

Italians are crashing all over the place as they tangle egos and share paint, with the bullish Rota being shunted hard from behind; I catch Frank making small gleeful punching motions with his hands. And then disaster: Rob has incurred a drive-through for speeding in the pitlane. As he drives through, he speeds

again, leading Rob to later surmise that his speedo was misreading. Hmm... The race finishes under yellows due to earlier crashes and general misbehaviour. Frank is pleased with his performance, Rob congratulatory but a touch miffed. They got ninth.

It's all over. A whole weekend for 40 minutes of fury, sweat and passion. An epic transcontinental drive for two hours of anticipation and a blur of red and white. When Rob and Frank change out of their overalls they become just blokes again, chatting away about the next race, where they might go faster and how to shave off that last second. It's a petrol-injected fairytale. With serious miles to cover before we hit the UK, we offer to drive our pair of Maseratis back to the UK while Frank flies. He won't hear of it. We started it together, we'll finish it, he says with a twinkle. I should really dislike this man. He has a very exciting lifestyle. But he also has the determination to take on a sport where he had no experience, and make himself competitive. We'll see him competing at Le Mans, because he's determined, committed and having fun; and that's where modern motorsport needs to be. This Mountain, it seems, hasn't quite reached its peak.* ▣ (*Sorry Frank).

Maserati **Coupe** Cambiocorsa

An everyday exotic

BY ANDREW BORNHOP • PHOTOS BY RON PERRY

R O A D **R&T** **T E S T** MASERATI IS MORE THAN JUST A GREAT NAME; IT'S a great marque with a storied racing history. Cars bearing Neptune's Trident have won the Mille Miglia, the Targa Florio, the Formula 1 World Championship, even the Indianapolis 500. Twice. And in the 1960s, the lightweight Birdcage Maserati left an indelible mark on the American sports-car racing scene.

In spite of these laurels, the Italian automaker has had a tumultuous history, dealing with, among other things, a succession of different owners. Further, its production cars haven't met with great success here in the U.S. Sure, the Ghibli, Khamsin, Merak and Bora qualified as exotics, but they never matched the stature or desirability of comparable Ferraris. Also, cars such as the large Quattroporte sedan of the early 1980s seemed a bit odd, whereas the Biturbo of the same era proved just plain unreliable. And then came a curious decision to build the TC by Maserati, a rebadged (and not particularly pretty) version of the front-drive Chrysler LeBaron.

But, as they might say in Florence, that's all *acqua* under the Ponte Vecchio now that Ferrari owns Maserati and is intent on making its longtime Modenese rival profitable.

Without a doubt, the heart of this handsome new Maserati is its dry-sump 4.2-liter V-8, which has a drive-by-wire throttle and is as attractive as it is potent. The prominent wrinkle-finish manifold feeds the alloy 4-valve heads, each carrying two chain-driven camshafts that operate the valves via hydraulic cups. Ignition and fuel injection duties are handled by Bosch.

The U.S. comeback, after an 11-year absence, started this year with the Coupe and Spyder, a pair of Giugiaro-penned machines now on sale at Ferrari dealers. Ferrari sees these Maseratis—which are built at the thoroughly modernized Maserati factory in Modena—as comfortable GT cars that aren't quite as extreme in performance, design and character as the steeds from Maranello.

And yes, after spending a couple of weeks with a Coupe fitted with the Cambiocorsa gearbox and optional Skyhook suspension system, we'd have to agree. This car isn't a 360 Modena. Nor is it a 575M. But it is a fine GT, a beautifully understated car that feels Italian not just in its driving position (which has the pedals a tad too close when

the reach to the steering wheel is optimized) but also in the mechanical fury of its 4.2-liter V-8 heart, its sumptuous interior and its superb driving manners.

Those manners can be traced in part to the not-so-svelte 3640-lb. Coupe's excellent 52/48 weight balance, made possible by having the 6-speed transaxle situated between the rear wheels and the battery in the trunk. Skyhook adjustable suspension damping also plays a role. Although we suspect a Coupe without the $2270 option would still work well, Skyhook does a commendable job of keeping the Coupe's ride relatively comfortable when traveling straight down the Interstate, and then automatically firming the damping when the road gets curvy. Six accelerometers

(on the body, the front hubs and on the right rear) monitor the motions of the chassis and suspension and communicate with a computer that makes continuous real-time adjustments to the coil-over shock absorbers at each double-A-arm corner. The Sport mode, accessible via a pushbutton on the center console, is significantly firmer than the Normal setting, but not so stiff as to prevent body roll in the corners. What's more, the Sport mode provides for a more aggressive Cambiocorsa shift strategy.

The Cambiocorsa system, which shifts the 6-speed transaxle hydraulically via paddles mounted behind the steering wheel, is a mixed bag. On one hand, we love it, because full-throttle upshifts have never been so easy, so quick, so precise. It

would be great to have in a racing car because there's no danger of ever missing a shift. And the downshifts, particularly in the Sport mode, are accompanied by perfect blips of the throttle that make it sound like we are all better than we really are at heel-and-toeing.

Around town, however, at mild to medium throttle openings, the Cambiocorsa's shifts border on being too clunky, in either the fully automatic or manual modes. With every upshift there's a momentary loss of momentum that's slightly unsettling right in the middle of the shift. Although the driver can minimize this by lifting the throttle at each shift, such tricks shouldn't be necessary in such a fine touring car. Also on a critical note, the

hydraulic linkage back at the transaxle makes what one editor called "a chorus of rattling thuds" as the car busily downshifts from one gear to the next while approaching stoplights. Not exactly confidence-inspiring, and it led one mechanically sympathetic editor to eliminate all that downshifting by pulling back on both paddles simultaneously to engage neutral every time he knew the car would be coming to a complete stop. One thing is for sure: The Coupe's vented and cross-drilled disc brakes—Brembos of more than one foot in diameter each—are more than up to the task of stopping the car without the help of engine braking.

In spite of the Cambiocorsa's good traits, and in spite of sales that show the public likes

it more than we do, we'd still rather have the 6-speed manual transaxle found in the Coupe GT. The reason is simple: We know it may not be cutting-edge technology, but its shifts are always as smooth as its driver.

With either gear-change system, however, you get the same fantastic engine—a dry-sump 90-degree 4.2-liter V-8 with four chain-driven overhead camshafts and a row of auxiliary pumps on the side of the silicon-rich aluminum block that looks like it's from Ferrari's F1 program.

And you know what? The beautifully exposed engine is in fact from Ferrari, although it is dyno-tested (like all Maserati engines) at Maserati. Benefiting from variable-intake cam timing and a forged crankshaft that rides in an F1-style full saddle of

■ Unlike other exotics, the Coupe has a spacious cockpit, but with all the expected craftsmanship. Note the suede backing on the paddle, above.

bearings, this screaming V-8 puts out 390 bhp at 7000 rpm, and 333 lb.-ft. of torque at 4500.

This is a fantastic engine, with all the fury you'd expect and an entertaining ability to plant the driver in his seat. Each upshift is accompanied by just a hint of squat, and wheelspin in the first couple of gears is the norm if traction control is switched off. At the same time this engine is smooth and amazingly tractable, able to pull strongly from 2500 rpm in all gears yet still able to rev so quickly and ferociously that we could be fooled into believing it has a featherweight flywheel.

The numbers at the track verify the engine's potency. The Coupe Cambiocorsa, in Sport mode, hits 60 mph in 5.0 seconds, and then reaches the quarter mile in 13.4 sec. at an excellent trap speed of 109.6 mph. These results are not quite up to Maserati's claims, but it's worth mentioning that our test car, with only 1800 miles on its odometer, perhaps needed some more break-in miles.

No matter—this performance still puts the Maserati quicker than an Aston Martin DB7, and on a par with the Porsche 911 and Chevrolet Corvette. And neither of these last two cars can come close to matching the elegant atmosphere found inside this sur-prisingly spacious Maserati, which accommodates drivers as tall as 6 ft. 4 in.—and back-seat passengers no taller than 5 ft. 4 in.

Once inside, you'll see that leather is everywhere. On the exquisitely stitched seats. On the door panels. On the dash itself. On the steering wheel. And it's most appreciated on the shift paddles themselves, where the suede backing helps keep the driver's fingertips from slipping.

In traditional fashion, Maserati's trademark clock graces the padded leather center console, which in our test car is a monochromatic black that doesn't show the rich texture of the leather the way some lighter colors do. Nevertheless, it's still handsome, with attractive chrome-trimmed Jaeger gauges looming beneath a prominent leather-covered instrument hood. Most of the controls are straightforward and where you'd expect them to be, and we found it refreshing to see a steering wheel devoid of controls for the radio and the like.

None of us, however, was particularly fond of the Maserati Info Centre, which condenses the controls for the climate control, stereo, trip computer and navigation system into one simple screen but doesn't seem to facilitate the operation of any of those systems. On a positive note, the CD slot located between the seats is very convenient.

On the road, the Maserati is a fabulous Grand Tourer that effectively blends the stability and substance of—let's face it—a heavier car with manners more befitting a lighter sports car. It also doesn't need to be babied. It can go up driveways without scraping its nose; it can idle in stop-and-go traffic without overheating; its climate control works like a charm and there's nothing the least bit finicky about the car's operation. Although the low-profile Michelin Pilots do thump a bit over Botts dots and other sharp bumps, the Coupe has a well-damped suppleness to its suspension that's readily apparent when crossing dips at intersections.

Timeless and understated, the Maserati Coupe is an everyday exotic, an Italian DB7 for two-thirds the price. It's attractive, not flashy. And let it be known that we'd rather have our Coupe as a GT, the model with the 6-speed manual gearbox in place of the automatic shifting of the Coupe Cambiocorsa.

In the meantime, the fruits of Ferrari ownership will be seen again late next year, when a new Maserati Quattroporte—a large V-8-powered rear-drive sedan with Pininfarina styling—makes its debut as a 2004 model. And around that time, Maserati has announced that it will go racing again, presumably with a hot version of its Coupe called the Trofeo. No series or country has been announced, but it's pleasing to see the Trident getting back into the sport that is such an important part of its legacy. ◉

THE COMPETITION

Jaguar XKR Roadster
Tested: 12/99

Porsche 911 Carrera
Tested: 3/02

■ Three expensive 2+2s, three very different characters. The 911 is the sports car of the bunch, which is no surprise given its lighter weight and racing heritage. The XKR, on the other hand, seduces us with its shape and tremendous torque. And the Maserati? It's an everyday exotic, a comfortable Italian GT that backs up its clean style with outstanding power.

	Maserati Coupe Cambiocorsa	Jaguar XKR Roadster	Porsche 911 Carrera
Current list price	$87,165	$86,330	$67,900
Engine	dohc 4.2-liter V-8	supercharged dohc 4.0-liter V-8	dohc 3.6-liter flat-6
Horsepower	390 bhp @ 7000 rpm	370 bhp @ 6150 rpm	320 bhp @ 6800 rpm
Torque	333 lb-ft @ 4500 rpm	387 lb-ft @ 3600 rpm	273 lb-ft @ 4250 rpm
Transmission	6-speed manual w/paddles	5-speed automatic	6-speed manual
0–60 mph	5.0 sec	5.3 sec	4.9 sec
Braking, 60–0 mph	118 ft	126 ft	117 ft
Lateral accel (200-ft skidpad)	0.87g	0.86g	0.91g
EPA city/highway	11/17 mpg	16/22 mpg	18/26 mpg
Length	178.1 in.	187.4 in.	174.5 in.
Width	71.7 in.	72.0 in.	69.7 in.
Height	51.4 in.	50.7 in.	51.4 in.
Wheelbase	104.7 in.	101.9 in.	92.6 in.
Track, f/r	60.0 in./60.1 in.	59.2 in./59.0 in.	57.7 in./58.3 in.
Curb weight	3640 lb	4015 lb	3215 lb

2002 Maserati Coupe **Cambiocorsa**

Maserati North America, Inc., 250 Sylvan Ave., Englewood Cliffs, N.J. 07632; www.maseratiusa.com

At a Glance

0–60 mph	5.0 sec
0–¼ mile	13.4 sec
Top speed	est 177 mph
Skidpad	0.87g
Slalom	64.7 mph
Brake rating	excellent

List Price: $87,165
Price as Tested: $99,158

Price as tested incl std equip. (front and side airbags, ABS, traction control, limited-slip differential, climate control, keyless entry, leather upholstery, heated seats; pwr seats, windows, mirrors & door locks), Skyhook suspension ($2270), gas-guzzler tax ($3700), navigation system ($1805), xenon headlamps ($1145), luxury tax ($1723), dest charge ($1350).

SCALE: 10 IN.(254mm) DIVISIONS
DRAWING BY TIM BARKER

SPECIFICATIONS

Engine

Type	aluminum block & heads, V-8
Valvetrain	dohc 4-valve/cyl
Displacement	259 cu in./4244 cc
Bore x stroke	3.62 x 3.14 in./ 92.0 x 79.8 mm
Compression ratio	11.1:1
Horsepower (SAE)	390 bhp @ 7000 rpm
Bhp/liter	91.7
Torque	333 lb-ft @ 4500 rpm
Redline	7550 rpm
Fuel injection	elect. sequential port
Fuel	premium unleaded, 91 pump octane

Warranty

Basic warranty	4 years/50,000 miles
Powertrain	4 years/50,000 miles
Rust-through	na

Chassis & Body

Layout	front engine/rear drive
Body/frame	unit steel
Brakes: Front	14.0-in. vented & drilled discs
Rear	13.0-in. vented & drilled discs
Assist type	vacuum, ABS, EBD
Total swept area	517 sq in.
Swept area/ton	273 sq in.
Wheels	alloy; 18 x 8J f, 18 x 9½J r
Tires	Michelin Pilot Sport; 235/40ZR-18 f, 265/35ZR-18 r
Steering	rack & pinion, vari power assist
Overall ratio	na
Turns, lock to lock	3.0
Turning circle	39.4 ft

Suspension
Front: upper & lower A-arms, coil springs, elect. adj tube shocks, anti-roll bar
Rear: upper & lower A-arms, coil springs, elect. adj tube shocks, anti-roll bar

General Data

Curb weight	3640 lb
Test weight	3790 lb
Weight dist (with driver), f/r, %	52/48
Wheelbase	104.7 in.
Track, f/r	60.0 in./60.1 in.
Length	178.1 in.
Width	71.7 in.
Height	51.4 in.
Ground clearance	4.5 in.
Trunk space	10.6 cu ft

Accommodations

Seating capacity	2+2
Head room: Front	36.3 in.
Rear	33.0 in.
Seat width: Front	2 x 18.0 in.
Rear	2 x 16.0 in.
Front-seat leg room	44.8 in.
Seatback adjustment	15 deg
Seat travel	8.8 in.
Rear-seat knee room	13.0 in.

Drivetrain

Transmission: **6-speed manual w/paddles**

Gear	Ratio	Overall ratio	(Rpm)	Mph
1st	3.29:1	12.26:1	(7550)	45
2nd	2.16:1	8.05:1	(7550)	69
3rd	1.61:1	6.00:1	(7550)	93
4th	1.27:1	4.73:1	(7550)	118
5th	1.03:1	3.86:1	(7550)	144
6th	0.85:1	3.16:1	est (7550)	177

Final drive ratio	3.73:1
Engine rpm @ 60 mph in top gear	2600

Instrumentation

200-mph speedometer, 8000-rpm tachometer, oil pressure, coolant temp, fuel level, volts, analog clock

Safety

front and side airbags
anti-lock braking
traction control
seatbelt pretensioners
(all standard equip.)

PERFORMANCE

Acceleration

Time to speed	Seconds
0–30 mph	2.1
0–40 mph	2.9
0–50 mph	4.0
0–60 mph	5.0
0–70 mph	6.4
0–80 mph	7.8
0–90 mph	9.2
0–100 mph	11.4

Time to distance	
0–100 ft	3.0
0–500 ft	7.5
0–900 ft	10.6
0–1320 ft (¼ mile)	13.4 @ 109.6 mph

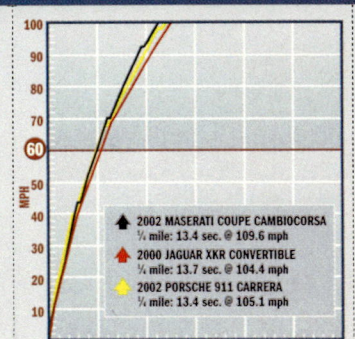

● 2002 MASERATI COUPE CAMBIOCORSA
¼ mile: 13.4 sec. @ 109.6 mph
▲ 2000 JAGUAR XKR CONVERTIBLE
¼ mile: 13.7 sec. @ 104.4 mph
■ 2002 PORSCHE 911 CARRERA
¼ mile: 13.4 sec. @ 105.1 mph

Braking

Minimum stopping distance
From 60 mph	118 ft
From 80 mph	211 ft
Control	excellent
Brake feel	excellent
Overall brake rating	excellent

Subjective ratings consist of excellent, very good, good, average, poor; na means information is not available.

Fuel Economy

Our driving	12.8 mpg
EPA city/highway	11/17 mpg
Cruise range	285 miles
Fuel capacity	23.2 gal.

Handling

Lateral acceleration (200-ft skidpad)	0.87g
Balance	mild understeer
Speed through 700-ft slalom	64.7 mph
Balance	neutral
Lateral seat support	very good

Interior Noise

Idle in neutral	59 dBA
Maximum in 1st gear	78 dBA
Constant 50 mph	70 dBA
70 mph	72 dBA

Test Notes:
Launching this Maserati is an exercise in throttle restraint—it's easy to spin the Michelins and not get much forward momentum. But with minimal wheelspin, the acceleration is outstanding. Equally impressive are the crisp, full-throttle shifts of the Cambiocorsa system. • Around the skidpad, the Coupe exhibits more body roll than expected, but it's not excessive, and it's easy to convert mild understeer into a bit of oversteer with the throttle. • Although this car isn't light, it stops exceptionally well from 60 and 80 mph.

Test Conditions:

Temperature	Humidity	Elevation	Wind
83°F	15%	150 ft	calm

Maserati Spyder

Just like the Coupe, only better looking, more exclusive and bloody near as quick!

If you're going to have a convertible, you might as well a) leave the roof down whenever animals aren't filing past on their way to the docks and, b) get the one with the biggest, baddest engine you can stuff into it.

At least, that's the overriding theory around here (along with an emphasis on chassis rigidity, but we'll get to that later).

The Maserati Spyder fits the bill on both counts – and it's got an exclusivity advantage over, oh, let's say, any Porsche.

While the Maser coupe has its odd odd angle, there are no such issues with the Spyder. The shape lends itself to dumping the back seat in favour of the roof mechanism and, if anything, it's cleaner, simpler and more integrated with the roof down.

That the wheelbase is a touch shorter than the coupe helps the drophead's look, and it also lends it a more enthusiastic air when you point it into second-gear corners and fire out again.

It's also pretty cosy with the roof up. Its lining is several layers thick, the sound deadening is also effective in disposing of unwanted road noise and the whole thing's dead sexy, from any angle.

The best angle, you'd reckon, is from the driver's seat when you've got that amazing 287kW 4.2-litre V8 pinned and its four exhaust tubes pumping their mischief. Crack the throttle in first gear and wait a nanosecond before, regardless of the revs, the Maser pins you into the seat. Then,

as it rips raucously towards the redline, snap the Cambiocorsa gearbox's right-hand paddle to snap up the shift and go again, at barely diminished acceleration, in second, then in third.

The mechanically empathetic may find it difficult to cope with the bang from the rear end every time you snap home a

Dammit! Missed the movie-star carpark!

flat shift, but it's precise and it's quick. What it isn't is a genuine alternative to an automatic gearbox, despite what Maserati Oz will tell you.

It's got an 'auto' mode (with a big brain on top of a six-speed manual 'box), but it still requires some fiddling about with throttle openings to organise smooth

upshifts and rapid downshifts.

The least comfy part, though, is trickling at low speed in first gear. A grand tourer *par excellence*, but you've still got to get the thing out of heavy traffic now and again. At low revs and low speed, the clutch is too eager to get into the action, which leads to jerky take-offs and, with it engaging, disengaging and engaging again, even jerkier trickling. Our tip? Save $12,000 and take the stock manual. You'll be happier.

Still, that's the biggest point of criticism with the Maser Spyder. While it isn't Boxster-rigid in the chassis, its suspension still has the ability to send and receive inputs with admirable accuracy.

The cabin is one of the most distinctive, classical and beautifully crafted in all of modern car-dom. From the curve of the leather dash to the little Maserati clock, from the gusseting on the seats to the craftsmanship of the carpet fitting, it's just one of the nicest places to spend time that we've seen in recent memory.

We've documented the changes to the Maserati driveline before (essentially a rejigging of the way it communicates its instructions between engine and clutch), and they've improved things, but it's still not as unfussed as the similar system in Ferrari's 575M Maranello. But it's half the money. And it's got no roof.

And, if everybody in your circle has a Porsche, the Maser has a degree of individuality your mates cannot hope to match. **CM**

STORY Michael Taylor PHOTOS Mark Bean

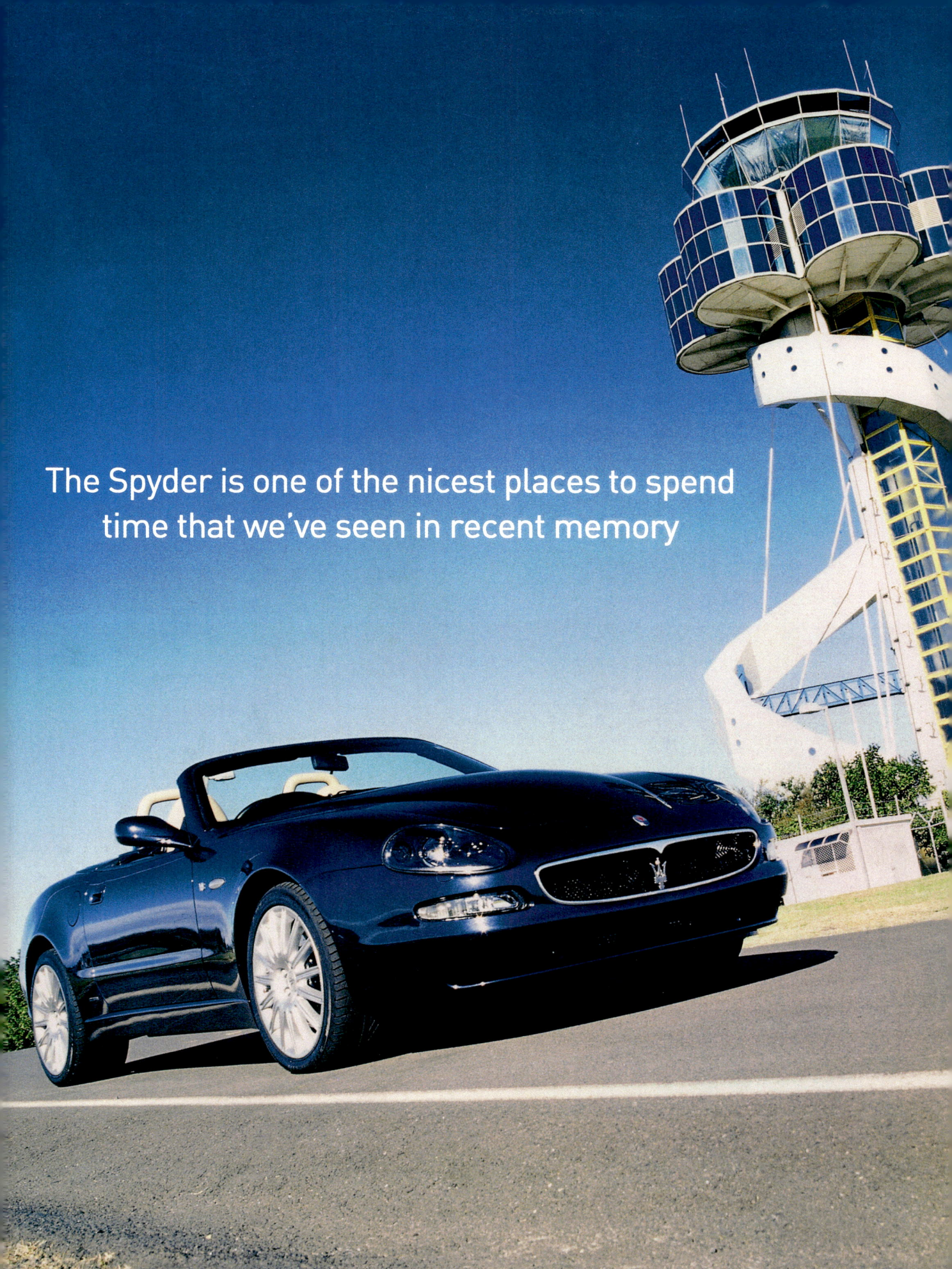

The Spyder is one of the nicest places to spend time that we've seen in recent memory

BACK TO FRONT

In a world where the Germans seem to have an armlock on what makes a large luxury saloon, Maserati's new Quattroporte promises an intriguing and charismatic alternative. But can Italy deliver?

Story Tom Ford
Photography Barry Hayden

D AWN IS MASSAGING golden fingers around the Florentine skyline as I descend the steps of the Hotel Villa Medici and stride confidently over to a line of new Pinifarina-penned Maserati Quattroporte, smiling gently at the concierge as he opens the glass door to the brisk slap of morning air. Dressed in my best corduroy jacket, I take the keys from the Maserati mechanic and breathe deeply, savoring the moment, smiling to myself. I put it all on black, and it came up gold. Shaking my head to clear the dreams of international playboydom I turn, catch my foot on the back of my leg and fall - with all the grace of a recently shot partridge - between two cars. Failing in any significant sense to react to gravity's sudden interest in my torso, my head cracks off the wing mirror with a bang.

Simultaneously cringing and bouncing back to the vertical as if propelled by rubber tarmac, I shoot my cuffs and finger the buttons on my jacket, looking left to right and unnecessarily smoothing hair that has the innate form of a burst sofa. Nobody sees. Packing photographer Barry into the car with a little more vigor than is

strictly necessary, we drive at speed from the scene. As we pass, the concierge taps the side of his nose and points at me from the doorway of the hotel, laughing.

Unfortunately, as I have just so colourfully demonstrated, being allergic to hip and suffering from a terminal deficit of style, I'm not sure that I'm entirely qualified to test this newest of Maseratis. Out on the road, the Quattroporte exudes that kind of visual arrogance that makes its slightly ungainly lines look like works of art. At first the hack in me questions front lights flanking that sucking great chromium mouth that look a bit like those from an Alfa 156/166, rear lights that somehow conspire to hint at those of foreign-market Lancias, tall tails and low noses and curves and vents that whisper of influence in form.

But then you just sit back and watch it roll past, you wonder where the Germans lost their passion, and why we all accepted it. It didn't look its best on the show stand, the pictures don't do it justice. Even the rear door's sensuous S-shaped curve smacks of tailoring, of attention to detail. The three rectangular air vents in the front

Now that's what we call a grille. Has a liking for krill and shellfish

Wood on test car not the best-looking option. Go for 'titanium'

wing like are little bits of jewelry hung from a challenging, but exciting shape. It grows on you. Like Savile Row fungus.

Looking forward to the drive and soaking up the attention of passing Florentines, we start to head out of town. The Quattroporte (it simply means 'four door' in Italian) has been designed - as boss Luca di Montezemolo himself put it - as a car that you are chauffeur driven in during the week that still prods swoopy butterflies in your stomach at the weekend. To that end, the big Maser is attempting to serve a broad palette of abilities to a wider range of people than the current Spyder and Coupe. It's a big car (over five-metres in length), based on a new chassis unique to the Quattroporte and boasting a transaxle layout with rear-mounted gearbox. Up front and driving the rear wheels is a development of the naturally aspirated 4.2 V8 in the Coupe and Spyder, tuned slightly to

400bhp and 333lb ft and geared more toward driveability with that prodigious low-down torque to designed to cope with a car that weighs 1930kg at the kerb.

Inside it's a trend-bucking swathe of leather-smell and single-function buttons. Our bronze-coloured test car came with a light interior leather and slightly MFI-looking wood - but the other cars on display had beautifully crafted interior combinations, including a rather tasteful black leather and 'Titanium' technical finish, that looks brilliant. The details get you hooked. The paddles behind the wheel are metal, with little tactile slivers of rubber set into their rear surface. The buttons all do one thing and one thing only - from switching modes for the traction control and gearbox (top buttons, left hand side of center console), to altering the brightness of the beautiful blue dial and instrument set (to the right and behind the steering wheel). It's a

refreshing and remarkably good-looking place to spend time.

The same can also be said of those in the back - adding credibility to di Montezemolo's comments. Two beautifully wide-beamed chairs luxuriate between a fold down central bolster that contains cup-holders and air-conditioning controls as well as a button that moves the passenger seat forward to leave more leg room for the chauffeuree. Not that they'll be lacking, because the rear accommodation in the Quattroporte feels to be at least as commodious as that of either long-wheelbase versions of the Audi A8 and BMW 7-series. Cunning stuff. The 'Quattroporte' legend is spelled out in chrome script between the front seats, reminding you of a trident heritage, even if you live in the rear compartment. It doesn't have quite the amount of toys present in either German limo, but there's an air of gentleman's club that the Maserati does so well. Long after

Quad pipes echo those of Coupe; heavy bumper the worst view

'As the engine blares into life a rosy glow envelops the Quattroporte'

gadgets are old hat, the Maserati will age gracefully. The instant the Ferrari-built engine blares into life, a rosy glow envelops the Quattroporte. The noise grinds home the *otherness* of this Italianate limo. Everything promises that this car is going to be one of the absolute greats.

Sadly, it isn't.

The issues begin with the 'Duo-Select' gearbox. Essentially a version of the six-speed Cambiocorsa sequential manual found in the Coupe and Spyder but with a less aggressive change during 'automatic' mode and tuned to cope with a bigger, heavier car. In automatic the Quattroporte can be driven on a light throttle and you won't really notice the changes because the torque loading on the gearbox is relatively light, but call for even moderate levels of throttle and the car will slam from one gear to the next and lurch around more than a particularly inebriate sailor.

A sequential manual has an electronically-actuated clutch that has no ability to 'slur' ratios like a traditional torque converter gearbox, leading to great gasping pauses between gears and throttle inputs at certain periods of the change cycle. Because the engine has so much torque, kickdown is somewhat abrupt and certainly not in the league of any auto on the current market. It's not relaxing for driver or passenger and even though you can learn to drive it smoothly, it still has very little appeal. Less of a problem in a sports car where you feel that the auto mode is an added extra - but not in a car that might well be driven like this 90 percent of the time.

Add to the jerksome 'box the 'Skyhook' adaptive suspension that seems incapable of filtering out even minor imperfections (and the roads around Florence have very few 'minor' imperfections), and you'll find the chauffeur has begun leafing meaningfully through

Serious expression undermined by pink T-shirt

Bronze colour sounds so 70s, but looks great on the big Maser

Jobfinder leaflets. Switch to 'manual' mode (the paddles) and you can mitigate some of the jerks with a little sympathetic throttle-lifting - but this is not the point for a £70k limousine. Unimpressed, we head out to interact with some scenery.

The engine starts to stretch, the volume and warmth swelling to become a proper V8 roar. This is more like it. Hit the 'sport' button and the gearbox changes more quickly and the Skyhook tightens up suspension damping even more, defining the edges of the Quattroporte's grip limits more sharply and removing the thump from the gearbox. There's a sweet spot for changing up in 'sport', a hefty 6500rpm up the revcounter, but the Quattroporte feels more alive, more vital when off the leash.

There's a deeper well from which the Maser can draw when speed and not comfort is the priority, disguising mass well, turning in from a direct-feeling wheel. Out on the damp and greasy roads, the Quattroporte slides around with MSP (Maserati Stability Programme) still switched on, the sport button releasing oversteer degrees for your delectation with which you can play without fear of a sudden forcible taste of pine tree. The gorgeous, fluent engine provides more than enough torque from very low revs to provoke gentle slides and the car is more than happy to provide this more juvenile excitement.

But the brakes are a disappointment, failing to stop the car without chirruping the front tyres, feeling all the time as if the brake bias is incorrectly set, the car pressing itself too deep into the corner despite being given more than enough opportunity to slow itself down. The Quattroporte amuses for a bit in a very specific set of circumstances and then just gets wearing. A couple of missed gears, a couple of stalls at hill junctions, a moment of slight panic

---

✱ CHAUFFEUR TO MR FERRARI

'The long way home, sir?'

If you were a chauffeur, you could do worse than being wheelman for the coolest boss in the automotive world; Luca di Montezemolo. Antonio Colfi is currently driving for di Montezemolo in the Quattroporte. Originally an F1 mechanic responsible for the left rear tyre on Schumacher's car, Antonio was sidelined with a back injury three years ago. One day he was dropping Jean Todt off at Fiorano, and Luca expressed a need for a permanent driver. The rest is history. Very cool. And no, Antonio swears he's never had an embarrassing prang with the head of Ferrari and Maserati in the back.

It's one way to get to drive a Maserati

'Slot in a six-speed auto and the car would definitely remove fabric foot coverings explosively'

Surprisingly low
Quattroporte
needs a proper
auto option

as the car draws inexorably toward an apex without slowing and the whole experience tarnishes like a brass buckle in salt spray.

Later, after we arrive back at the hotel and I've had another rosy-cheeked moment with the concierge, Roberto Corradi (technical head of Maserati SpA), pinions me with the kind of stare that's more usually used to hold cruise ships in port and asks The Question. I explain about the damping, the brakes, the recalcitrant gearbox. He suggests courteously that I might not be seeing the point. But I do. I do see what Maserati was attempting to achieve here. I just don't think it works.

I love F1-style transmissions and truly believe that they are the way forward for sportscars, but this one just doesn't gel with a car that looks - and feels - like a luxury limousine. As a result, the Quattroporte does not deliver as a car to be driven in; a car that is smooth and relaxed and comfortable. But it

also, crucially, isn't really a sportscar either. No near-two tonne saloon ever could be.

Slot in a six-speed automatic gearbox (the ZF unit from Audi following the recent link-up for example) and some decent dampers and it would remove fabric foot coverings explosively as a rapid, passionate alternative; a purchase that could base itself in the heart without too many high velocity compromises with the head. Corradi suggests that no other car in the sector provides the sporting intimacy of the Quattroporte. He's right. But I suggest that if you buy a four-door saloon with bonus rear legroom, your thoughts are more about comfort than ten-tenths balance.

This car is all about a trade-off. And the reality is the degree to which you can hammer along a fast, flowing road quicker than, say, an S-class is, at best, marginal compared with the time you'll spend wishing for a silkier gearbox, better brakes and a smoother ride. I'd also be

more than a little surprised if most potential owners don't have other things in the garage to play with should the mood take them.

The Quattroporte was supposed to be a car with two souls. It is. But in having a split personality it fails to have an identity. If only it drove as well as it looks Maserati would have cornered the market for all those people wanting to make an aesthetic, quirky choice in the sector. I wanted this car to be fantastic. I'm gutted to find it flawed.

SPECIFICATIONS

MASERATI QUATTROPORTE

Price: £69,995
Length: 5052mm **Height:** 1438mm
Width: 1895mm **Wheelbase:** 3064mm
Weight: 1930kg
Engine: 4244cc V8, 400bhp at 7000rpm, 333lb ft at 4500rpm
Transmission: 6-speed sequential manual rear-wheel drive
Performance: 5.2sec 0-62mph, 171mph
On sale in UK: Late spring

A car that almost meets the dreams of its maker.

BY PETER ROBINSON

It's styled by Italy's Pininfarina, it wears a price somewhere north of 100 large, and its name means "four doors."

Despite the commonplace moniker, the fifth-generation Quattroporte reeks of presence, individuality, classy conservatism, and drive-me desirability. It's clear that Pininfarina has achieved Maserati's ambition of creating a prestigious Italian rival for the Audi A8 and S8, Jaguar XJR, Mercedes E55 and S55, and BMW 745i.

With the four-cam V-8 located behind the front axle, the car looks big from the side. The 120.6-inch wheelbase (0.9 inch shorter than an S-class's)

and extended doors are clearly evident. Parent company Ferrari located the engine aft of the front axle to create a 47/53 front-to-rear weight distribution, as in the new Ferrari 612 Scaglietti.

The Maser's driving complexity begins with the fixed door handles. Behind each are two buttons. Touch the gray one, and it releases the door electrically; the black one, requiring more pressure, does the job manually, perhaps in case the electrics go fizz. The

cabin is Italianate—tasteful, chic—with all the luxury toys. There's a vast array of materials: rosewood, mahogany, or briarwood, or a titanium finish; 10 Poltrona Frau leathers using 13 stitching colors, 10 on the dash; and 15 exterior colors.

The power seats are as comfortable as they appear sporting. Rear-seat space is more E- than S-class, very relaxing for two. But that's not where we want to be. The nearly vertical steering wheel is adjustable for reach and height. Rather than go the infamous iDrive route, the Italians prefer dedicated dashboard buttons for the stereo, trip computer, telephone, dashboard monitor, and nav system.

Turn the key, and there's a moment's delay, followed by a long whirring sound from the starter before the V-8 fires with an automatic blip of the throttle. The transmission (there's no clutch pedal; it's a robotic manual with automated shifting and clutch) defaults to the automatic-shift mode. Select drive, press the accelerator, and go. Called Cambiocorsa in the Coupé and DuoSelect in the Quattroporte, it's the only transmission choice. On a light throttle, gearshifts are smoother than in the Coupé and almost as fluent as a conventional automatic. But as you add power, the shifting action becomes increasingly hesitant, and full-throttle shifts at the 7500-rpm redline are downright abrupt.

Flick a switch to engage manual mode, and gearchanging is done via paddles behind the steering wheel—left for downshifts, right for upshifts. There's more complexity: The "Sport" button on the steering wheel firms up the electronic dampers and quickens gearchanges—and it stays in gear, even as the engine hits its rev limiter, instead of upshifting. Learn to feather the throttle at each upward gearchange, and progress is smoother. The gearbox is slow from drive to reverse and back again. We can't help wondering how the Quattroporte would behave if it worked through a traditional torque converter

and six-speed automatic.

The 4.2-liter V-8's a belter. Maserati claims marginally more power here than in the Coupé or Spyder (394 horsepower versus 385) but the same 333 pound-feet of torque. Still, a new air filter, revised camshaft profiles, a modified engine-control map, and a new exhaust system have flattened the torque curve at low revs. No matter where you are on the rev counter, the engine never makes less than 221 pound-feet of twist.

These four-doors go from 0 to 62 mph in 5.2 seconds, according to the factory. The soundtrack is a rising crescendo of induction and exhaust music across the entire rev range. Top speed is 171 mph, Maserati says. Powerful though it is, the V-8 blends this stirring performance with terrific flexibility and refinement. Yet the combination of a weight

of about 4250 pounds and plenty of revs results in extreme fuel consumption: 9 mpg on Europe's city cycle.

The sports-car weight distribution, the new unequal-length control-arm suspension, and the mounting of the electrically assisted steering rack in front of the axle line are intended to endow the Quattroporte with exceptional agility. It failed to meet expectations. The car is clearly most comfortable on fast, open roads. There it feels settled, poised, and responsive. In tighter second-and-third-gear country, the steering feels comparatively slow, with 3.1 turns lock-to-lock. The leisurely turn-in worsens the mild understeer, but the speed-variable weighting is just right, with enough communication for the driver to feel a part of the action.

There's also plenty of grip, at least in the dry, and the car feels smaller and

lighter than the specs suggest. One theoretical advantage of the rearward weight bias is improved traction, but despite massive rubber—285/40ZR-18 tires at the rear—motoring over wet tarmac requires care, especially if you're brave enough to disengage the stability-control system.

The electronically controlled suspension is Maserati's second-generation Skyhook system. It adds throttle and steering angles to its range of senses. These help the suspension read road conditions and driver mood for the fast-adjusting shock absorbers to work out the best possible setting. The ride is always firm. Low-frequency wallows and road crowns are soaked up, but overall the ride quality is patchy. The suspension copes well with larger bumps and longitudinal ridges but lacks the ability to damp out small, sharp bumps. The big car sometimes feels skittish over transverse imperfections, such as railroad tracks.

The Quattroporte, due out in August, is close to being the great Italian sedan of Maserati's dreams, probably closer than we thought possible. Yes, it is flawed, but in so many ways the new sedan remains an irresistible combination, a viable alternative to German luxury sports sedans and to Jaguar's XJR. ∎

2005 MASERATI QUATTROPORTE
Vehicle type: front-engine, rear-wheel-drive, 5-passenger, 4-door sedan
Estimated base price: $105,000
Engine type: DOHC 32-valve V-8, aluminum block and heads, port fuel injection
Displacement. . . . . 259 cu in, 4244cc
Power (SAE net). . . . . . 394 bhp @ 7000 rpm
Torque (SAE net) . . . . . 333 lb-ft @ 4500 rpm

Transmission . . . . .6-speed manual with automated shifting and clutch
Wheelbase . . . . 120.6 in
Length/width/height. . . . . 198.9/74.6/56.6 in
Curb weight. 4250 lb
Manufacturer's performance ratings:
Zero to 62 mph . . . . 5.2 sec
Top speed (drag limited) . . . . 171 mph
Projected fuel economy:
European urban cycle . . . . 9 mpg
extra-urban cycle . . . . 18 mpg
combined cycle. . . . . 13 mpg

THE TRIDENT GETS STRIDENT

Fancied the Enzo but couldn't get your name on the order books in time? Well, well, well – something wicked this way comes...

Story by James Mills Photography by Tim Kent

ick-tock, tick-tock, tick tock. As far as announcing that you're sat in the most potent supercar ever turned out by Modena's lesser-known manufacturer goes, it's not what I'd expected. You know, sliding into the driver's seat, the hum of the ignition, whirr of the fuel pumps and, finally, the small explosions as every one of the 12 cylinders shudders into life.

Still, if there's one thing Maserati's road cars have been good at over the years, it's being anything but predictable. So an analogue clock fitted as standard to a car that is, by all intents and purposes, built to bring home the silverware from Le Mans, is the sort of quirky touch I should have seen coming.

Now I'm deviating. The hardcore car-porn you see before you isn't the actual car that's going to slug it out at the world's toughest, most high-profile motor race. The MC12, or MCS – Maserati Corse Stradale – is the road-going relative of the MCC (replace Stradale with the wonderfully Italian sounding Competizione)

and also the very, *very* big brother to Maserati's latest 911-sparring partner, the Gransport.

A run of 25 MC12s will be built this year, with a further 25 to follow in 2005. Why 25? Homologation. That's how many must be built to gain entry to the FIA GT Championship, with a race-car spin-off from the MC12. But even after committing to the hard sell of 50, £479,000 supercars (actually, *is* it that difficult to sell supercars these days?) Maserati awaits the FIA's decision this July.

Although the MCStradale supposedly came first, it's all a bit chicken and egg. After all, it wouldn't exist if the company didn't want to go racing. Scrap that. It wouldn't exist at all if it wasn't for the Ferrari Enzo, upon which it's based. There are crucial differences, though, with a reworked version of its carbon-fibre/aluminium chassis that's stretched by 10cm

and a new targa roof arrangement which required strengthening of the chassis, plus conventional, rather than scissor-style, doors.

Then there's the bodywork. Precious little is carried over from the Enzo. The all-carbon-fibre clamshell – any colour you like so long as it's classic Tipo 60-61 'Birdcage' blue and white – started off life as a proposal from Giugiaro, before Ferrari Maserati Group's director of design, Frank Stephenson (of new Mini fame) added the finishing touches.

Compared with the Enzo, the MC12 has more of a generic GT race car look about it. Of course, the architecture's the same as an Enzo, as are the seats and pedal box, but the sweeping dashboard in the same blue leather that's to be found in the latest GranSport model, blue starter button and, of course, that clock are uniquely Maserati. Oddly, after parting with a house-load

'If there's one thing Maserati's road cars have been good at over the years, it's being anything but predictable'

FACT FILE ▼

Engine 5988cc V12
623bhp @ 7.500rpm
480lb ft @ 5.500rpm

Performance 0-62mph
in 3.8secs. max 198mph

Weight 1.335kg

Economy Who cares?

Transmission Six-speed
paddle shift. RWD

Suspension Push-rod
double wishbones front
and rear

Cost 720.000 euros

On sale Now

Rivals Ferrari Enzo.
Pagani Zonda. Mercedes
SLR McLaren. Porsche
Carrera GT

Verdict Homologation
special. but with the
accent on special

of money, Maserati owners aren't deemed worthy of having the same F1-inspired steering wheel arrangement that's to be found in the Enzo. Petty in-house politics?

The 5998cc, 65-degree V12 engine is the same as the Enzo's only with Maserati-blue rocker covers and shrouded by the vast expanse of ducting from the roof-mounted air intake.

Ensuring owners get the best from each of the available 623bhp is an electro-hydraulic, paddle-shift operated, six-speed gearbox with Sport and Race modes. The latter is for those well blessed in the hairy castanets department – it cuts gearshift times and reigns back the traction control. Good luck to ya.

Double wishbone suspension with push-rod springs and dampers takes care of the corners in every sense, while Brembo ABS brakes ensure you don't get overenthusiastic with your half-million pound runaround.

Credit must go to Maserati Reparto Corse, the firm's race and performance road car division. It promises exciting spin-offs for the future, following on from the 400bhp GranSport which arrives this summer, with its body kit, sports suspension, distinctive blue-and-white interior and general unrepentant attitude problem.

At this stage, Maserati isn't quite certain of how and to whom it will sell the MC12. The company simply says it would prefer the cars to be bought by recognised friends and fans of the marque. Which could include you or me, er, if it weren't for the half-million pound asking price (more expensive, but then more exclusive than the Enzo). No-one knows how many will come to the UK, but with Europe-only type approval, the good news is that those philistines responsible for the Coupe and Spyder losing the elegant 'boomerang' tail lamps won't be getting any – the Americans. Payback had to come.

'Race mode cuts gearshift times and reigns back the traction control '

Roof air intake and push-rod suspension point to its role as a race car

For serious action, catch the racing MCC at the Spa 24 Hour GT race this August

CIAO BELLOW

A MORE PURPOSEFUL DYNAMIC RESOLVE, AGGRESSIVE NEW STYLING ELEMENTS, ENHANCED SNARL FROM ITS WONDERFUL V8 … IT ALL MARKS MASERATI'S NEW GRANSPORT AS AN ITALIAN TO LUST AFTER

WORDS PETER McKAY

OLD reputations fade as slowly as unwanted tattoos, so naturally there were sceptics who wondered if Ferrari ownership of Maserati could turn around the rough fortunes and questionable reliability of a brand that, 10 or so years ago, had been heading seriously south. These days, the concerns have shrunk away and sales continue to build. Happy owners have become the new positive marketing voice of the brand.

The new GranSport is the latest advancement of the coupe that started life in late 1998 as the twin-turbo 3500GT, a car that seduced with its looks and flick-a-switch performance. More recently, Maserati gave the Coupe and Spyder a stunning all-new 4244cc quad-cam V8 – the engine destined to power the Ferrari 360 Modena replacement, the F430.

This GranSport – the new, harder version of its V8 Coupe – gets an 8kW power hike, sportier handling, improved brakes, cabin trim that hollers athleticism, and aero body bits, all rolling on bigger 19-inch wheels and Pirelli tyres. It feels very taut dynamically and a little livelier; its stance is lower and more businesslike, and its sound irascibly racy.

In GranSport guise, the V8 now puts out 295kW at 7000rpm, up from 287kW, while torque remains unchanged at 451Nm. The extra grunt comes via a number of processes starting with finer tolerances in engine assembly, improved valve seating to help air exhaust, better breathing through the inlet manifolds, and revisions to the exhaust system.

Straight-line performance isn't shock-me superior compared with the Coupe, but does shade it by a slim margin. The factory claims zero to 100km/h in 4.9sec, to 400m in 12.8sec, times which sound only a little optimistic (we clocked a 5.2 and 13.4 when we ran the regular V8 Coupe Cambiocorsa in January '03). We should mention that the GranSport is not much lighter than the regular coupe – the bigger, heavier wheel and tyre package largely offsets the weight losses in other areas.

Bragging rights are muted until the GranSport gets on roads that demonstrate its dynamic qualities. On twisting bitumen in the hills above Palma in Italy, any concerns that this might be a too-tough, too-sporting car for daily use are dispelled in less than a kilometre. This is a very driver-friendly machine – not too hard, yet a real step up from the softness of the regular coupe, which floats and leans a little too much for absolute driving satisfaction.

The coils and anti-roll bars are no stiffer than before, but the ride height has been dropped 10mm and the Skyhook adaptive damping recalibrated most effectively.

Everything feels splendidly integrated. Along with the refined aerodynamics, the car's pitch and roll are very nicely controlled. Stability is enhanced, and there's a precision of placement on the road that earlier models didn't quite have. Remarkably, there doesn't appear to be any obvious trade-off in ride quality.

The cross-ventilated Brembo brakes with four-pot calipers (carried over from the Coupe, but with the addition of new braided lines)

Lower side sills are almost a nod to running boards; wheels are 19s with bespoke Pirellis

have a feel and progression previously lacking, certainly helped by the lower centre of gravity and firmer handling. (The optional yellow or red paint, however, probably doesn't make much difference to stopping distances…) They don't fade, though, as a day pounding around the Varano de' Melegari racetrack near Palma verified. More aggressive braking is tolerated by the chassis due to the minimal weight transfer and improved composure. (Gabrielle Tarquini, the former F1 driver and current Alfa Romeo works driver, confirms the GranSport is almost two seconds a lap faster than the V8 Coupe around Varano.)

The reduction in pitch and roll means less understeer, allowing the driver to carry more corner speed. The GranSport changes direction with less drama, and at slightly higher speeds.

There is understeer in the tighter stuff, but it's easily controlled with the throttle. And I love how a nailed right pedal forces the tail to squat, and brings a smidgin of power oversteer on the exit before those chunky Pirellis bite the bitumen and it fires itself into tomorrow.

Both traction control and the stability program can be switched off, yet the GranSport remains a relaxing car to punt with enthusiasm.

It's available only with the six-speed Cambiocorsa ('race change') gearbox in which the gears are shifted electro-hydraulically using paddles mounted behind the steering wheel. There's no conventional manual. Here, the Cambiocorsa has been recalibrated via improved software for shifting that's about 35 percent swifter than before. Also, sixth gear is four percent taller on GranSport, allowing the maximum speed to be pushed up to 290km/h (compared with a claimed 285km/h for the regular coupe; we achieved 276km/h at Avalon in Jan '03). The three-mode Cambiocorsa here has also lost much of its roughness. Normal mode gives smooth, fluid changes, although the fully automatic setting is often a little unsettling, especially when downshifting at low speed. Which does beg the question: who wants full auto anyway?

The sound of the V8's dramatic exhaust bark in Sport mode is irresistible, as is the

A little attitude, *grazie*

The GranSport is a response to a plea from some owners for a return to a car with the rambunctious nature of the original twin-turbo **Maserati 3200 GT**. That car was a more exciting drive than today's **V8 Coupe**, acknowledges John Fewings, the ex-BMW man now in charge of product marketing for Maserati. "The [V8 Coupe] is probably a little too soft, too smooth and too comfortable for some people. Some enthusiasts want a sharper drive – a car that's much more fun to drive, but sacrifices nothing in ride and cabin comfort. And with this they expect brasher styling." So the GranSport is no competitor for, say, the **Porsche 911 GT3**; rather a true gran turismo with a fine sports edge. It is Maserati's sales spearhead for 2005, and should take the Trident badge through to the next-generation **Spyder and Coupe**, expected to reach Australian shores around 2007.

computer-controlled blipping of the throttle on downshifts. The GranSport also does a nice version of exhaust-overrun cackling. Turn off the stereo, open the windows.

Above 4000rpm, and with more than 50 percent of throttle, a bypass valve opens to provide a sporty sound and to reduce back pressure. This exhaust bypass remains closed, though, if the Sport button is not active – this makes the exhaust quieter for city driving, while also delivering increased back pressure for more low-rev torque.

The steering – too vague and lacking the feel needed from a car of this performance capability – remains the GranSport's only major failing. New Maserati boss Martin Leach, a former karting champ whose background is engineering, is not unaware of this deficiency. "We're working on that – we know how to do good steering," vows Leach.

Ferrari/Maserati designer Frank Stephenson (formerly at BMW, where he did the Mini and X5) has made some subtle changes to differentiate the GranSport. He's given it a larger grille (for improved air ingress), now meshed-covered, while the front bumper is more aggressive, with an obvious lower spoiler to assist downforce.

A surprisingly subtle rear lip spoiler sits on the bootlid; a larger one was discarded after testing in Ferrari's Formula One wind tunnel.

Wheels are 19s, not dissimilar to those used on the one-make Trofeo track machines, and run specially developed Pirelli Rossos.

Stephenson has also visually removed weight from the cabin, adding a little more carbonfibre (the real stuff, naturally) to the slimmed-down tunnel, along with some pleasing metallic elements. More body-hugging seats, a Start button and a three-spoke steering wheel with a squared-off top also feature. All the luxury equipment remains – climate control, power seats, quality sound system – reinforcing the message that this is not a track stripper.

The GranSport retails in Australia for $242,500 – a neat price premium of $22,000 above the regular V8 Coupe GT. But Maserati claims it bears at least $30,000 of extra value.

We take the point. There's no good reason why any true Maserati enthusiast would want to pocket the change from the regular Coupe when a far more enjoyable, rewarding version is available. Essentially, the GranSport is the car the Coupe always should have been. ▼

MASERATI GRANSPORT
www.maserati.com

Body steel/aluminium, 2 doors, 2+2 seats
Drivetrain front engine (north-south), rear drive
Engine 4244cc V8, dohc, 32v
Power 295kW @ 7000rpm
Torque 451Nm @ 4500rpm
Transmission 6-speed sequential
Size l/w/h 4523/1822/1295mm
Wheelbase 2660mm
Weight 1680kg
0-100km/h 4.9sec (claimed)
Price $242,500
On sale Now

Three meshed air outlets expedite airflow from beneath the floorpan; quad oval tailpipes a trick sign-off

The Seductress

by WINSTON GOODFELLOW
photography by THE AUTHOR

The Germans may know how to make a sedan sporty, but it took the Italians to figure out how to make one sexy, as Maserati has done with its new Quattroporte.

Maserati's new Quattroporte is the world's most charismatic sedan. But when you consider that Maserati literally invented the luxurious-yet-fast fast four-door market four decades ago, it is simply a case of history repeating itself.

At the 1963 Turin Auto Show, Maserati displayed its first sedan, called, appropriately enough, the Quattroporte ("four door" in Italian). The body was designed by Frua, based in large part on a then one-off 5000 GT coupe the coachbuilder styled the previous year.

While the 1963 Quattroporte may have not been the first luxurious fast sedan—machines such as Facel Vega's Excellence and Lagonda's Rapide had earlier debuts— it was the Maserati that garnered worldwide attention and brought the segment into the limelight.

Left, clockwise from top: The first Quattroporte, powered by a 4.2-liter V8 and wearing a Frua-designed body, debuted at the Turin Auto Show in 1963; the fourth-generation Quattroporte from the 1990s featured a twin-turbo V6 and Gandini bodywork—it never came to the U.S.; the last Quattroporte for American consumption was the V8-powered, Giugiaro-designed third-gen version from the 1980s. Right: The new, fifth-generation Quattroporte brings the Italian four-door sport sedan into the 21st century with sumptuous Pininfarina lines, a 400-hp 4.2-liter V8 and a 171 mph top speed.

Powering the Quattroporte was a brawny 4.2-liter V8 with roots that could be traced directly back to the powerplant in Maserati's brutally fast 450S endurance racer that narrowly missed winning the GT championship in 1957. The Quattroporte could clear 130 mph with ease—a heady figure back in those days—and it handled and rode exceptionally well. It accomplished all this while cossetting the occupants in extreme comfort. The car was a testament to Maserati chief engineer Giulio Alfieri, who once said, "The driver is the guest of the car, and I liked the car to be a good host."

That first Quattroporte remained in production until 1970. Over the balance of the decade, Maserati made two other Quattroportes in extremely limited numbers. The first was a stunner by Frua in the early 1970s, of which two were made for the Aga Khan. Bertone made a 6-cylinder Quattroporte in the mid-1970s in response to the gas crisis, but only a dozen were built before production was canceled.

Maserati returned to the luxurious four-door market in 1979 with the Giugiaro-designed Quattroporte III. It did 140 mph, had an interior that any high-end bordello would have died for and remained in production for a decade. The late 1980s saw the smaller 425 and 430, which were then succeeded in the 1990s by the Quattroporte IV done by Gandini.

Still, of all the subsequent versions, the first Quattroporte has remained a benchmark, a car that put Maserati on the map and in the hands of an entirely new clientele.

Partnership Rekindled

Pininfarina received the commission to design the current version, and company chairman Sergio Pininfarina couldn't have been more pleased. The firm's last Maserati was a one-off 5000 GT in the early 1960s, but what thrilled Pininfarina was his chance to design a truly luxurious and fast four door for the Ferrari-Maserati Group.

"In 1980 we made the Pinin to celebrate our 50th anniversary," Pininfarina says, referring to a Ferrari sedan that was shown at the Paris Auto Show that year. Much to his dismay, Enzo Ferrari didn't want to take the company in that direction. Pininfarina views the Quattroporte as the successor to the one-off Pinin. "I couldn't be more delighted," he says. "I am thinking of ordering two for myself."

Pininfarina should be elated, particularly with the car's appearance. My first time seeing one in an outdoor setting was in Modena when picking it up at the factory, and there is no question the Quattroporte is a stunner.

It starts with the car's fabulous proportions and marvelous stance. The front is low, the hood long and the windshield is steeply raked, which all accentuate the sense of speed. A lovely hard line runs along the top of the doors, then curves up on the voluptuously muscular fender below the beefy C-pillar. The rear sits up slightly, as if to put an exclamation point on the Quattroporte's dynamic movement from front to rear.

Then there are details such as the hard lines on the hood, the Maserati Trident regally protruding from the C-pillar, the quad tailpipes and the portholes on the sides

that recall Pininfarina Maseratis from the 1950s. Unlike the sport sedan offerings from Germany, the Quattroporte makes me want to run my hands over its sculpted skin.

Maserati PR man Andrea Cittadini gives me a quick run-through on operations, then says, "Be back some time later today. I'll see you then." And off into Modena's bustling early morning traffic I went.

In a couple of kilometers it is clear this Maserati gets real respect from the locals, and the car's looks clearly have a lot to do with it. People turn and stare, bicycles part around it like a school of minnows and one attractive Italian woman gives a longing glance at the car and then sneaks a peek at

the tee-shirt-and-camera-vest clad driver. Sorry to disappoint you, *bella*!

The Maser handles itself well in traffic. Visibility is excellent in all directions and the steering is nicely weighted and quick responding. This, coupled with the V8's torque, makes it easy to squeeze through quickly disappearing holes in traffic.

Unfortunately, you'll most likely find yourself battling the electro-hydraulic 6-speed DuoSelect manual transmission in the stop-and-go, should this particular car's system prove to be the rule and not the exception. In automatic mode the 1-2 shift defines lethargic and proves so frustrating that I soon switch over to manual shifting. That lethargy was surprising in light of how well the 612 Scaglietti I tried last month performed in auto mode. Apparently Maserati will update the transmission software before the Quattroporte reaches American ports.

Inside Track

The sumptuous interior is seductively inviting. The dash is clean and simple, and all the controls are within easy reach and feel wonderful when you touch them. The steering wheel immediately jumps to mind on this last observation. The rim is the perfect diameter and size, there are subtle divots for your thumbs at 9 and 3 o'clock and the leather feels the softest of any I've run my fingers across since I drove the Sultan of Brunei's custom-built Ferrari F512M-based FX several years ago.

The Quattroporte's seats are great companions for a brisk or long drive. They are extremely comfortable with a cushion that fits my backside perfectly. The side bolsters provide excellent excellent lower back support without squeezing you like the deep buckets found in mid-engine machines. In fact, the seats fit me so well that the back aches I was experiencing in the morning before getting into the Quattroporte were all but gone by mid-day.

There are some faults with the interior. Surprisingly it is a bit small for a car this size. At 6-foot-3 I really wanted the driver's seat to go back another inch or two. When

It starts with the car's fabulous proportions and marvelous stance. The front is low, the hood long and the windshield is steeply raked, which all accentuate the sense of speed.

it is that far back, there was just enough room in the rear seat, though I had to sit with my legs splayed apart. Headroom front and rear was outstanding. The trunk wasn't as commodious as expected, another surprising discovery on a car this size.

Driving Dynamics

The Quattroporte's fully independent front and rear suspension features double wishbones and anti-dive and anti-squat geometry and Maserati's Skyhook adaptive gas-filled shocks which continuously react to driver inputs, road surfaces and the car's dynamics. The bit of body roll you feel in the normal setting is eliminated when switching to the sport setting, but the stiffer suspension makes sure you feel everything the handsome alloy wheels and 19-inch tires touch. That much information and a slightly harsh ride become a bit tiring after an extended run, so most of the time we kept it in the normal setting.

The only minor drawback in this mode is the absence of the sport setting's added crispness to the DuoSelect transmission's shifts. Using the delicious-feeling paddles mounted behind the steering wheel in sport mode the downshifts are particularly brisk, with the system perfectly matching revs. And with each shift, the tranny makes the most interesting hissing sound, like a boxer throwing punches while sparring.

The Quattroporte is sensational on the open road. It is is a large sedan—the car's overall length is 199 inches, and the wheelbase is 121 inches—yet the Maserati shrinks around you when driven hard, giving you the feeling that the back seats aren't there. The accurate, ideally weighted steering and an all-new, highly rigid steel unibody play a part in this, but perhaps an even bigger role is played by the engine's placement in the chassis. The all-aluminum 4,244-cc 400-horsepower DOHC V8 sits entirely behind the front axle. This combined with a rear-mounted transaxle result in 47%/53% weight distribution from front to rear.

Think about that distribution for a moment. When was the last time you heard of any sedan with a rearward weight bias?

You can really hustle the Quattroporte through turns, the car feeling neutral as you pile on speed, transmitting the right amount of information; it doesn't overwhelm you with data. The front wheels go exactly where they are pointed—understeer is hardly noticeable—allowing you to accurately clip apexes of corners and get back on the power early and listen to the music.

Not only does the V8 sing a great velvety song—particularly with the windows down

Right: V8 is shared with Maserati Coupe and Spyder, yet still delivers the goods in the larger Quattroporte.

on a confined road—but it is an absolute joy to use hard. The torque curve is relatively flat, with more than 75 percent of the 326 lb-ft of peak torque available at 2,500 rpm. However, you'll undoubtedly have the tach occupying much higher numbers most of the time. This intoxicating powerplant literally begs you to run it hard, truly coming alive and pulling with alarming alacrity above 4,000 rpm. And as impressive as that is, it is 2,000 rpm higher where, to your amazement, the real fun lurks.

Above 6,000 the engine is truly in its element, pulling as hard as can be. Think of immortal racehorse Seabiscuit looking back to taunt War Admiral in their match race, saying with his eyes, *You can't catch me*, and then simply running away from the vaunted horse from the East Coast. That is the attitude this charismatic V8 delivers as it whips towards its 7,500-rpm redline, feeling as if it will easily vanquish all comers without breaking a sweat.

Final Thoughts

So what to make of the Quattroporte? This is truly a sports car with four doors, with all the good and bad that the comparison invites. It is beautiful and emotional, providing an invigorating drive that really gets the heart pumping. It also has its shortcomings just like a sports car: the stiff ride in sport mode and the slightly small interior and trunk.

That makes it a most interesting alternative to Mercedes AMG and BMW's M offerings. These are not sports cars but superlative sedans developed as far as they can be to offer outstanding performance. They dazzle you with their completeness and competency, but don't pull at the heart strings like a car you would save to drive only on the weekends. The Quattroporte certainly has the beguiling character of such a weekend seductress, but this sports car just happens to have four doors. ●

2005 Maserati Quattroporte

GENERAL
VEHICLE TYPE	Front-engine, RWD 4-door sedan
STRUCTURE	Steel unibody
MARKET AS TESTED	Europe
MSRP	$90,000 (est.)

ENGINE
TYPE	V8
DISPLACEMENT (cc)	4244
COMPRESSION RATIO	11.0:1
POWER (bhp)	400 @ 7000 rpm
TORQUE (lb-ft)	326 @ 4500 rpm
INTAKE SYSTEM	EFI
VALVETRAIN	DOHC, 32 valves

TRANSMISSION
TYPE	6-speed paddle-shift manual
FINAL DRIVE RATIO	n/a

DIMENSIONS
CURB WEIGHT (lbs.)	4246
WHEELBASE (in.)	120.6
TRACK, F/R (in.)	61.4/62.5
LENGTH (in.)	198.9
WIDTH (in.)	74.6
HEIGHT (in.)	56.6

SUSPENSION, STEERING, BRAKES
FRONT SUSPENSION	Double wishbones, coil springs, gas shocks, anti-roll bar
REAR SUSPENSION	Double wishbones, coil springs, gas shocks, anti-roll bar
STEERING TYPE	Rack and pinion
WHEELS, F&R	8.5x18, 9.5x18 alloys
TIRES, F&R	245/45ZR18, 285/40ZR18
BRAKES, F&R	13.0-inch, 12.4-inch discs
ABS	Standard

PERFORMANCE
0-62 MPH (sec.)	5.2
TOP SPEED (mph)	171

CONTACT
	www.maserati.com

Gran
daddy

The Maserati Coupe has always been a 'nearly' car; the
new GranSport finally realises the four-seater's full potential ➔

Maserati's distinctive Coupe has been perpetually on the brink of greatness. Launched as the 3200GT back in 1998, it appeared on the cover of the very first issue of **evo** and since then we've charted its evolution; the surprise switch to a normally-aspirated 4.2-litre V8 from the original's twin-turbo 3.2, the redesign of the once-defining boomerang rear lights, the introduction of the Convertible and, latterly, the various iterations of the 'Skyhook' adaptive damping and Cambiocorsa auto-clutch manual.

For six years the Coupe has charmed us but failed to convince us fully, the positives of a superb engine, sling-shot performance, beautifully crafted interior and rarity tempered, mostly, by sharp handling, numb steering, an indifferent ride and an unsatisfactory gearshift, especially in Cambiocorsa guise.

The invitation to drive the new range-topping GranSport contained no indication that something rather remarkable had happened to the Coupe. There were no great claims about stealing sales from Jaguar and Porsche, no boasts that Maserati had created a better GT than the XJR or a sports car as involving as the new 911. To be honest, even if there had been, after so many re-workings it would have sounded like well-intentioned PR bravado. Yet the GranSport really is very good. Maserati has hit the bullseye.

The specification details of the GranSport certainly didn't suggest such a transformation. Instead they painted a picture of an even more aggressive and uncompromising experience: lowered, stiffened suspension with bigger wheels and lower profile tyres; power up 10bhp to a respectable 400; Cambiocorsa transmission (no manual option) with faster shifts, and some aerodynamic tuning. 'The GranSport is designed as a sportier, edgier alternative to the current Coupe and has been designed to express the powerful temperament at the heart of the car,' ran the press release. Knowing the current car, the words 'edgier' and 'powerful temperament' sounded vaguely menacing.

The charm offensive starts as soon as we clap eyes on the colourful grid of ten GranSports basking on the startline of the Autodromo Riccardo Parletti, 20 miles from Parma. The Giugiaro-styled four-seater has never looked better, the subtle additions and tweaks lending it extra muscle and sharpening its stance.

Overseen by recently installed Maserati/ Ferrari chief designer Frank Stephenson (he of New Mini fame), the styling changes are both aesthetic and functional. The most obvious elements are the curved sill extensions and the sliver of a boot spoiler, but the front grille is deeper, too, more like the Quattroporte's, with a chunkier spoiler below. The lower ride height helps enormously, the tail in particular appearing to hunker down much more than the

Above: deeper grille and front bib-spoiler distinguish GranSport from regular Coupe. Quad exhaust tailpipes make great noise

10mm drop would suggest.

Inside, the changes are pretty much all positive, too. New, deeply sculpted seats offer a welcoming embrace as you slip into them, and the facia, wheel and centre console treatment are all sportier. The dials have simpler white-on-blue markings, while the wheel is more ergonomically shaped and also features an unusual non-circular, carbonfibre top edge that is raised to give full sight of the dials. There's a carbon surround for the heater controls and radio, too, while the upper section of the centre console is now shorter and groups together four buttons, including those for the 'Sport' mode and the starter. The extended console between the seats is now in carbon, much like that of the 360 Stradale, and carries the stubby little T-bar forward/reverse gear selector lever and sundry switches. Only the new 'technical' cloth jars slightly; it looks like the tight-webbed material some training shoes are made from. Leather is an option.

Twist the key, thumb the blue starter button and the V8 fires up with a glorious, resonant, rolling rumble. The new exhaust back-boxes feature valve flaps that open above 4000rpm in regular mode and are open all the time in Sport but, rather neatly, are also programmed to open on start-up. The sonorous burble sets the tone beautifully.

Pull on the felt-backed right-hand paddle, squeeze the throttle and we're off, very soon encountering the first dynamic test – a pair of speed humps on the feeder road from the circuit. Buttock-clenching proves unnecessary as the GranSport traverses them with impressive suppleness. On the open road, the absorbency of the ride continues to impress. At moderate speeds there's noticeable roll, squat and pitch, which I hadn't expected, but it all feels comfortable, natural, and as we'll soon discover, the Sport button sharpens up its demeanour considerably.

Another aspect of the GranSport that impresses within the first few miles is the steering. The Coupe has never lacked directness but feel and feedback are another matter. Here, though, there are no such concerns; it is still keenly responsive but no longer unsettlingly sharp, and there's a real sense of knowing what is happening at the treadblocks. The tyres themselves – Pirelli P Zero Rossos, 235/35 ZR19 and 265/30 ZR19 front and rear – are acknowledged by Maserati to be a significant factor in the improved dynamics. Compared with the 18in Michelins or Dunlops fitted to the Coupe and Convertible, they are an inch bigger in diameter, a section lower in profile but the same width, yet with the revised Skyhook tuning seem to provide increased suppleness and feel.

The Cambiocorsa gearbox has been roundly criticised in these pages in the past but each new generation of software brings improvements. Its action feels more refined than before in regular mode, slipping between ratios smoothly, though ambling through town in auto mode there's still the feeling that there's too much clutch slip than is good for the friction plate. Maserati's

engineers shrug when this is pointed out and say that they doubt GranSport owners will use auto much. By implication, they'll be more interested that the GranSport's shift speed in Sport mode has been reduced by up to 35 per cent and that on downchanges there's a generous heel-and-toe-style flourish of revs.

The V8's rumbling exhaust note evaporates as the revs climb into the mid-range, replaced by a smooth, light, creamy whirr. The V8's modest gain in horsepower comes at the top end of the rev-range, the tuning centred on finer build tolerances, including reworked valve seats and more accurate connections between the intake piping and cylinder head ports. The back-box flaps also contribute to the extra 10bhp. The full 400bhp is delivered at 7000rpm; torque remains

at 333lb ft at 4500rpm, the same as the Coupe.

Pressing the Sport button restores the low-rev rumble, and it's there on the overrun, too, a delicious low, powdery popping and pulsing. Out on more demanding roads, it's the change in the damping and shift speed that the Sport mode brings that are more significant. You can make pretty good progress without it, but the downchanges are a little too sluggish and, laden with driver, passenger and a bootful of camera gear, the continually adaptive Skyhook damping doesn't grab hold of the mass as firmly as you'd want as soon as you'd want. That said, the GranSport still feels very good, poised and responsive, with terrific turn-in and exceptional traction, but in Sport mode it rises to another level, becoming taut, confident and rarely wrong-

footed. Body movement is more tightly controlled, with roll and pitch resisted in the early stages, yet the ride remains supple. Securely and comfortably restrained by the well-shaped seat, you feel perfectly placed to exploit the strong grip the chassis generates. Braking is confident, with good pedal feel, and now when you request downshifts, the Cambiocorsa 'box delivers swiftly, with a blip-perfect swell of revs helping the ratio slip sweetly home.

These are difficult roads, mainly second- and third-gear, throwing up complex sequences of corners thick and fast, and the Maserati is devouring them with a seemingly insatiable appetite. The whole car is working hard but feels as if it has plenty still in reserve. The front end slices for the apex accurately and keenly and it takes a really early throttle to get the traction control warning light flickering – mostly the GranSport simply digs in and goes.

The V8 isn't over-burdened with torque, it's true, but the drive the GranSport finds makes you wonder if it couldn't cope pretty well with the original twin-turbo 3200GT's spiky delivery. The 400bhp, short-stroke 4.2 is a bit soft below 2000rpm but picks up strongly thereafter, bellowing its way through to 4500rpm, the point of peak torque, before the note quietens into a smooth, light eight-pot whirr right through 7000rpm and on to the limiter. Power keeps on building and you can spend most of a testing road with the V8 singing urgently between 4000 and 7500rpm.

If you're the sort who thinks a manual with no clutch pedal should shift as smoothly as a regular auto, the jolt when the gears go home if you keep the throttle pinned will disappoint you. Personally, I've never objected to helping smooth the process by lifting the throttle slightly on upshifts. For me, the speed of the shift is more important going down the 'box, especially when braking hard, and here the Cambiocorsa system is faultless. It surely can't be beyond the ingenuity of the software manufacturers to build in a slight ignition cut to ease upshifts in a similar way. On the upside, there is an automatic handbrake action that holds the car when pulling away or when you're manoeuvering and going between first and reverse, so you don't have to dial in as many revs as you might.

Short-cutting back to the circuit so as not to be late for the afternoon exercises, photographer Shepherd finds some wicked little roads, and I mean wicked in the traditional sense – horrendous, narrow, writhing, part-subsided asphalt. Despite our hurry, the GranSport never loses its cool. At the pace we're maintaining I could imagine a Mini bouncing like a pogo stick and a Jaguar XJR running short of answers, while an Aston DB9 would be all at sea. It's not the sort of drive you'd expect a GT to relish but the GranSport is quite unfazed by it all. Stability control rarely intervenes. Even with it switched out, at the limit of front grip the nose edges progressively wide, and if mid-corner bumps excite the tail when it's driving hard, the resultant slide is small and catchable. If you're thinking

SPECIFICATION

MASERATI GRANSPORT

■ **Engine**	90-degree V8
■ **Location**	Front
■ **Displacement**	4244cc
■ **Bore x stroke**	92mm x 79.8mm
■ **Cylinder block**	Aluminium alloy, dry sumped
■ **Cylinder head**	Aluminium alloy, dohc per bank, four valves per cylinder
■ **Fuel and ignition**	Bosch integrated ignition/injection system, fly-by-wire throttle control
■ **Max power**	400bhp @ 7000rpm
■ **Max torque**	333lb ft @ 4500rpm
■ **Transmission**	Six-speed manual with 'Cambiocorsa' paddle-shift, rear-wheel drive, lsd
■ **Front suspension**	Double wishbones, coil springs, 'Skyhook' adaptive damping control, anti-roll bar
■ **Rear suspension**	Double wishbones, coil springs, 'Skyhook' adaptive damping control, anti-roll bar
■ **Steering**	Rack and pinion, power-assisted
■ **Brakes**	Cross-drilled and ventilated discs, 330mm front, 310mm rear, ABS, EBD, ASR, MSR
■ **Wheels**	8 x19in fr, 9.5 x 19in rr, al alloy
■ **Tyres**	235/35 ZR19 fr, 265/30 ZR19 rr, Pirelli P Zero Rosso
■ **Fuel tank capacity**	19.4gal/88 litres
■ **Weight (kerb)**	1680kg
■ **Power-to-weight**	239bhp/ton
■ **0-62mph**	4.9sec (claimed)
■ **Max speed**	180mph (claimed)
■ **Insurance group**	20
■ **Basic price**	£66,600
■ **On sale (UK)**	Autumn 2004

evo RATING ★★★★★

'New 997 Carrera S versus GranSport? I wouldn't put money on the outcome'

that sounds not unlike a certain German sports car with the engine in the wrong place, I'd agree.

If Maserati hadn't provided a circuit, the GranSport's very outer limits would have remained a mystery. Let loose on this entertaining little track, whose corners are mainly second- and third-gear, it's easy to soon get to grips with. Safe understeer awaits unless you're prepared to get on the throttle hard and early, having got the nose tucked in. The tail is keen to regain grip so you have to keep the throttle planted until there's some momentum behind the swing; once the tail is out about half a turn, you can determine the trajectory with small modulations of the throttle.

It's the GranSport's engaging performance on the road that stays uppermost in the mind, though. It has the sort of responsive, feelsome steering and dynamic composure we always wished the Coupe had, combined with a superb ride, excellent seats and a deliciously sweet-

revving and potent engine. Best of all, it works on two levels, both as a cosseting four-seat GT and a sports car, something the DB9 tried but has so far failed to do.

So, how good is the GranSport? Well, the regular Coupe now looks expensive at £56K (£59K with Cambiocorsa) while the GranSport seems like a bargain at £66,600. In fact, I can't see why anyone would want the standard Coupe. The GranSport isn't just the car that keen drivers like us have always wished the Maserati was, it's now a GT that has the measure of the Jaguar XJR and BMW 645i. And even if I was considering a 911, the stylish and much rarer Maser would be very tempting. New 997 Carrera S versus GranSport? That's a twin-test whose conclusion I wouldn't put money on, and you could add Aston's forthcoming AMV8, which is expected to be similar money. The Maserati really is that good, and after six years it's a pleasure to be able to write it. ■

Maserati
QUATTROPORTE

Luxury con brio

BY JOHN LAMM • PHOTOS BY THE AUTHOR

IF YOU'RE BORED WITH so-called "traditional" luxury cars, sedans that deliver about as much excitement as a Barcalounger in full recline, then you're in for a treat: the Maserati Quattroporte, an upmarket Italian 4-door that bows to tradition while breaking it.

Ferrari took control of Maserati in 1997 and began to remake the company, modernizing its traditional factory in Modena and creating a new Italdesign-styled Coupe and Convertible. Perhaps the best example of the Maserati-Ferrari blending is the Maser's V-8. Designed by the two automakers, the block and heads are machined and the engines assembled at Ferrari's ultramodern facilities in Maranello.

Several years ago we heard rumors Maserati would revive its famed 4-door, the Quattroporte. The United States had been spared the Biturbo-based version of this sedan, so our memories are fond ones of a great hunk of a car that could seat four in luxury and went like the hounds of hell, thanks to its rumbling V-8. We saw scale models of possible Quattroportes at one auto show, heard more whispered hints at another and then, at Frankfurt in 2003, the real thing appeared.

It's a gutsy move. By positioning its automobile in the high-end luxury sedan market, Maserati leaps with both Gucci-loafer-clad feet into one of the toughest segments in the business. Its $95,500 price slots the Quattroporte above most of its competition: Mercedes' S-Class, BMW's 7 Series, Audi's A8 L and Jaguar's XJ. To justify that jump over the established models, Maserati needs to demonstrate a clear difference from the others.

Not surprisingly, its answer is to be truly Italian, with styling by Pininfarina, an attractive leather-and-wood interior, a front mid-engine/rear-transaxle layout and sporty suspension. Nice package on paper, but how well does it work? Let's see.

One of the first things you notice is that the Maserati has different proportions, more of a cab-rear stance, thanks to the forward-mid-engine layout that puts the V-8 behind the front axle. Large wheels and minimal front and rear overhangs visually plant the Maserati solidly on the ground.

The Quattroporte's overall shape has a

different look from the others in its class. It's rounder, a bit more voluptuous and prettier than the other models except, perhaps, for the Jaguar. There are touches of Maserati tradition, particularly the grille and a trio of side vents.

One thing the Pininfarina shape seems to do is camouflage the size of the Quattroporte, which at first appears smaller than its competition. But it's not. The Maserati's wheelbase, at 120.6 in., is almost as long as the Audi A8 L's and 7.2 in. longer than the Mercedes S500's. Its overall length is about the same as the Mercedes and almost 6 in. shorter than the A8 L.

Interior dimensions are difficult to compare because of the various long- and short-wheelbase versions of some luxury cars. What you can count on is that the Maserati can accommodate four six-footers for some distance in comfort. And in Italian style.

The difference? The German cars are more formal. Their seats are a bit flatter, as are the dashboards, which are often needlessly complex. In contrast, the Maserati is less reserved, with more shapes across the dash. The blue-face gauges—a big tach and speedometer with an info screen between them and flanked by small fuel-level and coolant-temperature dials—are in a pod you might expect to find in a sports car. The steering wheel is a classic hands-at-three-and-nine design with control buttons for features like the sound system. Behind the wheel are transmission shift paddles, which force the lights and wiper stalks a bit farther forward.

Atop the center stack is an elegant analog clock above a modern readout screen for navigation and the Blaupunkt-Bose sound system. Below are the heating/air-conditioning/vent controls on a dedicated panel. Although the controls aren't as ergonomic as some might like, they fall readily to hand once learned.

Below the dashboard is the center console with the gearbox reverse lever and an armrest/bin that cools drinks. On the console's back side are air vents for the rear passengers plus door lock and sunscreen switches.

But it's the seats that might be the best in this class. Thanks to careful sculpting, the four individual seats—as luxurious in back as up front—snuggle up to your backside, cushioning it and holding you in place during hard cornering. The fronts are electrically adjustable—14 ways—while those in back have a control to move each seat cushion forward about 4 in., tilting the seat back. Additionally, the rear right-side passenger has electrical fore-aft control of the front passenger seat.

All the seats are covered in Poltrona Frau leather with attractive piping and, like the entire interior, are beautifully finished.

The Quattroporte's V-8 built at the Ferrari Maserati engine-building facility in Maranello has a dry-sump oil system and sits low and to the rear in the engine bay. A classic design, with four cams, four valves per cylinder and no supercharger, the powerplant displaces 4.2 liters and produces 394 bhp at 7000 rpm and 333 lb.-ft. of torque at 4500 rpm, three-quarters of that from 2500. A 6-speed manual transaxle with electrohydraulic actuation is located in back and is connected to the engine via a torque tube.

Like the V-8 and the gearbox, the suspension and running gear of the Maserati sedan are what you might expect to find in an exotic sports car. There are upper and lower A-arms front and back, with coil springs and Skyhook automatic shock regulation. The steering has speed-variable assist. Not surprisingly the brakes are big Brembos, vented and cross-drilled, the fronts with 4-pot calipers and all with anti-lock and electronic brake distribution. Encircling them are Pirelli tires on 18-in. alloy wheels, though our test car had the optional 19-in. wheels with P Zero Rossos, 245/40R-19s front and 285/35R-19s at the back. An electronic yaw-control system called the Maserati Stability Program has two thresholds, Normal and Sport, enabling the driver to choose the degree of skid correction desired.

With a curb weight of 4280 lb., Maserati puts the Quattroporte's weight distribution at 49 percent front/51 percent rear. And because of the front-mid-engine layout, the major masses are confined within the wheelbase.

The subject of so much discussion is the Quattroporte's DuoSelect transmission, the first Formula 1-type paddle-shift system offered in a luxury car. Although Ferraris and the Maserati Coupe and Spyder use essentially the same type of transmission, the transmission is now in a luxury sedan, and that requires you to adjust your thinking.

Here's how it works: Insert the key, plant your foot on the brake and start the V-8. The transmission will be in neutral, an "N" displayed in the center of the instrument cluster. If you prefer to drive in

"It's rounder, a bit more **voluptuous** and prettier than the other models."

■ Poltrona Frau leather and handsome wood define the Maserati's interior. A central readout identifies gears of its DuoSelect paddle-shift transmission. Even rear seats are adjustable.

The Quattroporte's 4.2-liter V-8 is a joint Maserati-Ferrari product. Our test car's 19-in. wheels are part of the Sport package.

automatic, push the T-handle on the center console forward to the drive position or pull back on the right upshift paddle; a "D" will replace the "N" and you drive away. That's it, though you will also have the option of manually shifting up and down.

Push the M/A Shift button and you're in the Manual mode. Upshifts are made with the right paddle, downshifts with the left, and the gear number is displayed in the center window.

Push the Sport button and you raise the shift points, firm up the clutch action, put the suspension in its firmer mode and raise the threshold of traction control. Choose the "Ice" setting and the transmission starts in 2nd gear, with lower shift points and softer clutch engagement for slippery surfaces.

For reverse, grip the T-handle, lift up and back and an "R" appears in the middle of the instrument cluster. Push the same handle forward or tap the right paddle and you're again in forward.

In Automatic, the transmission certainly does the job, particularly in light driving and cruising on the freeway. But it just isn't satisfying and feels out of place—like a 6-speed manual in a Rolls-Royce.

On freeways or winding roads, the Ma-

serati V-8 is always satisfying, its sound subdued, but never stifled, the power delivery smooth and willing right up to the redline. With the transmission in Manual/Sport, our test Quattroporte clocked a 0–60 time of 5.1 seconds and covered the quarter mile in 13.6 sec. at 103.6 mph. That's 1.0–1.2 sec. quicker to 60 than the S500, which weighs about as much as the Quattroporte, and the 745i, which weighs about 400 lb. more. The Audi A8 L needs 6.7 sec. to reach 60 mph.

Around the skidpad, the moderately understeering Quattroporte generated 0.88g, which bested all its competition—the S500 (0.76g), Jaguar XJR (0.81g), BMW 745i (0.87g) and the Audi A8 L (0.78g). Then it carved through the 700-ft. slalom at 65.8 mph versus the S500's 58.1 mph, the XJR's 64.8, 745i's 64.9 and the A8 L's 65.3, with the Maserati showing mild understeer. Braking was particularly impressive for the Brembo-equipped Italian, 60–0 in 109 ft. against the S500 at 138 ft., the XJR's 115 ft., the 745i's 121 ft. and the A8 L in 121 ft.

Those Maserati numbers translate directly to fine road manners, allowing you to thread the needle with the big sedan, which isn't upset by road surface imperfections or poor weather conditions. As one driver said with a smile, the Maserati "likes to be a little bit faster than everyone else."

This is all part of the Italian style that blends a fashionable exterior and interior with a sporty drivetrain and chassis. On the Quattroporte, Maserati makes no excuses and few compromises. The company is charting its own course in the luxury automobile business, searching for customers who want to not only cushion their backsides but also satisfy their driving souls. ◉

2005 Maserati Quattroporte

Maserati North America, Inc., 250 Sylvan Ave., Englewood Cliffs, N.J. 07632; www.maseratiusa.com

At a Glance	
0–60 mph	5.1 sec
0–¼ mile	13.6 sec
Top speed	171 mph
Skidpad	0.88g
Slalom	65.8 mph
Brake rating	very good

List Price: $95,500
Price as Tested: $105,350

Price as tested incl std equip. (ABS, dual front, side & curtain airbags, traction & yaw ctrl, paddle-shift trans, adj damping, auto. dual-zone climate ctrl, AM/FM/CD Bose sound sys, nav sys, wood trim, lthr, sport seats, tilt & telescope strng wheel; pwr seats, windows, mirrors & door locks). Sport pkg (19-in. wheels, tire-press. monitoring, revised damping software, perforated lthr, vented & cross-drilled brakes, titanium-colored brake calipers & braided-steel brake lines) $4500, gas-guzzler tax ($3700), preparation & delivery ($1650).

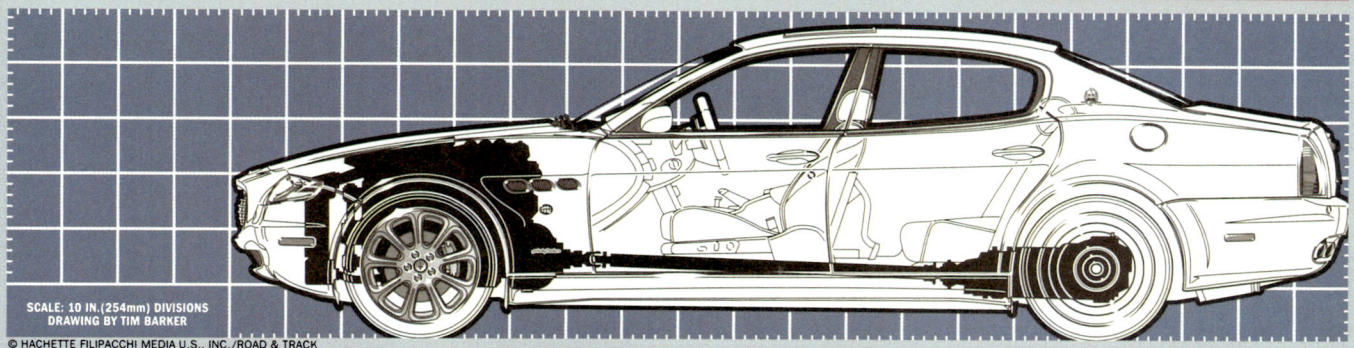

SCALE: 10 IN.(254mm) DIVISIONS
DRAWING BY TIM BARKER

© HACHETTE FILIPACCHI MEDIA U.S., INC./ROAD & TRACK

SPECIFICATIONS

Engine

Type	aluminum block & heads, V-8
Valvetrain	dohc 4-valve/cyl
Displacement	259 cu in./4244 cc
Bore x stroke	3.62 x 3.14 in./92.0 x 79.8 mm
Compression ratio	11.1:1
Horsepower (SAE)	394 bhp @ 7000 rpm
Bhp/liter	92.8
Torque	333 lb-ft @ 4500 rpm
Redline	7500 rpm
Fuel injection	elect. sequential port
Fuel	premium unleaded, 91 pump octane

Warranty

Basic warranty	4 years/50,000 miles
Powertrain	4 years/50,000 miles
Rust-through	4 years/50,000 miles

Chassis & Body

Layout	front engine/rear drive
Body/frame	alum., steel/unit steel
Brakes: Front	13.0-in. vented & cross-drilled discs
Rear	12.4-in. vented & cross-drilled discs
Assist type	vacuum, ABS
Total swept area	524 sq in.
Swept area/ton	235 sq in.
Wheels	cast alloy; 19 x 8½J f, 19 x 10½J r
Tires	Pirelli P Zero Rosso Direzionale; 245/40R-19 98Y f, 285/35R-19 99Y r
Steering	rack & pinion, pwr asst
Overall ratio	na
Turns, lock to lock	3.0
Turning circle	40.4 ft

Suspension
Front: upper & lower A-arms, coil springs, elect. adj tube shocks, anti-roll bar
Rear: upper & lower A-arms, coil springs, elect. adj tube shocks, anti-roll bar

General Data

Curb weight	4280 lb
Test weight	4460 lb
Weight dist (with driver), f/r, %	49/51
Wheelbase	120.6 in.
Track, f/r	62.5 in./61.8 in.
Length	198.9 in.
Width	74.6 in.
Height	56.6 in.
Ground clearance	na
Trunk space	15.9 cu ft

Accommodations

Seating capacity	5
Head room: Front	36.5 in.
Rear	35.0 in.
Seat width: Front	2 x 19.0 in.
Rear	54.0 in.
Front-seat leg room	42.5 in.
Seatback adjustment	65 deg
Seat travel	8.0 in.
Rear-seat knee room	28.0 in.

Drivetrain

Transmission: 6-speed manual paddle-shift

Gear	Ratio	Overall ratio	(Rpm)	Mph
1st	3.29:1	13.74:1	(7500)	44
2nd	2.16:1	9.02:1	(7500)	67
3rd	1.61:1	6.73:1	(7500)	90
4th	1.27:1	5.31:1	(7500)	114
5th	1.03:1	4.32:1	(7500)	141
6th	0.85:1	3.55:1	est (7500)	171

Final drive ratio ... 4.18
Engine rpm @ 60 mph in top gear ... 2600

Instrumentation

200-mph speedometer, 9000-rpm tachometer, multifunction LCD, fuel gauge, coolant temp

Safety

dual front, side & curtain airbags
seatbelt pretensioners
ABS, traction and yaw control
(all standard equipment)
tire-pressure monitoring (optional)

PERFORMANCE

Acceleration

Time to speed	Seconds
0–30 mph	1.7
0–40 mph	2.5
0–50 mph	3.9
0–60 mph	5.1
0–70 mph	6.9
0–80 mph	8.4
0–90 mph	10.6
0–100 mph	12.8

Time to distance	
0–100 ft	2.8
0–500 ft	7.4
0–900 ft	10.7
0–1320 ft (¼ mile)	13.6 @ 103.6 mph

▲ 2005 MASERATI QUATTROPORTE
¼ mile: 13.6 sec. @ 103.6 mph

Braking

Minimum stopping distance
From 60 mph ... **109 ft**
From 80 mph ... **197 ft**
Control ... **excellent**
Brake feel ... **very good**
Overall brake rating ... **very good**
Subjective ratings consist of excellent, very good, good, average, poor; na means information is not available.

Fuel Economy

Our driving	15.6 mpg
EPA city/highway	11/17 mpg
Cruise range	356 miles
Fuel capacity	23.8 gal.

Handling

Lateral acceleration
(200-ft skidpad) ... **0.88g**
Balance ... **moderate understeer**
Speed through
700-ft slalom ... **65.8 mph**
Balance ... **mild understeer**
Lateral seat support ... **good**

Interior Noise

Idle in neutral	49 dBA
Maximum in 1st gear	77 dBA
Constant 50 mph	67 dBA
70 mph	72 dBA

Test Notes:

Best launch of the Quattroporte is to fully depress the gas pedal with the traction control turned off. After that, upshifts are quick, except for the slight hesitation going from 1st to 2nd gear. • Through the slalom, the chassis responds nimbly. However, the body does roll modestly before taking a set. • Circling the skidpad, the car exhibits moderate understeer, but can be corrected easily with throttle modulation.

Test Conditions:

Temperature	Humidity	Elevation	Wind
91° F	36%	350 ft	light

MASERATI MC12

It was as if we'd travelled back in time. When the first pictures of Maserati's stunning MC12 supercar GT racer appeared last year, it seemed the clock had been turned back to 1997. Squint a little, and you could easily be looking at one of the GT1 contenders that created a golden era for sportscars. The problem was the self-same cars almost killed off top-level GT racing in the space of two seasons. Which begs the question: will the Maserati do the same?

The answer is almost certainly 'yes' if Maserati is left unchecked, both in terms of the performance of its rear-engined carbon-chassis supercar and the amount of money it has to spend going racing. The MC12 may be based on the Ferrari Enzo, but it has been designed not as a road car but an out-and-out racing car.

That fact alone sets it apart from the opposition in a class predominantly fought out by front-engined, spaceframe chassis contenders, such as the Ferrari 550 Maranello. Put simply, Maserati has moved the goalposts, and that's without considering a budget that dwarfs any of its rivals, with the possible exception of the factory Chevrolet team.

Only, the goal may not end up where the Maserati left it. The governing bodies that control the arenas in which the MC12 will race, the FIA and the Automobile Club de l'Ouest at Le Mans, have revealed their intent to pick up the posts and put them back where the Italian supercar maker found them. FIA president Max Mosley has categorically stated that the Maserati will not be allowed to dominate FIA GTs, a series in which it has already won in two of its four appearances so far. And in a departure for the Le Mans organisers, the performance of individual GT cars will be pegged back if they dip below a pre-determined race pace in the 24 Hours.

The difference between success and failure for the FIA championship and the health of GT racing at Le Mans – not to mention the series that take its name on either side of the Atlantic – will be down to the ability of the rule makers to even things up between the differing types of car in a class that's been confusingly renamed GT1. "This is the big issue," admits FIA GT boss Stéphane Ratel. "Either we prove we can balance performance or we'll be back to a situation we had in 1997-98."

The arrival of more and more exotic cars in the second half of the '90s destroyed GT racing. Porsche's 'parts-bin' special 911 GT1 rendered the original McLaren F1 GTR, a true road-based contender, obsolete in 1996 and was then leapfrogged itself by a succession of cars starting with the Mercedes CLK-GTR. The FIA GT series effectively died in the space of two seasons, while the escalation in technology, and therefore costs, in the same period precipitated a major shift away from GT machinery to prototypes at Le Mans.

Not everyone is convinced that the FIA will stick to its guns and penalise a marque that, until last year, was under the control of Ferrari, the team, incidentally, that wields the most political clout in Formula 1. Scuderia Italia was one of the doubters, so much so that the winner of the past two FIA GT titles quit the series over the winter. Officially, it has taken its 'unofficial' Ferrari 550 Maranellos, built and developed by Prodrive in Britain, to the Le Mans Endurance Series to seek a new challenge after cleaning up in the FIA championship. Behind the rhetoric, however, is a fear that the Maserati will be allowed to dominate in 2005 and beyond.

Ironically, Prodrive is not among the sceptics. The British motorsport engineering firm is the driving force behind Aston Martin's return to top-flight sportscar racing, and thinks its ➡

IS THIS CAR TH
DEATH OF GT R

Maserati's MC12 is controversy on wheels. GARY WATKINS looks at the consequences f

FIRST, THE world didn't like the fact the thing was based on the Ferrari Enzo and then, when we saw the pictures, it was more race car than road car. Controversy has never been far away since Maserati revealed in 2002 it was going GT racing.

Yet the wrangling that has dogged the MC12 isn't entirely of the Italian company's own making. The car has been the unwitting victim of a major rules reshuffle that brought the disparate regulations of the FIA and the Automobile Club de l'Ouest together, but almost resulted in leaving Maserati frozen out.

The MC12 was built to embryonic supercar rules drafted by the FIA to not only allow the likes of Maserati, which didn't have a suitable front-engined car in its stable, to compete, but also to bring the likes of Saleen and its rear-engined S7R into the FIA GT series. Yet by the time the MC12 was ready to roll those rules had vanished as the two governing bodies harmonised their rule books.

"THE MC12 HAS BEEN THE VICTIM OF A RULES RESHUFFLE"

That didn't help Maserati's cause when it was time to homologate the car last June and the MC12 was turned down, although series boss Stéphane Ratel was charged with finding a compromise. Subsequently, Ratel got the approval of all teams taking part to let the Maserati run, but not for points and with a smaller rear wing by way of a penalty, in three end-of-season races.

The FIA reckoned it had learnt enough to ensure the car could be controlled, and the MC12 was duly homologated in October, although not in the form it raced last year. That would be far too simple.

The 2005-spec Maserati has a flat-bottom and has been reduced in length from 5180mm to five metres, as per the new joint GT1 rules. The car is just outside the new maximum width of two metres, which was taken from the Le Mans rule book, so the FIA has granted the MC12 a waiver because it was penned before this came into effect.

The men in blazers at Le Mans are sticking to their guns, however. The MC12 will not be allowed at the 24 Hours until it is narrowed, nor is the ACO happy with the way the car has been shortened. It wants the all-important rear overhang and the nose reduced.

It would be foolish to expect anything other than further controversy in the season ahead. Watch this space...

Main: The MC12 has had to be modified to make sure it doesn't run away with the FIA GT championship

Below: Maserati sports boss Claudio Berro will oversee the MC12 project

MASERATI

E
ACING?
he radical car is allowed to compete unchecked

MASERATI

MASERATI MC12

new DBR9 will not be left trailing in the wake of the MC12.

"The playing field can be controlled; it's just a matter of school boy physics," says George Howard-Chappell, who heads up the Aston project at Prodrive. "The only question is, 'will it be controlled properly?'. And on that [company boss] David Richards has the absolute assurance of Max Mosley."

The man in charge of making sure Mosley's promises are kept is Peter Wright, one of the pioneers of ground-effect aerodynamics and now a technical consultant to the FIA. Each car in the FIA series now has a 'black box' data recorder and the information these provide, with lap and sector times and speed traps, will help Wright model the performance of each car.

A bogey mark has been set around the level of the Prodrive 550 Maranello. FIA officials will then be able to reduce the performance of cars back to that level through a combination of weight penalties, aerodynamic tweaks and changes to the diameter of the air-restrictors that control power outputs in GT racing. The same system could also be used to 'help' cars the FIA would like to encourage into the series, particularly less exotic machinery such as the V10-powered BMW M6.

"The object is to stop manufacturers spending stupid money," says Howard-Chappell, "either by making outlandish cars or undertaking massive development programmes. You won't be able to spend your way to success. That is the message coming loud and clear from Max."

The situation at Le Mans is less clear. The ACO has already slapped a 35kg penalty on the 550 Maranello and the Chevrolet Corvette C5-R for 2005 because these cars regularly lapped under 3m55s in last year's race. How it will deal with the Maserati is unknown because the Italian manufacturer has yet to build a car that conforms to the Le Mans regulations, nor even commit to doing so. That, says Maserati sports boss Claudio Berro, "is a matter of time and money".

ACO sporting director Daniel Poissenot is insistent that the MC12 will be controlled if, as it surely will, Maserati decides to contest the jewel in the crown of worldwide sportscar racing. "We have to make sure," he says, "that this car is at the same level of performance as the other cars." Comments he's made about the Maserati in the past – "this car is like a prototype", "it is not a car to take to the supermarket" – suggest the ACO thinks the MC12 has not been built in the same spirit as its competitors. Don't expect it to pull any punches in its attempt to keep a lid on the pace of development in its top GT class if the cars arrive on its turf in 2006.

There should be an MC12 racing in an ACO series this year. The organisers of the American Le Mans Series have brokered a deal to allow a solo factory-entered MC12 to compete, albeit not for points, even though it doesn't conform to the regulations. Just as in Europe, its performance will be strictly monitored and penalties applied if it proves too fast.

The efforts to which series bosses have gone to ensure the MC12 will race proves the Maserati is not all bad news. The process leading to last week's confirmation that one factory Maserati would be present on the grid for the series opener at Sebring isn't entirely clear. The ALMS has even put its relationship with Le Mans (from which it licenses its name) on the line to bring the car into the series, because the likes of series boss Scott Atherton know just how important the car could be in the development of GT racing.

"There is no question the Maserati is a spectacular car," says Atherton. "Everyone knows about Maserati, but even I was surprised when I read through its resume. It has so much history in America as well as in Europe."

Atherton is not alone in believing that the Maserati is an essential ingredient in a mix that could bring sportscar racing to a new level of awareness. Ratel points out that the arrival of the MC12 at the same time as the return of Aston Martin, plus the presence of other key marques, could herald a golden era for GTs. "Come Silverstone in May we will have a grid of cars I believe is unprecedented in the history of GT racing," he says. "We'll have Aston Martin, Maserati, two types of Ferrari, Lamborghini, Chevrolet and Lister racing together. People talk about the glory days of GTs in the late '60s and early '70s, but there were never so many big names involved."

The involvement of these big hitters could draw other major manufacturers in. "If we can prove we can balance the MC12 with the other cars, then I believe others will come," Ratel goes on. "There is already more good news for this year that I can't reveal yet and we know BMW is looking at doing something with the 6-Series at some point." Others known to be eyeing the GT1 class are Mercedes, Peugeot and Toyota.

The Maserati could be the catalyst that takes GT racing to new heights or it could kill it stone dead. Only time will tell.

Maserati's drivers romped to a 1-2 in the FIA GT finale at Zhuhai last year – a sign of things to come maybe?

F. De Simone

J. Herbert

"EVERYONE KNOWS ABOUT MASERATI. IT HAS SO MU

The crew that helped the MC12 dominate in its few outings last year

PAST ERRORS

A RIVALRY THAT GOT OUT OF CONTROL

▶ **PORSCHE 911 GTI** 1997

▶ **MERCEDES CLK-GTR** 1998

PICS: LAT

NEARLY 10 YEARS on, Stéphane Ratel admits he made a mistake. The Global Endurance GT Series was growing quite nicely when Porsche decided it wanted a bigger slice of the action. It had produced the purpose-built 911 GT1 for the Le Mans 24 Hours and now wanted to take on the McLaren F1 GTRs in the pan-European series. Letting them in was wrong, reckons the Frenchman today.

Ratel held the casting vote when it came to whether or not the car should race. His partners in the BPR Organisation that ran the Global series were split on the subject. Patrick Peter was 'against' while Jurgen Barth was 'for' — hardly surprising given that he was also Porsche's customer sport boss.

"Looking back, it was a mistake," says Ratel. "It was a mistake in that we destroyed what we had created very rapidly. The cars became more and more extreme and things quickly got out of control."

Ratel is being harsh on himself. Equally important in that spiral was a late rule change in the run-up to the 1997 season, by which time the Global series became the FIA GT Championship after annexation by the sport's governing body. That allowed in the Mercedes CLK-GTR, a car that barely paid lip service to the idea that cars should be true road-going machines.

Porsche was subsequently forced to do a new car in the form of the 911 GT1-98, failed to win a round of the 1998 FIA series and promptly pulled out. The FIA GT Championship collapsed, limping on as a GT2-only series.

Part of the reason was that BMW, which backed McLaren's GT campaign, had pulled out at the end of 1997 and built an open-top prototype for the following year instead. Audi followed its lead, and a new era at Le Mans began.

HISTORY IN AMERICA AS WELL AS IN EUROPE" SCOTT ATHERTON

Mika Salo has tasted race-winning glory behind the wheel of the MC12

Bumper to bumper in Zhuhai – the MC12 blitzed the opposition

AUTOCAR ROAD TEST

MASERATI QUATTROPORTE

Maserati desperately needs this fifth-generation Quattroporte to sell well. But can its dynamics possibly match its peerless beauty?

PHOTOGRAPHY STAN PAPIOR

MASERATI

Model tested QUATTROPORTE
List price £74,550
Top speed 161mph
0-60mph 5.3sec
70-0mph 46.6m
Average test MPG 14.1
For Surprising agility, sound, spacious cabin, looks, exclusivity
Against Restless ride, thirst, transmission in automatic mode

THESE ARE uncertain times for Maserati. In the Fiat Group's post-General Motors reorganisation, the Trident has been separated from Ferrari and linked instead with Alfa Romeo in an effort to extend the Modena company's range and – eventually – return it to profitability.

Because at the moment Maserati is haemorrhaging cash. Despite last year recording a 60 per cent increase in sales over 2003, the 4600 cars shifted are still well short of the 10,000 annual target it needs to turn a profit. Replacements for the ageing 4200 Coupé and Spyder are still a way off, and any fruits of the union between Maserati and Alfa Romeo are still further into the future.

Which means that this flagship Quattroporte – despite the name's exotic ring, it translates simply as 'four door' – is the car to tempt much-needed new money to Modena. To outpoint the likes of Mercedes' supercharged AMGs (E55, S55 and CLS55), Jaguar's (cheaper) XJR and BMW's breathtaking M5, it must combine sports car handling and limousine luxury while retaining the unique character of a Maserati. If that's not hard enough, this fifth iteration of the mighty saloon must cement Maserati's credibility as a maker of one of the most opulent and desirable saloons in the world.

DESIGN & ENGINEERING

★★★★☆

Packed with electronics, wrapped by Pininfarina

Traditionally, the four-door Maserati hasn't been a beautiful car, lacking the elegance of its GT brethren. The original was fair, the second dull and the third resembled a bloated Hyundai Stellar. At least the fourth-generation car was striking, in a square-edged way. It has taken

HISTORY The Frua-styled 260bhp quad-cam V8 Quattroporte 1 was 1963's fastest four-door. With a heavy Bertone body and 190bhp V6, its 1975 successor attracted just five buyers in two years. A year on and the Quattroporte 3 revived V8 power and rear-drive. With a new name – Royale – the ItalDesign-penned car soldiered on until 1987. There followed a seven-year wait for the Quattroporte 4 designed by Gandini, whose turbocharged V6 and V8 engines kept it alive until 2001.

Pininfarina to deliver a truly attractive Quattroporte with this model.

There is no bold styling theme – instead lithe, flowing lines cleverly mask its considerable 5052mm length and incorporate cues from Maseratis past – noticeably a thick, Quattroporte 1-echoing rear pillar and A6-style square wing vents and jutting nose. It's a shape without an unattractive angle, clearly glamorous yet understated enough to invite no malice from fellow road users.

Maserati has ploughed over £140m into development of the Quattroporte and its M139 platform. The steel monocoque is conventional, only the bonnet and bootlid being made of weight-saving aluminium, but the tiny front overhang and long area aft of the front wheels subtly betray the effort that has been made in optimising the car's mechanical balance.

The front/mid-mounted engine is the same 4244cc V8 that powers the Coupé and Spyder, but with revised camshafts and modified mapping to boost low-end torque. With twin cams for each bank and 32 variably timed valves, the dry-sump unit produces 394bhp at 7000rpm (9bhp more than in the Coupé) and the same 333lb ft of torque at 4500rpm. Those are peaky numbers and outgunned by every one of the Maserati's rivals.

To further improve weight distribution, drive heads to the back wheels through a rear-mounted six-speed transaxle. The transmission offers fully automatic gearchanges or clutchless sequential manual operation via paddles mounted either side of the steering column.

Suspension is by coil springs and double wishbones all round, controlled by Maserati's 'Skyhook' electronic adaptive dampers. A button on the dash switches between normal and Sport modes, adjusting the aggression of the damping and gearshift speeds, as well as the degree of intervention from the stability control.

PERFORMANCE/BRAKES

Engine needs revs to perform; poor gearbox and pedal feel

The V8's character is apparent from start-up. There's lengthy starter whine before it fires with a yelp and settles to a subdued rumble, a surprising amount of vibration sneaking into the cabin.

Select manual gearchanges, switch off the MSP stability control and select Sport mode to engage the transmission's most aggressive shift mode, floor the throttle and there's a split-second delay as the revs rise before the huge saloon lunges forwards. Our two-way average 0-60mph time of 5.3sec could have been bettered by further runs, but we were keen to preserve the car's twin-plate clutch.

With rivals such as the benchmark BMW M5 toting 500bhp, the 394bhp V8 was always likely to suffer by comparison, particularly as our test car's 2017kg was nearly 100kg over Maserati's 1930kg claim. The Quattroporte trailed 0.7sec behind the M5's 4.6sec 0-60mph time, despite its 53 per cent rearward weight bias giving brilliant traction ▶

◆ and a 0.2sec advantage to 30mph. By 100mph the Italian's 12.8sec performance was 3.0sec behind the German's. A comparative lack of torque (333lb ft plays 384lb ft) also hampers the Maserati, though 75 per cent of that peak (250lb ft) is available from 2500rpm and the 8.4sec it took to go from 50-70mph in top gear was just 1.0sec behind the M5.

And the Maserati's V8 is magical, with a thicker songbook than even the M5's V10. Low-rev woofle and mid-range induction growl are trumped by a scream that transports you straight to Monte Carlo's infamous tunnel, mid Grand Prix.

Short gearing – sixth offers just 23.0mph per 1000rpm – means a lot of gearchanging. Which is fine when driving hard, the robotised manual gearbox giving fast (150 millisecond) changes in Sport mode without the kidney-bruising abruptness of the M5's SMG. And as long as you're happy to swap ratios yourself, then the third-generation DuoSelect system works well in normal use, too. It's in Drive mode that it trips up. With light throttle openings there's a perceptible nodding from the occupants as each automated shift occurs, but press on and it's a real pain, with a long wait as the software decides which gear to provide, and a reluctance to upchange when you've finished accelerating. It never lets you relax in the way that an auto-made-manual such as the Aston Martin DB9's ZF six-speeder does.

The cross-drilled and ventilated Brembo brakes disappointed, too. Unlike the M5's, they suffered no fade and put in an impressive 46.6m 70-0mph performance. But the pedal has an alarmingly long 'dead' travel followed by a confidence-robbing spongy feel that contribute to some scary moments when slowing from speed.

HANDLING & RIDE

★★★★☆

Sports car handling but firm and fidgety ride

The challenge that faced Maserati's engineers with the Quattroporte was not an enviable one. This car needs to combine two opposing talents to deliver the Mercedes S-class comfort levels and Porsche 911 agility that buyers are looking for. Maserati was a maker of racing cars long before it ventured onto the road, so an excellent handling balance should be a given. It's not always so, but the Quattroporte demonstrates an appetite for corners that its size would never lead you to expect.

Exceptional body control plays a big part in shrinking the Maserati, its adaptive dampers sensing body movements and reacting in an instant to all but eliminate roll, pitch and dive and provide nimble turn-in. Even when you expect a left-right sequence of bends to set up a pendulum motion it never arrives.

The Quattroporte works best on open, fast corners, where the grip of the 245mm-wide front and 285mm rear tyres is rarely called into question. But the

Luxurious cabin has uniquely Italian feel; 'titanium' plastics work well with blue leather; CD changer loads beneath steering wheel

Quad-cam 4.2-litre V8 is magnificent

Noise ranges from woofle to scream

Tactile paddles provide swift changes

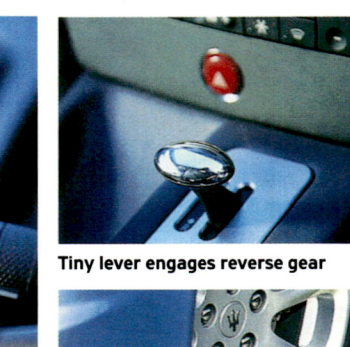
Tiny lever engages reverse gear

19-inch wheels part of Sport Package

53 per cent rearward weight bias gives good traction, but easily broken with 394bhp and 333lb ft; Quattroporte very agile

effects of 2017kg are impossible to mask completely, the Maserati's heft exposed by lurching through tight corners, though the ensuing understeer can be neutralised or turned into a predictable tailslide with a burst of throttle.

The speed-variable electric steering is precise if a little light, and gives a better simulation of feel than most of its genre to ensure the driver always feels involved.

But there's a price to pay for the Maserati's handling and that's a very un-limo-like ride. Our test car was fitted with the £3055 Sport Package, which offers harder settings for the adaptive dampers and lower-profile 19-inch tyres (albeit the same width as the standard 18-inchers). It's a chassis that never settles, with a continual fidget on the motorway that becomes more intrusive as the speed drops. By the time the car has to deal with town Tarmac it's downright uncomfortable, turning skittish over cats eyes and potholes and occasionally producing an alarming crash from the back over speed humps – though this is reduced with a couple of passengers in the rear.

COMFORT, SAFETY AND EQUIPMENT

★★★★☆

Stylish and spacious with a generous specification

If the ride disappoints those looking for comfort, then at least the cabin won't. There's huge space front and rear and a finish that's exudes a restrained opulence – the Maserati's Italianate character is more individual than the sober approach of the Germans, and its quality, fit and finish beats that of the Jaguar XJR.

Most Quattroporte buyers are likely to want to drive themselves, but the few who opt to be driven will have little to complain about, the two rear seats providing similarly sporty accommodation as the fronts. There's bags of legroom and not only does each outer seat adjust for height, but they move fore and aft as well, altering the angle of the backrest at the same time. Just don't expect room to carry five passengers for any distance, because the central rear seat occupant will find themselves close to the roof on an uncomfortably hard base.

Up front the seats are comfortable, though the steering wheel could do with a little more adjustment for the perfect driving position. Behind the slender three-spoke wheel are simple white-on-blue instruments in an elegant binnacle flanked by a bewildering number of buttons and switches.

Our test car featured no-cost optional 'Titanium' (silvered plastic) finish on the dash, central console and doors in place of the usual high-gloss wood, and it combined well with the Poltrona Frau blue leather, though we couldn't help feeling that real aluminium would better suit the cabin's classy finish.

Standard equipment includes effective climate control, which can be adjusted separately to suit the needs of driver, passenger and rear passengers. The ◗

DIMENSIONS

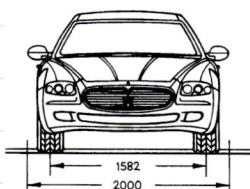
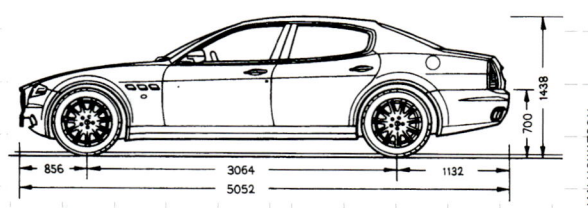

IAN HOWATSON

Min/max front legroom 920/1110mm **Min/max front headroom** 920/950mm **Min/max rear legroom** 690/890mm **Rear headroom** 890mm **Front/rear cabin width** 1550/1510mm **Boot volume** 450 litres/dm³ **Min/max boot width** 1040/1310mm **Boot length** 710mm **Boot height** 450mm **Front/rear tracks** 1587/1560mm **Kerbweight (claimed/tested)** 1930/2017kg **Weight distribution (front:rear)** 47:53 **Width inc/excl mirrors** 1895/2000mm

SPECIFICATIONS

Layout V8, 4244cc
Power 394bhp at 7000rpm
Torque 333lb ft at 4500rpm
Max engine speed 7600rpm
Specific output 93bhp per litre
Power to weight 204bhp per tonne*
Torque to weight 172lb ft per tonne*
Installation Longitudinal, front, rear-wheel drive
Construction Alloy heads and block
Bore/stroke 92.0/79.8mm
Valve gear 4 per cyl
Compression ratio 11.0:1
Management Bosch

Type Automated 6-speed manual
Ratios/mph per 1000rpm
1st 3.28/5.9 **2nd** 2.16/9.0
3rd 1.61/12.1 **4th** 1.27/15.4
5th 1.03/18.8 **6th** 0.85/23.0
Final drive 4.1

Type Rack and pinion, electro-hydraulic power assistance
Turns lock to lock 3.0
Turning circle 12.3m

Front and rear Double wishbones, coil springs, anti-roll bar, electronic dampers

Four-door saloon, steel and aluminium unibody construction

Front/rear wheels 8.5J x 19in/ 10.5J x 19in
Made of Alloy
Front/rear Tyres 245/50 ZR19/ 285/35 ZR19 Pirelli P-Zero Rosso

Front 330mm ventilated discs
Rear 316mm ventilated discs
Anti-lock Standard, with electronic brakeforce distribution

Driver, passenger, side and curtain airbags, traction and electronic stability control

ROAD TEST RESULTS

6th 161mph/7000rpm
5th 143mph/7600rpm
4th 117mph/7600rpm
3rd 92mph/7600rpm
2nd 69mph/7600rpm
1st 45mph/7600rpm

True mph	sec	speedo mph
30	2.0	30
40	2.7	40
50	4.2	50
60	5.3	60
70	6.9	71
80	8.5	81
90	10.6	92
100	12.8	103
110	15.1	114
120	19.1	124
130	23.2	135
140	28.3	145
150	–	–

Standing qtr mile 13.8sec/105mph
Standing km 24.9sec/134mph
30-70mph through gears 4.9sec
30-70mph in fourth gear 8.3sec

mph	6th	5th	4th	3rd	2nd
20-40	11.0	8.8	4.9	3.5	2.4
30-50	8.6	6.5	4.4	3.1	2.2
40-60	8.4	6.2	4.0	2.9	2.2
50-70	8.4	5.8	3.9	2.9	–
60-80	8.2	5.5	3.9	3.1	–
70-90	7.9	5.7	4.0	3.4	–
80-100	8.2	5.9	4.3	–	–
90-110	9.0	6.3	4.7	–	–
100-120	–	6.9	–	–	–
110-130	–	–	–	–	–
120-140	–	–	–	–	–
130-150	–	–	–	–	–

Average/track/touring
14.1/8.7/18.9mpg
Urban/combined 10.1/14.9mpg
Tank capacity 90 litres
Theoretical range 295 miles
Real-world range 279 miles

30/50/70mph
8.7/23.6/46.6 metres
60-0mph 2.9sec
Pedal feel /fair/good/excellent
Fade poor/fair/ /excellent

Normal driving
Balance understeer/oversteer/
Steering feel poor/fair/ /excellent
Body control poor/fair/good/
Ride quality /fair/good/excellent
Grip poor/fair/ /excellent
Hard driving
Balance /oversteer/neutral
Steering feel poor/ /good/excellent
Body control poor/fair/good/
Ride quality poor/ /good/excellent
Grip poor/fair/ /excellent
Test notes Skyhook adaptive dampers help disguise massive bulk. Ride similarly fidgety in normal and Sport modes. Poor pedal feel (dead travel followed by spongy feel) but excellent braking performance.

Idle/max revs in 3rd 46/74dBA
30/50/70mph 61/66/69dBA
Sound quality poor/fair/good/

Dipped beam poor/fair/good/
Full beam poor/fair/ /excellent
Test notes Despite small headlamps, xenon bulbs give particularly good projection on dipped beam.

AUTOCAR ROAD TESTS... are the most exhaustive published in the UK. Each car is measured, then performance tested on a neutral proving ground using Racelogic VBOX equipment and weighed using scales provided by Intercomp Europe. We also cover at least 500 miles on all types of road, and measure economy in all conditions.

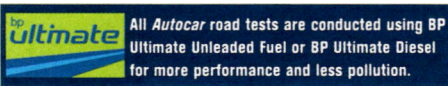

* Power- and torque-to-weight figures calculated using manufacturer's claimed kerbweight. The performance figures were taken with the odometer reading 6538 miles. **AUTOCAR** test results are protected by world copyright and may not be reproduced without the editor's written permission

♦ standard Blaupunkt entertainment system is rather less satisfying, with fiddly control menus and satellite navigation that is easily confused. And you'll need to pack carefully because that neat tail styling, and the need to package a sizeable 90-litre fuel tank, results in a boot of only 450 litres – 10 fewer than the new BMW 3-series provides. Go for a full-size spare wheel and this drops even lower.

In addition to the standard anti-lock brakes with electronic brakeforce distribution and stability control, the Quattroporte serves a full complement of safety gear with six airbags, ISOFIX child seat mounting points in the rear and seatbelts with pretensioners and load limiters all round.

RUNNING COSTS

★★★½☆

Comparatively fair pricing; massive thirst for unleaded

Lined up alongside cars offering a similar combination of space, pace and prestige such as the £76,000 Alpina B7 or £88,540 Mercedes S55 AMG, the £74,550 Quattroporte looks well priced. Only the £60,970 Jaguar XJR and (smaller) £61,755 BMW M5 make it seem expensive.

It won't be cheap to run, occupying the highest bands for both insurance (20) and company car tax (35 per cent). After a week of varied driving, our test car returned an average of 14.1mpg, giving a range of just 279 miles.

Option prices are also ludicrous, with a five-CD autochanger at £488 and heated front seats £459.

The list price does include a three-year 'peace of mind' service-inclusive package with roadside assistance. A good thing, too, the numerous electrical glitches our test car suffered gave us fears for its long-term reliability. Chief of these was the gearbox refusing to engage gears on four separate occasions until the ignition was turned off and on again.

Fiddly Blaupunkt sat-nav not accurate enough

Elegant steering wheel houses one of six airbags

Mass of small buttons; at least they're accessible

Steering wheel could do with further adjustment for taller drivers; seats comfortable and supportive; good interior finish

Trademark oval clock in centre of dash

Trident logo adorns fifth Quattroporte

Delightful square vents hark back to A6

Lots of rear legroom; comfortable seats

Rear passengers get own ventilation

Extra space or spare wheel – you decide

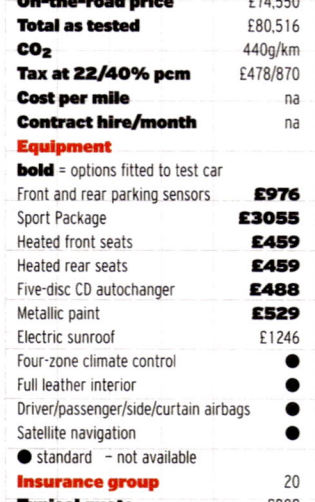

WHAT IT COSTS

On-the-road price	£74,550
Total as tested	£80,516
CO$_2$	440g/km
Tax at 22/40% pcm	£478/870
Cost per mile	na
Contract hire/month	na
Equipment	
bold = options fitted to test car	
Front and rear parking sensors	**£976**
Sport Package	**£3055**
Heated front seats	**£459**
Heated rear seats	**£459**
Five-disc CD autochanger	**£488**
Metallic paint	**£529**
Electric sunroof	£1246
Four-zone climate control	●
Full leather interior	●
Driver/passenger/side/curtain airbags	●
Satellite navigation	●
● standard – not available	
Insurance group	20
Typical quote	£809
Warranties	
Three years/60,000 miles	

Pininfarina-styled Quattroporte the best looking so far; performance not outstanding: 0-60mph in 5.3sec, 161mph

THE CLASS

Maserati Quattroporte £74,550 ★★★☆☆

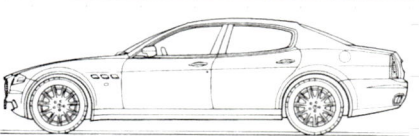

Capacity	4244cc
Output	394bhp/333lb ft
Max speed	161mph
0-60mph	5.3sec
CO_2	440g/km
Date tested	29.3.05

Beautiful looks, a rev-hungry V8 and agile handling that belies its 2017kg kerbweight, but slow automated manual gearbox, restless ride and considerable thirst peg Quattroporte back. A flawed diamond.

Alpina B7 £76,000 ★★★★☆

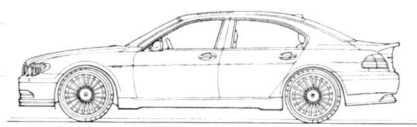

Capacity	4398cc
Output	493bhp/515lb ft
Max speed	186mph
0-60mph	4.8sec
CO_2	308g/km
Twin test	1.2.05

It might be a tuned car, but Alpina's touches work wonders on the controversial BMW 7-series. Supercharged 4.4-litre V8 is a belter and the revised suspension settings provide a more communicative drive.

Audi A8 W12 £75,775 ★★★☆☆

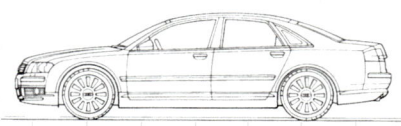

Capacity	5998cc
Output	444bhp/427lb ft
Max speed	155mph
0-60mph	5.2sec
CO_2	331g/km
First drive	15.6.05

Visually and ergonomically a success, but a disappointment on the move, mainly due to firm ride. The W12 engine is marginally quicker than the 4.2-litre V8, but is noisier and struggles to justify the £17k premium.

BMW M5 £61,755 ★★★★★

OUR CHOICE

Capacity	4999cc
Output	500bhp/383lb ft
Max speed	161mph
0-60mph	4.6sec
CO_2	357g/km
Road test	2.11.04

Technically advanced with a fabulous engine, entertaining chassis and brutally effective gearbox. Restricted touring range and brakes that fade with hard use are the only weaknesses. The M5 is back, and how.

Jaguar XJR £60,970 ★★★☆☆

Capacity	4196cc
Output	400bhp/408lb ft
Max speed	154mph
0-60mph	5.2sec
CO_2	299g/km
Group test	30.3.04

The XJR puts the emphasis on refinement, with ride and steering insulating the driver and passengers alike from the road. Aluminium construction keeps weight down to 1814kg, boosting touring range.

Mercedes-Benz S55 AMG £88,540 ★★★★☆

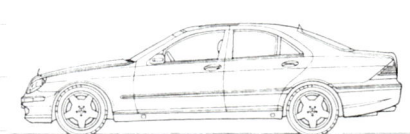

Capacity	5439cc
Output	500bhp/516lb ft
Max speed	155mph
0-62mph	4.8sec
CO_2	317g/km
First drive	23.10.02

AMG modifications turn the brilliant S-class into a hot rod. Suspension changes help keep the 2005kg body in check, but the ride suffers. Powered by a wild, if slightly unrefined, supercharged 5.4-litre V8.

THE AUTOCAR VERDICT

WE WANTED THIS to be a five-star car. All of the elements were in place: stunning looks, incredible chassis balance and a truly inspirational engine. But the Quattroporte isn't that car, and it's more than just a few tweaks away from those elusive extra stars. Because although we have little doubt that this is the finest saloon Maserati has ever made, our concerns centre on some fairly fundamental facets of its make-up – namely the occasionally slow-witted gearbox, fidgety ride and questionable reliability. Few cars manage to be so beguiling yet completely exasperating at the same time.

TESTERS' NOTES

Glad to see that Maserati still persists with its characteristic ornate clock. As well as being embedded in the dash of this Quattroporte, it also makes an appearance in the new MC12 supercar **Chas Hallett**

Early designs featured a grille even more protuberant than this model's. The end result is bold, but could have been bolder. **Richard Bremner**

If you're in the right mood and on the right road, the sensations picked up by your ears, backside and fingertips give a tingle like no other saloon, save perhaps the BMW M5. But this is a car that has a narrow focus. It's too unrefined and restless for 95 per cent of driving conditions, be it a long motorway drive in the rain or a daily city commute.

A saloon like this needs to be good enough to use every day, all year round but, as it stands, the Quattroporte is going to be hard work for all but the most committed Maserati enthusiast.

Flawed but fabulous ★★★☆☆

White
HEAT

GranSport scorches through the Alps on its way home to Modena
Story Chris Chilton Photography Mark Bramley

THE THUNDER RATTLES octogenarian sash windows in their well worn frames, rouses dogs from dreams of genital-licking and angry neighbours from drool-covered pillows. Its source, a GranSport bound for the Maserati factory in Modena, comes to a halt, hunkering menacingly, mid-street, over delicately spoked graphite wheels, canary yellow paint taking on an eerie fluorescence in the pollution of London's streetlighting.

By the time I reach photographer Mark Bramley's front door, the noise has increased four-fold to a Spector-esque barrage. Not the laconic rumble of its equally cylindered late-'60s Buick namesake for this V8 coupé, but a leaner, hard-edged sound whose urgency is matched only by my own need to get the hell out of here: it's 5am on a Saturday and at this volume the Maserati is just one more curtain twitch away from getting me an Anti-Social Behaviour Order.

Resisting the temptation to slot straight back behind the wheel I drop into the passenger seat of our left-hook Italian-registered ride, leaving Bramley to play chauffeur for the first few miles. Chassis experts like Ford's Richard Parry-Jones will tell you that you can understand 80 percent of a car's dynamic ability from the non-steering seat but my motives are more selfish. Bramley has coerced me into this ungodly start with promises of ice go-karting in the Alps tonight. I rose at four and the two cups of coffee I downed five minutes ago have yet to kick in. He can drive while I plan the route.

It's probably better that way – we're in a hurry and can't afford to get lost. Though *CAR* has been a surrogate home to more than its fair share of gifted Aussie expats, I'm disinclined to trust the directional sense of anyone who sets off from a land of grunty V8s, cheap petrol and 20deg winters and ends up in England's grey and often unpleasant land, as Bramley has done.

Not that much planning is called for. Folkestone, Calais, Reims, Troyes, Lyon, Dijon – earn your crust putting together a magazine like this and it soon becomes a mantra, something as integral to the job as a permanently glowing engine warning light is to the authentic exoticar experience. And there it is, less than 15 miles into the journey, beaming back at us from the dash. Anxious to make our date with the ice karts we press on. If a rod appears through the side of the crankcase we'll know to stop.

Map stowed, I settle back into the deeply contoured bucket, noting the irritating wind whistle from the window over my right shoulder while orbs of orange light streak over the bonnet and windscreen as Surrey blends into Sussex, Sussex into Kent. The thin smattering of traffic and long, inviting stretches of camera-free M20 are just begging us to straighten a right leg but we resist the temptation, tying the needle just ↘

Traction is immense, but try hard enough and you can leave some rubber on the hairpins

below 100mph for now. That's fine: providing the weather holds there should be ample opportunity across the water to chase the speedo's 320km/h (199mph) extremity.

Sun-up as we near Folkestone adds light to the proceedings and another kind of dawn – the realisation that what had earlier looked vaguely like smart carbon trim adorning the dashboard and seats is actually a soft synthetic material whose aesthetic and tactile delights precisely mirror those of a football shirt. The yellow piping framing this pyro-accelerant delight is questionable too. I'm in my dream bedroom, circa 1985.

Time being of the essence we're bypassing the dubious pleasures of the floating bingo

THIS ONE'S FASTER!

Maserati's Trofeo championship is more than just another one-make series - competitors race all over Europe, supporting major events. The '05 season kicks off at Monza on 10 April and is open to novice and experienced racers alike.

Freeflowing exhausts and some mapping work help the GranSport engine punch out 425bhp, suspension and brake revisions tie the chassis down and Plexiglas side windows and lightweight body panels slice 35kg off the kerb weight.

You can rent a racer from Maserati for 128,000 euros (plus flights and taxes) a season. This includes mechanics, spares, transport, meals, accommodation and hospitality for your sponsors. You can even lunch the car once for free.

What's it like to drive? Imagine sitting in a bin while it's hit by bats. The reverberations of undamped body panels echoing around the carpet-free cabin seem to double with every extra millimetre of pressure exerted on the throttle, the wonderfully communicative steering puts the road car's to shame and the mechanical grip from this year's new Pirelli slicks is staggering. When warm.

Strangely, Maserati has left the MSP stability system in place; model and Trofeo racer Jodie Kidd reckons it's a boon in the wet but saps time in the dry. Find out more about Kidd's Maseratis on p86.

halls commuting between Dover and Calais for the Germanic efficiency of the Channel tunnel. On a trip such as this the Channel is nothing more than a watery inconvenience which the train shrinks to a minor delay.

Tucked up on one of the Chunnel's identikit carriages we've time to soak up some of the details that help a regular Coupé earn the GranSport tag that Maserati first used on the '50s A6. Those wheels, styled to resemble the Trofeo racecar's rims and echoing the company's trident design in their spokes, measure 19 inches across, an inch bigger than the Coupé's. The ride height is down 10mm. New front and rear bumpers add aggression and cut the air more cleanly. But it's the ugly sill extensions that grab the attention. They ruin the original's waisted look.

As we near France, I relegate Bramley to the passenger seat. Leaving the Maser's windows open, I thumb the GS-only console-mounted starter button and wait for the quad tailpipes' music. Flicking the right hand paddle to engage first gear in the Cambiocorsa sequential manual 'box I nose the car along the carriage and out on to French tarmac for the long drive south. Derided as clunky and unsophisticated when launched, this F1-style transmission has received regular software updates, and it shows. While still no match for a conventional auto it seems to give smoother shifts than the earlier cars and is less of a hindrance in town. Just as well given that it's the only 'box available on the GranSport.

A prudent prod of the loud pedal dispatches the local southbound traffic, leaving the locals to bemoan the loss of the old 3200 GT's boomerang rear lights. The GranSport's pie-quarter lamps are a clue that our car isn't one of the beautiful but evil handling 3200s, but rather a derivative of its Coupé successor. They don't begin to hint at the differences between the 3200 and the Coupé beneath the skin. The Coupé has eight naturally aspirated cylinders rather than eight force-fed, an extra 1000cc of swept volume to make up any deficit, and the gearbox is further back, fusing ⇲

'The GranSport wins us a reprieve from the polizia with a blip of the throttle'

GranSport's 19-inch wheels are styled to resemble the Trofeo racer's

Freer breathing GS has another 10bhp and a few extra dB on the Coupé

Starter button is unique to GranSport. Engine sounds great. Mesh trim almost as loud

There's no shortage of spectacular sights in the Alps, but ours is yellowest

with the differential to form a Porsche 928-style transaxle for a near perfect weight distribution. There's 20bhp more, at 385bhp, and 333lb ft of torque, which is down by a similar number, but the straightline numbers are fractionally better: sub five seconds to 62mph and knocking on three miles a minute flat out. No slouch.

GranSport spec doesn't signify any great engine changes bar a reduction in internal friction, plus work on the intake manifolds and valve seats and the addition of a sports exhaust, enough to liberate another 10bhp and an extra few dB, slimming the 0-62mph sprint to 4.85sec and making it a genuine 180mph car.

FRANCE PASSES IN A BLUR OF food and fuel stops, dodgy CDs and bad jokes. Warning light apart, the Coupé doesn't miss a beat, and with Sport mode off to soften the suspension, exhaust note and gearchanges, it plays the GT role with conviction. By the time the traditional dash-mounted clock passes 5pm, we're deep into the Alps and Bramley's hyping of the ice karting experience has reached fever pitch. Flat through the chicane, late entry and full noise on the second corner: I haven't seen the circuit but he's plotted every nuance of its twists and turns in my mind, talked me through an entire race. And there it is up ahead, under

that enormous sign. Ice karting: Closed'.

Dejected, despondent, deflated, we're every miserable d-word as we rumble on through the town like a rudderless ship. Until, that is, BTCC ace Yvan Muller saves the day, not to mention Bramley from a kicking. Remembering a visit to the Alps the previous year, when I'd come to see ice racing champion Muller in action, I grab the map to see how near we are to the track. A quick scan shows it's not far, and better still, getting there involves negotiating a Stelvio Pass-style sequence of hairpins.

Hands clasping what must rate as one of the finest shaped steering wheels currently fitted to a car, I scythe up and down the Maser's 'box, racing between switchbacks, marvelling at the composure and stomping on the Brembo-equipped brakes. Even with the stability control disengaged, the 333lb ft of torque is not enough to break traction in second, so a tap down to first serves up the requisite blip of the throttle and enough grunt to liquefy the rear boots in an instant. Hard to resist though, so well balanced is the chassis even beyond the tyres' lofty limits.

Perhaps it's the trumpet of tortured rubber and screaming V8 heralding our arrival, or merely the shocking hue of our Giallo Granturismo paint, but the Maserati is causing ripples in Alpe d'Huez as we pick our way through the après skiers en route to

the ice track. This crude looking circuit with its terrifyingly tall and unforgiving white walls is home to a round of ice racing's Andros Trophy as well as the base for an ice driving academy. Sadly we've arrived too late to hoon about in the school's battered and sinister looking fleet of mid-'80s 325i BMWs so we settle on 20 minutes of sideways quad biking instead on a neighbouring circuit.

Juvenile fun quotient filled, we banish the Alps to a speck in the rear-view mirror and knuckle down for a serious autostrada workout on the final leg to Modena. The frequent toll booths hinder our progress, but not enough to stop us hitting 290km/h (180mph) at just shy of the red line in sixth on one lightly trafficked stretch.

We're lucky enough to avoid a run-in with the feds on that occasion but Modena is teeming with polizia when we roll into the beautiful but pedestrianised cobbled streets to take some pics. The GranSport is a natural charmer, though, and wins our reprieve with a blip of the throttle. I've long held a perhaps irrational fondness for the standard Coupé, but a recommendation for the GranSport comes with far fewer caveats. Sensible money will always choose a 911 but there's something beguiling about the Maser's less straightforward character. In GranSport form, the Coupé's the car it always promised to be. car

MASERATI GRANSPORT
Price: £66,000 **Engine:** 4244cc
V8, 395bhp @ 7000rpm, 333lb ft @ 4500rpm
Transmission: Six-speed Cambiocorsa, rear-wheel drive
Performance: 4.85sec 0-62mph, 180mph, 15.1mpg,
434g/km CO₂
On sale in UK: Now

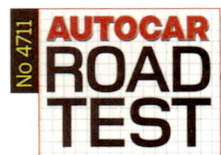
Maserati GranSport

Maserati coupés have always appealed to the heart, but can the GranSport, with its tuned V8 and revised chassis, make the Italian GT a logical choice?

QUICK FACTS

Model tested	GranSport
Price	£66,600
On sale	Now
0-60mph	4.9sec
Top speed	180mph
70-0mph	50.4m
Skidpan	na

DEFINE A CAR'S performance by its name and the new Maserati GranSport should be able to out accelerate just about anything on the road. Such emotive names have always been part of the mystique of Maserati, along with style, passion and racing success. Of course, in the past 20 years that little lot has been balanced by financial strife and an often less than perfect product, but the name still carries tremendous kudos, even though Maserati's last F1 victory was in 1957.

Nevertheless, it's been many years since Maserati had a genuine contender in the driver-oriented GT class – a car to lock horns with the Porsche 911 – but the GranSport could be the car to give the regular 4200GT coupé the mechanical edge it needs to complement its undeniable emotional appeal. You only need to stand next to this pearlescent white car to appreciate the latter; the bassy rumble from the exhaust at tickover promises much of the former.

Now, the shape of the car looks about right. Although there are many who still lust for the rear boomerang lights that disappeared with the 3200 GT, the GranSport's subtle but purposeful front chin spoiler, rear lip spoiler and pronounced side skirts and 19in alloy wheels all alleviate the slightly bloated look of the standard 4200 GT, drawing it closer to the ground and improving the stance. Although this is a shape that can still appear ill-proportioned from certain angles, the GranSport looks hungry, either for air to feed its V8 through that classic gaping mouth, or for the rear bumpers of unsuspecting Porsches.

It's not surprising to learn that the V8 requires a serious lungful when you appreciate its vital statistics. With a classic 90 degree layout and a cubic capacity of 4244cc, it features twin chain-driven overhead camshafts with variable timing on the inlet side, four valves per cylinder, a dry sump and a fly-by-wire throttle. It makes 395bhp at 7000rpm – an increase of 10bhp over the standard car – and the maximum 333lb ft of torque is developed at 4500rpm.

Maserati says the gains in performance are down to careful tuning of the induction tracts and the valve seats, and plenty of hard work in the engine room to reduce internal friction. There is also, as it rapidly becomes apparent, a sports exhaust fitted, with four rather ostentatious gold tailpipes. And in the GranSport, you have no choice but to take the semi-automatic Cambiocorsa gearbox, the hydraulically-controlled transmission also found in Ferraris and the Aston Martin Vanquish. Sixth gear is lengthened to enable a new top speed of 180mph.

Press the big starter button and the V8 whumpfs into life before settling down to a deep, murmuring idle. Extending your toes to flex the accelerator pedal produces a whoop of revs from the engine and a clearer understanding of what 'reduced internal friction' means in reality rather than on the spec sheet: angry just about describes it. For the full GranSport effect you'll need to press the button labelled 'sport'. This opens a pneumatic valve in the exhaust and ramps up the decibels from 'cultured' to 'centre of attention'. It's a very nice noise. But the sport button isn't just a way of making new friends (and enemies); it also gathers several of the GranSport's other →

RANGE AT A GLANCE

PETROL		
4200 GT	385bhp	£56,650
4200 Spyder	385bhp	£61,995
V8 GranSport	395bhp	£66,600
Variants	Coupé/Spyder	
Transmission		
6-speed automated manual,		
6-speed manual		

PHOTOGRAPHY STAN PAPIOR

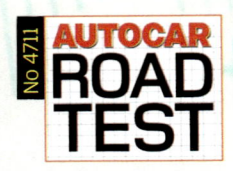

GranSport a highly entertaining drive in sport mode; oversteer on demand

Looks great, sounds amazing – 395bhp V8 is very much at the heart of this car

STEERING WHEEL

Unusual part leather, part carbonfibre wheel is good to hold and it has an expensive, bespoke feel.

STEREO

Single-slot Becker system with sat-nav is difficult to use at first but very effective once learnt. Decent sound quality, in the unlikely event you don't want to hear the engine.

HEATING & VENTILATION

Air conditioning system is straightforward to operate, and performed without a problem during our test.

TRANSMISSION

Along with the manual mode, you can switch the gearbox to fully automatic via a button on centre console,

SEATS

Leather seats use nautical-look fabric on centres for extra grip, but it doesn't really work during hard driving and chairs don't drop low enough for tall drivers.

Ferrari-style T-bar selects reverse. It's fiddly and awkward to use

Oddly-sited switches include the hard-to-reach window controls

Paddles behind wheel operate six-speed Cambiocorsa transmission

These are proper seats for proper human beings, not just for luggage

HISTORY MASERATI GRANSPORT
FIRST TIME AROUND

THE GRANSPORT name originates from a rare coupé version of Maserati's first road car, the 1954 A6G. Like many sports cars of the era, the A6G appeared in many different guises, with specialist coachbuilders (eg Pininfarina, Zagato, Vignale and Allemano) fitting their own designs over the independent tubular chassis. Today's GranSport extends the

life of the Maserati Coupé, which has done much to restore the fortunes of the company. First appearing in 1999 as the 3200, the coupé has been gently evolved ever since. The biggest change came in 2002 with the addition of a naturally aspirated V8 power and the 4200 name. Following Maserati's recent split with Ferrari, the GranSport, originally planned as a run-out model, now faces a longer lifespan. Given its performance, that's no bad thing.

← systems. Pressing it changes the damping to a firmer setting, pulls back the MSP stability control threshold and speeds up the gear-change software. And as we shall see later, this has a fundamental effect on the character of the car.

The V8 feels like it's been at training camp once you're on the road. It's quite happy to amble around at low revs, but its forte is pulling hard from the mid-range, where it lugs with fantastic purpose and a menacing growl. There's a real burst of power between 5000 and 6000rpm that's hard not to resist tapping into once you've experienced it, and then the performance tails off marginally along with the noise before you reach the cut-off at 7600rpm. At the test track we recorded a 4.9sec run from 0-60mph, charging on to 100mph in 11.7sec and still pulling with fervour at 140mph (26.3sec). So the GranSport is quick, but not

WHAT IT COSTS

MASERATI GRANSPORT

On-the-road price	£66,600
Price as tested	£74,581
Retained value 3yrs	na
Typical PCP pcm	na
Contract hire pcm	na
Cost per mile	na
CO$_2$ 437g/km	
Tax at 22/40% pcm	£410/£746
Insurance/typical quote	20/£809

EQUIPMENT CHECK LIST

Steering adjust reach/rake	■	
Airbags front/side	■	
Alloy wheel upgrade	£470	
Dual-zone climate control	■	
Anti-whiplash head restraints	na	
Auto headlights/wipers	na	
Xenon headlights	£964	🖒
CD multichanger	£540	🖒
Ceramic brakes	na	
Cruise control	£341	🖘
DAB Radio/iPod plug-in	na	
Emergency brake assist	na	
ESP/Traction Control	■	
Heated seats	£530	🖓
Metallic paint	■	
Multi-function wheel	na	
Keyless go	na	
Sat-nav/GSM phone	£2465	🖘
Rear parking sensors	£447	🖒
Run-flat tyres/spare	na/£441	🖒
Electric leather seats	■	
Sports exhaust	■	
Sunroof	na	
Trip computer	■	
Tyre pressure sensors	na	
Adaptive suspension	■	

Options in **bold** fitted to test car
*denotes option as part of a package
■ = Standard na = not available
🖒 Buy it 🖘 Consider it 🖓 Forget it

ridiculously so, which is as much a reflection of the 1672kg kerbweight and the difficulty of getting traction off the line as anything else. With this much character in an engine, you're not inclined to quibble about a few tenths against the clock.

After being spoilt recently with the semi-automatic gearboxes found in the Ferrari F430 and the BMW M5, operating the Maserati's paddles comes as a reality check. The most telling comparison is with the Ferrari, as they share the same basic 'box but with new generation software and technology in the mid-engined car. Gearchanges in normal mode suffer from that slightly uncomfortable pause between shifts that used to be a trademark of paddle-shift systems. It's a trait you'll learn to live with, as the actual change is pleasantly smooth, but it can be an irritant in fast but relaxed A-road driving.

Once in sport mode, the shift is urgent, but brutal. Now changes are whacked through with a slam through the structure that makes you wince. In fact, the best technique is to lift between shifts, which doesn't seem to have any effect on the speed of the change, but smooths the process considerably. Try the same in normal mode and the 'box gets confused. As with many similar systems, if you value precision and sportiness in your car, you'll prefer the speed and added control of the gearchange in sport mode, along with the unrestrained exhaust note. It's just a shame that in the Maserati all that good stuff is linked with the sport mode's significantly harder ride.

In normal mode, however, the ride is actually quite absorbent. For all the road-racer connotations, this Maser is comfortable enough for everyday use and, although it feels unyielding around town, it never allows as much thump and bump into the cabin as you expect. However, drive in the manner in which you're encouraged to by the rest of the GranSport package, and you'll soon reach its limitations down a challenging road.

PUSH THE BUTTON

At 2.1 turns lock to lock the steering is now extremely quick – almost too quick, as it makes the car feel more nervous than it actually is – but it doesn't communicate a great deal to the driver. You quickly sense the car's weight and the body control disapppears, allowing the Maserati to hit the bump stops over compressions and generally squirm over poor surfaces at speed. So far then, a disappointment, and far from the 911-chaser we hoped it would be. But then you hit the sport button and the Maser gets a firm grip of its →

←underpinnings, reapplying itself to the task of going quickly and proving the worth of the retuned double wishbone suspension and bespoke new tyres. Now, you've not only got the vastly better gearshifts and the bark from the exhaust encouraging you, you've also got a chassis that actively wants to be really driven.

Although it's firm, and occasionally jars over potholes, the suspension works hard to contain the car's mass and you soon find yourself enthusiastically piloting the GranSport in a flamboyant manner. Keen application of the throttle pedal exposes the car's ultimate lack of rear-end traction – which can really give you something to think about over a bumpy or wet road – but the resultant slide is nicely controllable and great fun, with a good sense of balance to the chassis. Power oversteer in a Maserati is a good feeling, you are forced to conclude after such behaviour. The GranSport is perhaps a car without the supreme cross-country pace of some of its peers, but one which is tremendously rewarding and involving as an experience. You have to work for your entertainment, but you'll be glad you made the effort.

ITALIAN STYLE

You could never confuse the interior of a GranSport with that of a car from anywhere but Italy. The use of colour, texture and tone is a million miles away from the sombre, dark cabins of German performance cars. Hence getting into the GranSport is always an event for all the right and, in some cases, the wrong reasons. Once you're seated

it's disappointing to realise that the driving position comes very much from the old school of long-arm short-leg Italian ergonomics.

The fascia is upright, and covered in a mixture of fine leather and a coarse nautical-look fabric that's definitely an acquired taste. You still get an analogue clock, in true Maserati style, and the steering wheel is a fine concoction of leather and carbonfibre, but the details around the cabin are starting to show the age of the basic design. The most obvious sensation is of sitting in a big car, looking out through a relatively narrow glasshouse, something that makes the GranSport less confidence-inspiring when you're trying to place it at speed on narrow roads.

And you'll feel like that because the Maserati is a big car for its class, and that means the two rear seats are a lot more than just a couple of cubby holes for overnight bags. Even the boot is useable.

At £66,600 the GranSport is swimming straight into the perilous waters occupied by the formidable Porsche 911 Carrera S. It does so with a decent level of standard equipment, and there are pleasing ways to personalise your purchase including specifying a bespoke colour, but it will still take a brave buyer not to make the obvious German choice. Part of this quandary is caused by the way the Maserati still feels a little too creaky: this test car developed a number of squeaks, rattles and groans that you wouldn't expect in a 911 or a BMW M6. Until Maserati can imbue its cars with a deep-set feeling of integrity, buying one will always carry a greater sense of chance about it.

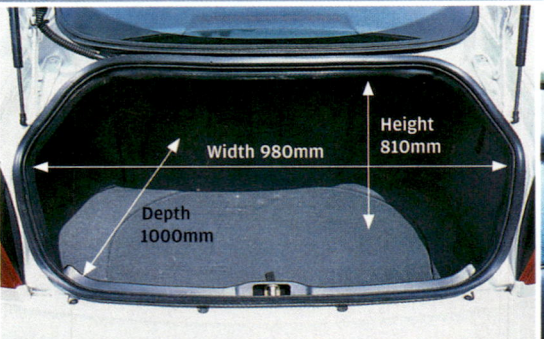

Height 810mm
Width 980mm
Depth 1000mm

At 315 litres, the boot is a lot bigger than you may expect

Very characterful cabin uses unusual materials, but driving position and ergonomics poor

GranSport is quick but not super quick – it will dispatch 60mph in 4.9sec, and makes one hell of a noise doing so

INSTANT GROUP TEST Italian character takes on its cheaper rivals

OUR CHOICE

MAKE	MASERATI	PORSCHE	JAGUAR	CHEVROLET
Model	GranSport	911 Carerra S	XKR	Corvette C6
Price	£66,600	£65,000	£59,995	£45,850
Power	395bhp at 7000rpm	350bhp at 6600rpm	400bhp at 6100rpm	400bhp at 6000rpm
Torque	333lb ft at 4500rpm	295lb ft at 4600rpm	408lb ft at 3500rpm	400lb ft at 4400rpm
0-60mph	4.9sec	4.6sec	5.4sec	4.3sec
Top Speed	180mph	182mph	157mph	186mph
Fuel consumption	10.4mpg	20.9mpg	16.7mpg	21.7mpg
Kerbweight	1672kg	1420kg	1723kg	1517kg
Boot space	315 litres	135 litres	327 litres	295 litres
CO₂/Tax band	434g/km / 35 per cent	227g/km / 35 per cent	304g/km / 35 per cent	310g/km / 35 per cent
We think	GranSport is good fun, and has plenty of character, but it's still overshadowed by the 911.	It's still the benchmark driver's car in this segment, and the 911 remains our choice.	Not much longer for this world, but the elegant Jaguar's opulent charm still appeals.	Vette isn't as complete as some rivals, but this American icon is loveable and very good value.
VERDICT	★★★½☆	★★★★★	★★½☆☆	★★★½☆

Little body roll under hard cornering; four fat exhaust pipes not just for show

TEST SCORECARD

ENGINE ★★★★☆
GranSport's subtly-tweaked V8 is as charismatic as they come. At its best through the mid-range and sounds fantastic.

TRANSMISSION ★★★⯪☆
Cambiocorsa transmission now showing its age. Shifts are fast in sport mode, but require a lift of the throttle to smooth them out.

STEERING ★★★⯪☆
Quick, but so much so it makes the car nervous and feel through the thick steering wheel rim is poor. Requires delicate inputs for smooth progress.

BRAKES ★★★⯪☆
Slow the car convincingly, but if you're driving hard you're always aware of the momentum you have to shed.

HANDLING ★★★⯪☆
Much more nimble than you would imagine when in sport mode. Plenty of power oversteer available on demand.

RIDE ★★★⯪☆
Impressive ride with dampers in normal mode. Very stiff in sport mode for town driving, but essential to maintain body control in hard driving.

ECONOMY ★★⯪☆☆
As thirsty as you would imagine a thoroughbred V8 to be; it managed just 6.8mpg at the test track.

DRIVING POSITION & VISIBILITY ★★☆☆☆
Driving position and ergonomics still suffer from typical Maserati flaws. Slender glass area and long nose reduce wieldiness.

INSTRUMENTS & CONTROLS ★★★☆☆
Attractive dials and nice details partly make up for ageing switchgear and its odd locations; for instance, electric windows switches are a stretch.

EQUIPMENT ★★★⯪☆
A fair deal from Maserati, with most of the technical specification thrown in. Personalisation options expensive.

LIVEABILITY ★★★⯪☆
More practical than you would imagine, with room in the rear and a fair-sized boot.

QUALITY ★★⯪☆☆
GranSport's details feels nicely bespoke, but too many worrying squeaks and groans on our test car to instil confidence.

VALUE ★★★⯪☆
A considerable price hike over the regular 4200GT coupé, but a much better car. Right in Porsche 911 Carrera S territory.

SAFETY ★★★☆☆
Four airbags and a raft of active safety systems like MSP stability control and EBD, but the basic design is getting old.

AUTOCAR VERDICT

The changes to the GranSport over the regular car not only make it much more focused, but also a far better all-round proposition. Objectively, it still doesn't get close to offering the all-encompassing talents of a Porsche 911, but it's more of an event to look at, sit in and drive. A car to buy with your heart, and now partly with your head.

A great Maserati, a fine sports GT ★★★⯪☆

MASERATI GRANSPORT DATA

TESTERS' NOTES

Love the styling, and the white paint. But what's going on with the blue interior? It looks completely out of place in a car as sophisticated as a Maserati.

The updated Cambiocorsa 'box may be the best performing version yet, but still requires patience when parallel parking. You need to be very careful on the throttle and very quick on the brakes.

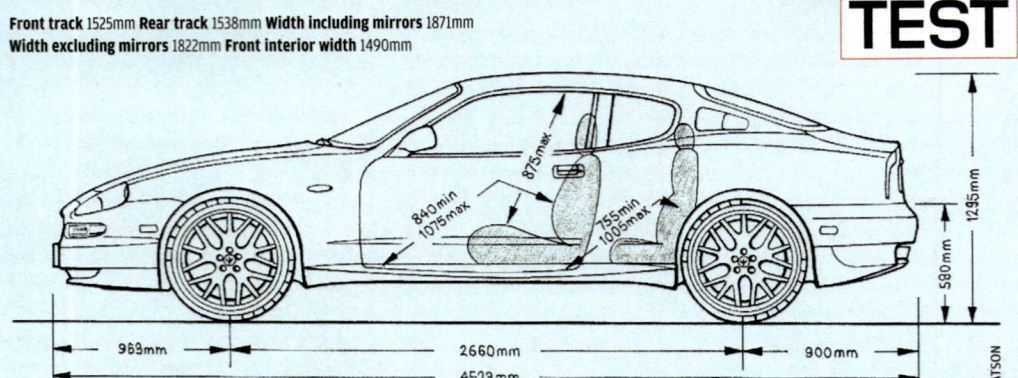

Front track 1525mm **Rear track** 1538mm **Width including mirrors** 1871mm
Width excluding mirrors 1822mm **Front interior width** 1490mm

873max
840 min 1075max
755min 1005max
1295mm
580mm
969mm 2660mm 900mm
4523mm
front 54% Weight distribution 46% rear

IAN HOWATSON

SPECIFICATIONS

ENGINE

Type	V8 ,4244cc
Made of	Alloy head and block
Installation	Front,
Power	395bhp at 7000rpm
Torque	333lb ft at 4500 rpm
Red line	7600rpm
Power to weight	238bhp per tonne
Torque to weight	198lb ft per tonne
Specific output	94bhp per litre
Bore/stroke	92.0/79.8mm
Compression ratio	11.1:1
Valve gear	4 per cyl
Management	Bosch
Fuel type	Petrol

CHASSIS & BODY

Construction	Steel unibody construction
Weight	1680kg
Weight as tested	1671.5kg
Drag coefficient	0.33 Cd
Wheels	Front 8.0J x 19in, rear 9.5J x 19in
Made of	alloy
Tyres	265/30 R19, Pirelli P-zero
Spare	Opt 185/60 17in spacesaver

TRANSMISSION

Type	Rear-wheel drive
Gearbox	6-spd automated manual, lsd
Ratios/mph per 1000rpm	
1st 3.29/6.1 **2nd** 2.16/9.3 **3rd** 1.61/12.5	
4th 1.27/15.9 **5th** 1.03/19.5 **6th** 0.82/24.7	
Final drive ratio	3.73

SUSPENSION

Front Double wishbones, coil springs, anti-roll bar adaptive dampers
Rear Double wishbones, coil springs, anti-roll bar adaptive dampers

STEERING

Type	Rack and pinion, hydraulic power assistance
Turns lock-to-lock	2.1
Turning circle	12.0m

BRAKES

Front 330mm cross-drilled ventilated discs
Rear 310mm cross-drilled ventilated discs
Anti-lock Standard with EBD

SAFETY

Driver, passenger and side curtain airbags, ESP with ASR (traction control)

ROAD TEST RESULTS Dry weather, minimal wind, 21 degrees

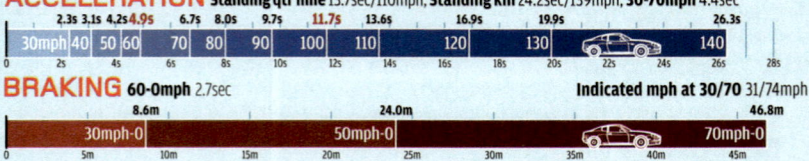

ACCELERATION Standing qtr mile 13.7sec/110mph, Standing km 24.2sec/139mph, 30-70mph 4.4sec

2.3s	3.1s	4.2s	4.9s	6.7s	8.0s	9.7s	11.7s	13.6s	16.9s	19.9s	26.3s
30mph	40	50	60	70	80	90	100	110	120	130	140

BRAKING 60-0mph 2.7sec   Indicated mph at 30/70 31/74mph

8.6m	24.0m	46.8m
30mph-0	50mph-0	70mph-0

POWER & TORQUE

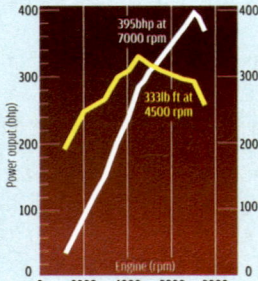

395bhp at 7000 rpm
333lb ft at 4500 rpm

ACCELERATION IN GEAR

	2nd	3rd	4th	5th	6th
20-40	2.0	3.0	6.0	9.5	
30-50	1.9	2.7	3.6	5.3	8.3
40-60	1.9	2.5	3.5	4.7	6.9
50-70	-	2.5	3.3	4.6	6.7
60-80		2.6	3.3	4.3	6.6
70-90	-	2.7	3.4	4.2	6.5
80-100	-	-	3.5	4.5	6.3
90-110			3.8	4.7	6.6
100-120				5.0	7.2

MAX SPEEDS IN GEAR

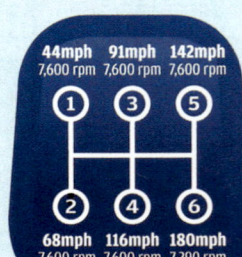

① 44mph 7,600 rpm	③ 91mph 7,600 rpm	⑤ 142mph 7,600 rpm
② 68mph 7,600 rpm	④ 116mph 7,600 rpm	⑥ 180mph 7,290 rpm

HANDLING

Lateral acceleration	na
Balance	Oversteer
Seat support	Average

ECONOMY

TEST	**Average**	12.1mpg
	Touring	14.2mpg
	Track	6.8mpg
CLAIMED	**Urban**	10.0mpg
	Extra-urban	21.7mpg
	Combined	15.2mpg

Tank size 88 litres **Test range** 275 miles

CABIN NOISE

Idle 56dBA **Max revs in third gear** 80dBA
30mph 69dBA **50mph** 71dBA **70mph** 73dBA

HEADLIGHTS

Dipped beam Poor **Full beam** Average
Test notes Not enough for the car's performance

VERDICT & RIVALS p148▶

PETER LIDDIARD

	FIAT PUNTO
MASERATI QUATTROPORTE	

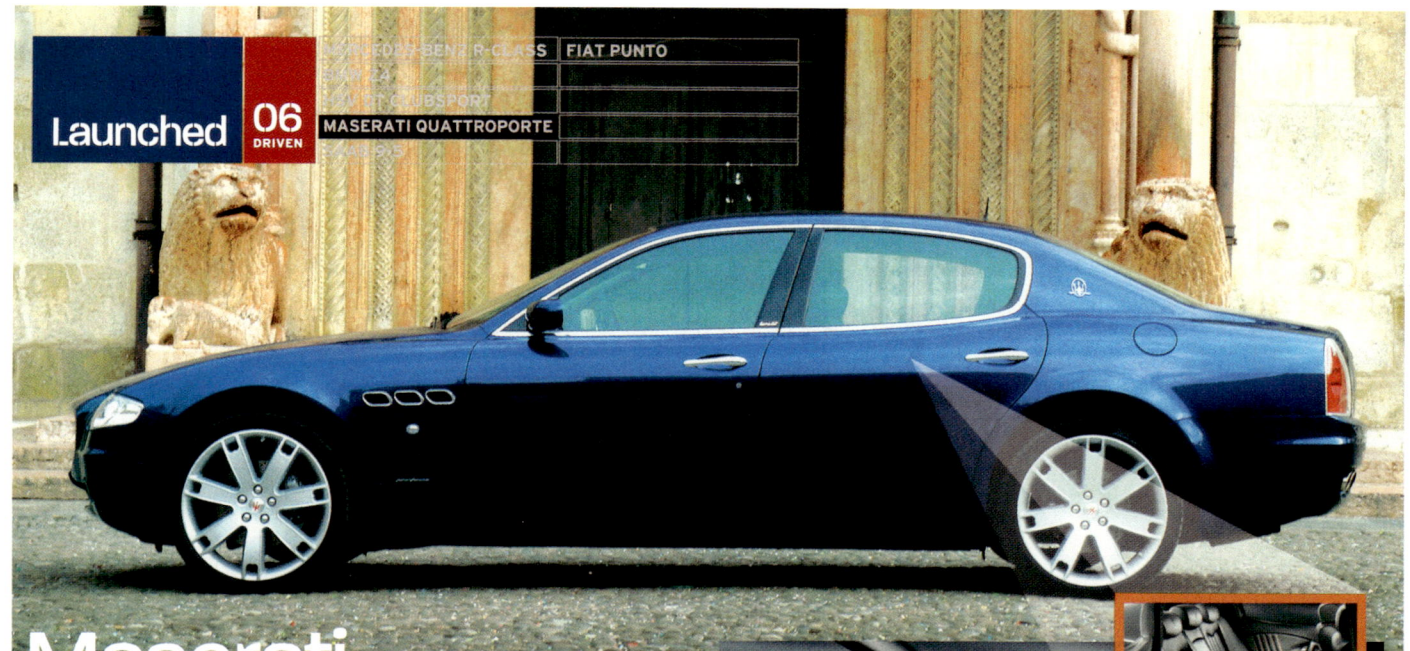

1. Rear seats beautifully deep and sculpted, but legroom only sufficient; not substantial

2. Lashings of carbonfibre trim and red stitching differentiates Sport from regular Quattroporte

3. Sequential manual now shifts 35% faster in Sport mode

Maserati Quattroporte Sport GT

Italian express now with keener edge

IF YOU'RE wondering how the Sport GT differs from the standard Quattroporte launched back in 2003, the answer is: not significantly. It runs the same 4.2-litre V8 good for 295kW, the same slinky sedan body, the six-speed sequential gearbox is still mounted as part of a rear transaxle, and most of the hardware is likewise unaltered.

Look a little closer, though, and fat 20-inch alloys (up from 19s) really fill the wheel-arches, the shiny mesh grille suits the Quattroporte's stick-out nose rather well, but the new badge tacked onto the B-pillar seems a bit, well … tacked on.

Dig a bit deeper, and changes to the gearbox software become apparent. Maserati claims the paddleshift manual has been improved with faster gearchanging, amounting to a maximum 35 percent quicker upshifts in manual mode with the Sport button depressed. There's no conventional auto offered for now (nor a proper manual), although ZF's six-speed will be available by year's end.

The adaptive damping system has been given firmer settings, and there's a beefier exhaust note over 4500rpm, but overall it's a mild re-work of the existing theme, not a focused effort to match and beat Mercedes' and AMG's finest, let alone the brilliance of BMW's M5.

Or so you'd think. Put down the brochure, clamber behind the wheel, fire up the Ferrari-designed V8, give the Quattroporte a big prod, and it doesn't take long to understand this is one big sedan that doesn't follow rules invented by German manufacturers.

The engine has a delicious snarl, and delivers hearty straight-line acceleration, despite the hefty 1800kg-plus kerb weight. However, more than half that is rear-biased, aiding traction, just as the mechanised gearshift aids a perfect launch. The V8 works noticeably better at higher revs, but a lack of pull below about 4000rpm is only relative to the sheer, howling hell that breaks loose above it.

The Sport GT is beautifully balanced, too. There's amazing traction battering out of tight, second-gear corners, an eagerness to turn in to the next one, and oodles of grip the whole way. It's difficult not to compare it favourably with the nose-heavy tendencies of most AMG Mercs and their twitchy rear ends.

Hit the Sport button and the suspension stiffens, gearshifts slam home quicker and there's no doubt about it: this Quattroporte simply urges the driver onwards towards delinquent activity all the way to an unlimited 275km/h.

The only downside is electrically assisted steering that lacks much in the way of loading up as lock increases, or self-centring on the way back. And the ride that's acceptable for a sports car on very low-profile tyres, but choppy for a limo. Boot space is also only adequate – that transaxle and a fuel tank had to go somewhere, also forcing a space-saver under the floor.

In short, the Quattroporte is a rip-roaring drive with finesse as well as thunder. Instead of rivalling, or at least being an alternative to, the usual German suspects, it could well be a precursor to the kind of four-door luxo-sport to which the Porsche Panamera or a production version of the Aston Martin Rapide will aspire. I have a funny feeling they'll have to be pretty good to beat this Maserati.

JONATHAN HAWLEY

Model	Maserati Quattroporte Sport GT
Engine	4244cc V8, dohc, 32v
Max Power	295kW @ 7000rpm
Max Torque	451Nm @ 4500rpm
Transmission	6-speed sequential manual
0-100km/h	5.2sec (claimed)
Price	$275,000
On sale	Now

☑ Addictive blend of performance and luxury
☒ Not overly roomy in back seat or boot. Needs an auto

RANGE FINDER

Maserati is a small company: last year, it sold just 5659 cars. In an effort to increase that, there's a Quattroporte for every occasion, starting with the standard car for $258,000, rising to the Sport, Sport GT, Executive GT, and topping out at the $295,000 Executive. All have the same engine and transmission, but different equipment levels.

French Connection

There's a French ancestor in the Maserati family tree, and it has more
in common with the latest Quattroporte than you might imagine

Words: Dale Drinnon   Photography: Martyn Goddard

Standing at the bathroom mirror on Sunday morning, razor in hand, eyes a trifle bleary, and suddenly there's an almighty *whoop!* of revs from somewhere downstairs. First thought from wine-dulled brain: Good God, is there a Grand Prix on television? Surely I haven't slept that late, have I? Sounds like they're cranking up for the formation lap...

Then I remember that photographer Martyn was getting up early to do some close-ups; the mighty rip of racing engine was him moving our four-door Maserati across the driveway.

No wonder we've turned every head we passed since setting out from Martyn's place in London – and at five o'clock in the bloody ay-em, to boot; his neighbours must have been delighted. From inside the car, the noise is stirring but unobtrusive; outside it will stand your hair on end. It isn't the volume that grabs you, for the Quattroporte isn't terribly loud: it's the tone

'Running at 100mph, the SM's ride quality is better than a limo trip through the park; comfort and control from the hydropneumatic suspension are phenomenal'

and intensity. Somehow, the Ferrari engineers responsible for the latest rebirth of the famous *Four Doors* have managed to build a traditional Maser V8 with an added dose of full-race V10. Imagine shoving a microphone up the tailpipe of Michael Schumacher's F1 car, adding a little bass, and playing it back at 'two' instead of 'eleven'.

Of course, this car would be a traffic-stopper on its Pininfarina looks alone: it's aggressive, elegant and simple, and there's just enough nostalgia to tell the world I Have History. In black-on-black with tinted windows, the effect is deliciously ominous, too, and even down here on the Cote d'Azur, where the latest Merc draws about the same notice as a white van in an industrial park, passers-by will wait in turns just to run their fingers over the Quattroporte's sexy, sculpted door handles.

Add some reflected glory from the original Quattroporte of the '60s and the ailing Fiat Empire's entry into the prestige super-saloon category would seem to have an early leg-up; nothing from Audi, BMW, Jaguar or anybody else can drop an envious jaw quite like the Trident. But to see how it rates as a working automobile, we've brought it to the south of France for a comparison with its long-lost cousin, the Citroën SM.

Which isn't as far-fetched as you're thinking. You see, among the many owners of the Maserati name since the Brothers went belly-up in the 1930s was none other than Citroën, 1968 to 1975. Like Ferrari when Fiat handed them the Maserati reins, Citroën decided this was the perfect opportunity to explore new market segments, to tap into a lucrative customer base outside their normal product range. What could be better than their own avant-garde chassis combined with the magic of a thoroughbred Italian engine?

That's where the Citroën *Série Maserati* comes in, along with our travelling companion and Maserati and Citroën expert, Andrew

Brodie. Andrew specialises in these V6, quad-cam French techno-GTs, particularly in making them quicker, and one of his very best belongs to Michael Quinlan. Michael is an expatriate Brit who lives in Monte Carlo, loves interesting and unusual cars, and keeps an outstanding cellar. Hence the wine-dulled brain, hence the Cote d'Azur. Yes, it's a tough old life, isn't it?

Anyway, Michael bought this 1972 model in 1990 and drove it happily until about three years ago, when he finally decided it needed a touch more oomph and rang Andrew. It isn't an uncommon complaint; thumping great French taxes on engines over 2.7 litres held the Maserati engineers down to only 2670cc and 170bhp, not a lot for a ton-and-a-half of Citroën that uses an engine-driven hydraulic pump to run the power steering, brakes and self-levelling suspension. Andrew's answer was the hot-rodder's time-honoured universal fix – drop in a bigger motor. In this case it's the 3-litre edition of the same V6, the big-valve version exclusive to the Maserati Merak SS. That gives this SM a boost of 50 extra horsepower, and Andrew built it using all the lessons he's learned about keeping these once-finicky engines together under pressure.

But first, a few words about driving the beautiful, exciting new Quattroporte south along the wide, sweeping motorways of France. Frankly, it was kind of a mixed lot. First of all, this was Bastille Day weekend, the busiest of the year for French traffic and French traffic cops, and there was absolutely no way we could give the car its head. (Besides, the first rule of automotive journalism is: 'Don't crash the car until the photographs are done.')

Furthermore, for a vehicle that aspires toward state-of-the-art, some things are rather behind the competition. The nav' system/multi-function display, for example, is ponderously awkward (I never did figure out how to turn off the radio) and

SPECIFICATION
1972 CITROËN SM
Engine
2965cc V6, four chain-driven overhead cams, two valves per cylinder, three 44mm Weber DCNF carburettors
Power
220bhp @ 6500rpm
Torque
199lb ft @ 4400rpm
Transmission
Five-speed synchromesh manual gearbox, front-wheel-drive
Suspension
Independent, via self-levelling hydropneumatic spring and damper units, pressurised by engine-driven pump
Brakes
Discs all round
Performance
0-60mph 7sec (est)
Top speed 146mph

Above
Citroën SM is much better on tight, twisty roads than it has a right to be, but Quattroporte proves a real sports car.

Facing page
Quattroporte looks great, sounds great, and goes very, very fast; interior is well appointed but refreshingly simple.

if the navigator is wearing polarised sunglasses, the screen disappears. There is no all-wheel-drive, no soft-close doors, the turning circle is a stately 40 feet, ride quality around town is choppy, and the brake pedal has that squishy ABS feel.

The biggest puzzlement, though, is the 'DuoSelect' gearbox. (They call the active suspension 'Skyhook'. Go figure.) It's the only box offered, and it's a six-speed sequential manual that can be shifted F1 fashion with steering column paddles, or left to its own devices via computer control. Upshifts are sluggish in manual mode; in automatic, they're glacial, and the system is easily confused in slow manoeuvering situations. To engage reverse, there's a tiny fiddly lever on the centre console to lift and pull, followed by an idiotic warning beeper that leaves you feeling like a lorry driver squaring up to the dock with a delivery of bananas.

On the other hand, when you get an opening the Quattroporte is awesome for carving up an Autoroute, and any shifting you do out there is strictly for your own amusement. With 400bhp on call, there isn't much you can't leave for dead merely by rolling on the throttle. The 'Skyhook' feels firmly planted and secure, and trundling along between the caravans through those interminable parts of French farmland that look like southern Indiana without the exotic charm, the front armrest refrigerator and the double-adjustable lumbar support are manna from Heaven. Still, for 80 thousand quid, you'd think

they could at least offer you the option of a nice five-speed...

So when the close-ups were finished, the coffee downed and we hit the road for the mountain sections, I made sure I got the first stint in the SM. This would start out with motorway before jumping off for the climb into the hills, and I was dying to see how the Citroën-Maserati's reputation as one of the great highway cars stood up against the far newer Ferrari-Maserati. The answer is: not bad at all, thank you, and with not many allowances for the age difference, either. In fact, three decades on, the SM still does some things better than almost anything else going.

The key to the Citroën-Maserati is that it is first of all a Citroën, with the funky, functional mannerisms that implies. Yes, the mushroom brake pedal will throw you against the windscreen. Yes, the arse end jumps in the air when the engine starts and the turn indicators don't self-cancel and the steering wheel always returns to centre position, even if you switch off the ignition. Running down the A8 from Nice at 100mph, though, the ride quality is better than a limo trip through the park, and a sudden lane change is, well, only another lane change. The combination of comfort and control from the legendary hydropneumatic suspension is phenomenal and the rear seat passengers have it just as easy as the front – as long as they're not too tall. That roofline does slope down a bit.

Past Cannes, off the Autoroute and swinging around toward

'Don't be fooled by that premium luxury crap, it's only clever window dressing. Underneath it the Quattroporte is monumentally, shockingly fast'

SPECIFICATION
2005 Maserati Quattroporte
Engine
4244cc V8, four chain-driven overhead cams, four valves per cylinder, dry sump, fuel injection
Power
394bhp @ 7000rpm
Torque
333lb ft @ 4500rpm
Transmission
Rear transaxle, six-speed sequential gearbox, limited-slip diff, rear-wheel-drive
Suspension
Independent, via coils and wishbones, active adaptive damping
Brakes
Discs with ABS
Performance
0-60mph 5.1sec
Top speed 171mph

'The Quattroporte and SM are cars made by and for people more concerned with their own opinions than those of customer focus groups'

Above
In the Southern French mountain passes, where the tourists fear to tread, there's still some room to run...

the village of Mons, the single-carriageway turns twisty and starts to rise. This is where a normal 2.7-litre would be getting breathless, and where Andrew's engine upgrade is worth its weight in gold. As I get more accustomed to two turns lock-to-lock and the surprisingly flat torque curve under that forest of Webers, it becomes increasingly obvious the long, wide Citroën can be hustled along the back roads far faster than you'd think. Plus, it has a wonderful, conventional five-speed with a fantastic gated shifter. Hallelujah.

More photographs on the road along the way, a few shots against the backdrop of scenic Mons, and lunch in the village: fortunately, far enough off the main tourist routes to be relatively quiet and unmolested. Perhaps not so quiet, though, with the four of us waving hands through the air like Spitfire pilots after a dog-fight, replaying the morning's drive and debating each car's place in the ultimate scheme of things. At the end, I'm still not sure I know exactly what Maserati intends for you to have in exchange for 80 large ones, whereas the SM's Grand Touring message seems straight and to the point.

Back into the Maser, then, for the afternoon session, the last of the photographs, and maybe a chance to stretch it out a tad on some open road. With that in mind, we jiggle up the goat-path D563 to the N85, a lovely smooth thoroughfare running along the ridges toward Grasse, which has today apparently attracted every estate car with an overloaded roof rack in the entire country. Might as well find a quiet track off to the side and finish the shoot with the car-to-car pictures. This involves Andrew leading in the SM, while Martyn snaps me driving down one of those bumpy Monte Carlo Rally roads about half-a-lane wider than the car, with a bottomless drop-off opposite a sheer

wall of rock. It's nerve-wracking stuff, and it's a relief when Martyn says 'That's all. See you back at the main road.'

Naturally, it's only after they disappear that I discover I've got about twice too much car for this turnaround, I have no idea where they're going, and my mobile is in their car. With the huge turning circle and the stupid joystick reverse, my three-point turn has eight points, and by the fifth, I am officially Fed Up. On the final ungainly, frustrating lurch that gets me pointed the right direction, I punch the button for manual shifting and stomp my right foot to the floor. The next several miles are what you might call a life-changing experience...

...And I think I know now what Maserati is offering for your 80 grand. Don't be fooled by that premium luxury crap, it's only clever window dressing. Underneath it the car is monumentally, shockingly fast, and an absolute 400-horsepower hooligan. On tight turns, you'd swear the car gets smaller, and no matter how narrow or rough the surface, you can place it like a kart. The harder you use the brakes, the firmer they feel; the shifting gets better the higher you wind, and, on full-bore downshifts, the computer even throws in a glorious, arrogant throttle blip. It is a car to be driven, as they say, like you stole it.

Screaming down a French mountainside at 7000rpm with the exhaust bouncing off the stone face, you realise that, in their own different ways, the Quattroporte and the SM are just as marvellous as each other: cars made by and for people more concerned with their own opinions than those of consumer focus groups. Stuff the on-board navigation system: I'll buy a map.

Thanks to Michael Quinlan and Andrew Brodie. You can contact Andrew Brodie on +44 (0)20 8349 2260 or visit website www.brodie.cc.

2007

MASERATI Quattroporte Sport GT

A wonderful matter of taste

BY DENNIS SIMANAITIS

WHEN IT APPEARED IN 2004, we liked this exoti-luxury sedan giving the well-heeled enthusiast a decidedly Italian alternative to top-line German sedans. Think *Filet all'Aceto Balsamico,* beef steak sauced with vinegar di Modena (get the Tradizionale!), in lieu of *Schweinhaxe,* that succulent rotisserized pork from Bavaria.

But (see our First Drive, May 2004) we also sensed some less-than-successful execution in this car's first iteration.

And so apparently did Maserati. The Quattroporte Sport GT I recently drove in and around Modena combined its inherent brio with significant improvements in several areas.

The fit and finish of the cars I drove and examined were first-rate. Panel gaps are now uniform. The paintwork is superb, profiting from major investment in the Ferrari paint facility where Maseratis are also invited. (True, the two marques went through a recent divorce, but it seems to have been a reasonably amicable one.)

A walk down the Maserati assembly line showed a real challenge in improving something like panel gaps: Maseratis continue to be built by artisans, with nary a robot in the place. Artisans have never been known for disci-

pline, but Maserati has achieved a neat blend of organizational structure and manufacturing technology that resolves this.

Mechanical changes are primarily embodied in the Quattroporte's DuoSelect sequential gearbox. Unlike its Germanic counterparts' hardware, DuoSelect has a 6-speed manual underlying its electro-hydraulic controller. The system offers modes that are purely automatic, purely paddle, or a blend of the two, with improvements in all three.

The original DuoSelect behaved perfectly well, whether paddled or left to its own choices—but only in aggressive driving. In light- or moderate-load conditions, its shifts could be drawn out or clunky or both.

Revisions to the software take care of light-load driving very well indeed, whether you've chosen Normal or Sport setting. (Damping as well as shift schedules are affected.)

By its very definition, though, moderate load is something of a catchall, and hence it's more challenging to optimize effectively. DuoSelect holds its lower gears longer than I'd like in automatic mode, even with a liftoff of its drive-by-wire accelerator pedal. I can take an active role by tapping the right-hand paddle

to force the upshift. However, at moderate load, there's a delayed reaction to the tap.

Some people, I suspect, would have a philosophical objection to this mixed-mode "automatic" operation. With this in mind, you can bet Maserati is looking hard at a planetary-based alternative for those set-and-forget types who aren't into paddling.

Of course, set-and-forget isn't brio. And the Quattroporte has the latter in gobs, with road behavior that sets the Maserati distinctly apart from German counterparts (even from the BMW we usually blather on about).

The GT comes with a 20-in. wheel/tire package, about which I have mixed feelings. Pimp though they are, the 20's sidewalls look a bit dwarfed in the Quattroporte wheel wells (though I confess "pimp" and "dwarf" hardly belong in the same sentence). More to the point, once or twice in cornering exuberance, I thought I sensed those fat rear tires at less than an optimally perpendicular orientation with the

road surface (reminding me that the lowest profile doesn't always offer the best handling).

Comfort issues, though, are nonexistent. Despite these ultra-low-profile tires (245/35ZR-20s front, 285/30ZR-20s rear), the GT's ride is well nigh ideal. It is superbly controlled, utterly without float yet never harsh or jiggly, even on indifferent surfaces of Italian snow-country roads.

The Quattroporte Sport GT's poise, style—and warmth of execution—make it a most desirable automobile, even at its $112,200 list price. In fact, it's this warmth that sets the Maserati quite apart from equally lofty Germans. In fact, these may not even *be* competitors: If you want a Maserati, you're likely to find these others a bit too cold, too analytical in their mechanical and stylistic solutions.

I'm quite happy (and lucky!) to celebrate both. Truth is, I like *Filet all'Aceto Balsamico* and *Schweinhaxe.* ◉

» **Black-mesh grille, 20-in. wheels/tires, carbon-fiber trim, special wheel and pedals set Sport apart from other Quattroportes. DuoSelect shifting is sharper; 4.2-liter 400-bhp V-8 is Ferrari-sourced.**

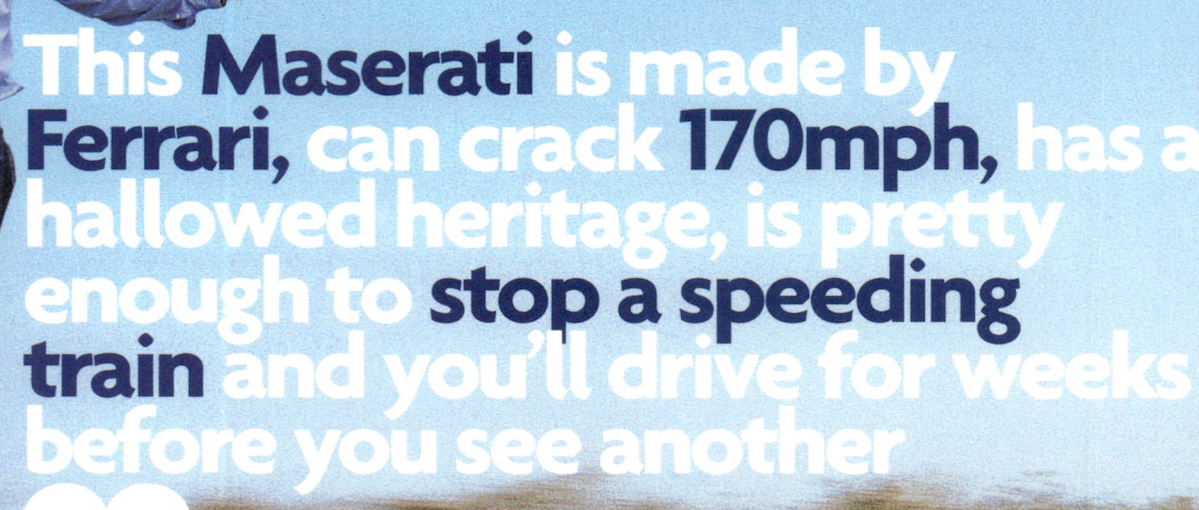

> **This Maserati is made by Ferrari, can crack 170mph, has a hallowed heritage, is pretty enough to stop a speeding train and you'll drive for weeks before you see another**

Quentin Willson

The most important Maserati for years can be a temptingly cheap and outrageously fast luxury GT. Just make sure you buy the right one

THE MASERATI 3200 GT has always bothered me. I've fancied one for years. I adore its upmarket elegance and understatement, the wholly wonderful pleasure of being able to say 'I drive a Maserati', and the fact that it really is frenziedly fast, has four decent seats and used ones are crazily cheap. And those gorgeously delicate boomerang rear lights are pure automotive art. But I do this all the time: carefully construct a cogently compelling argument for buying one, and then minutes later convince myself I shouldn't. Why? Because the first time I drove a 3200 I loathed the thing.

You see, the early UK cars were all manuals, had massive dynamic issues and drove like dogs. I remember a press car making me apoplectic with rage because of its driveline shunt, over-sharp brakes, stiff Getrag gearbox and hair-trigger throttle. One minute I was unleashing an uncontrollable blizzard of torque and the next madly dabbing the middle pedal and standing the whole car on its nose. What should have been a blissful day, testing Maserati's most important car for years, was literally spent kangarooing along like a green and callow learner. The PR suits from Modena insisted the appalling lack of harmony between the controls >>>

PHOTOGRAPHY LYNDON MCNEIL

So special: the Maserati 3200 GT provides power, luxury, and exclusivity for a quarter of the price of its equivalent Ferrari

You'll be pressed back into the seat as you hit 60mph in five seconds, but slowing down wears out the brakes. Don't slow down

was just a temporary quality glitch, but I came away hugely disappointed. Since then, most of the issues seem to have been sorted and the 2001 model year cars are leagues better. Drive a Y-plate auto and you'll wonder why the press was so lukewarm.

The 3200 GT appeared in 1998 and was the first Maserati to be made by Ferrari, new owner of the troubled trident. Originally destined to be called the Mistral, there were red faces all round when it was discovered that VW had trademarked Maserati's hallowed old model name. The rather less sexy numerical moniker was chosen to pay homage to the 3500 GT of the Fifties. Styled by Giugiaro, the 3200's sweeping silhouette was a refreshing change from the cubist edginess of the previous Gandini-designed cars, which had all the visual appeal of an Eighties Nissan Cedric. Most critics hailed the new GT's looks, but initial sales were slowed by criticisms of the clunky driving dynamics. In June 1999, a four-speed automatic gearbox became an option and UK deliveries hit record numbers. Progressive refinement followed (the factory warranty was extended from two to three years to bolster confidence) and in 2001 a new steering rack, different dampers, re-mapped engine management unit and changes to the ABS and traction control software made the 3200 much less psychopathic to drive.

Fire up the twin turbocharged, 370bhp V8 and there's a muted burble. Hit the throttle and the cultured rumble turns into a barking howl as you're snapped back into the seat. The acceleration is electrifying – 60 comes up in five seconds – and the quoted 174mph maximum becomes an urgent and very real possibility. And those three years of mechanical and electrical refinements have paid off, because the new steering rack feels alert, the massive vented Brembo brakes much more progressive and the power delivery from the twin turbochargers infinitely more controlled. The ride feels polished, there's little body roll and turn-in is

> **The acceleration is electrifying. 60 comes up in five seconds and 174mph is a very real possibility**

exemplary. Only the manual gearbox still feels stiff and baulky (a malady still present in the current 4200 coupé), so those without masochistic leanings should really opt for the slightly slower (168mph) but much smoother self-shifter. That said, this isn't a car for softly spoken boulevardiers and a well-driven 3200 GT can lap Ferrari's Fiorano test track quicker than a 550 Maranello. Not many people know that.

The 3200 may offer similar levels of heave to the Jaguar XKR and Porsche Carrera but it feels much, much more exclusive. Only nine cars left the Modena factory each day and yearly UK deliveries rarely exceeded 350 units, all of which makes every other coupé feel ordinary and mass-market. That's this Maser's most compelling virtue – it oozes charisma from every orifice. Every time you open the garage door and see that glinting trident badge or those sexy rear light clusters, you'll feel you own a machine that's genuinely rare and special. What's more, two adults can sit in the back comfortably and you can accommodate most of their baggage. For an Italian car, the driving position is surprisingly good and the opulent leather-clad cockpit is the best Maserati has ever stitched. In fact, as cabins go, the GT's is indulgently sybaritic, with soft hide gracing the seats, door cards, dashboard and centre console. Some of the minor switches and air vents are from the Fiat parts bin, but the quality of interior fittings and furniture is way above that of Maseratis of old.

But the GT is still a flawed gem. Major mechanicals may be robust, but clutches can last as little as 15,000 miles and you'll get through front brake discs and pads

The twin turbocharged 370bhp V8 powers a ride that's as polished as it is fast as you sit in a roomy and luxurious leather-stitched cockpit

Cool enough to give you shivers, courtesy of Giugiaro styling. Pick a pre-2002 car for those slick boomerang rear lights

Thanks to owner Robbie Webb

at the same rate. All cars seem to have an appetite for oil, electrics can be wayward, (especially the engine management light) and if its not wearing Pirelli, Michelin or Bridgestone tyres it'll handle like a wayward supermarket trolley. Service intervals are once a year or every 6000 miles, cambelts should be changed every 18,000 and the tappets need regular adjustment too. The 1999 models had a couple of recalls – brake reservoir hoses and the ABS unit – so make sure these have been sorted before you do the deal. And only buy one that's had unstinting Maserati dealer servicing with a reassuring parade of rubber stamps to prove it. If you're prepared to spend around £2000 a year and be fussy about hitting the maintenance intervals, a 3200 should be reasonably reliable.

The best news of all is that a used GT is a quarter of the price of the equivalent Ferrari. £25,000 buys a mint 02-plate with tiny miles, and a Y-plate auto with 30,000 miles could be sitting in your garage for £19,000. That's silly money for something that radiates so much class. Find a cherished post-2000 auto, make sure it's stacked up with options like sports suspension, electric heated seats, sat-nav and air-con and you'll own one of the coolest coupés on the block. The 3200 GT may be frustratingly compromised, but in many ways it's also very nearly brilliant. Learn to understand its foibles, accommodate its appetites and treat it like the thoroughbred it is, and you won't rue the day you chose a Maserati. In fact, as car brands go, I'd say that the three-pronged trident has more kudos, charisma and desirability than even Aston Martin. Look at this way: this is a car that's made by Ferrari, can crack 170mph, has a hallowed heritage, is pretty enough to stop a speeding train and you'll drive for weeks before you see another. And you can own a decent used one for just twenty-five grand. Now you know why the 3200 GT has always bothered me and why, one day, I'll probably end up owning one.

ESSENTIAL NUMBERS, SMART ALTERNATIVES

MASERATI 3200GT

Engine 3217cc, V8, dohc per bank, twin turbochargers **Power and torque** 370bhp @ 6250rpm; 362lb ft @ 4500rpm **Transmission** Six-speed manual or four-speed automatic, rear wheel drive **Steering** Rack-and-pinion, power-assisted **Suspension** Front and rear: independent, double wishbones, coil springs, telescopic dampers **Brakes** Vented discs front and rear, anti-lock **Weight** 1500kg (3300lb) **Performance** Top speed: 174mph; 0-60mph: 5.1sec **Cost new** £60,575 **Value now** £25,000

Pick of the range

Find a limited edition Assetto Corsa run-out model made from 2001 and you'll get a special handling package with lowered ride height, stiffer springs, bigger front anti-roll bar, uprated brakes, and softer compound Pirelli P Zero rubber. Well worth a premium of a couple of grand over the standard car.

Annual running costs

Reckon on around £2000 a year for a mix of servicing, tyres and brakes. Pads, by the way, won't leave much change from £300 a set.

RIVALS

JAGUAR XKR
The supercharged XK8 is a very fine motor indeed with proven quality, searing grunt and great dealers. Only trouble is you'll have to pay ten grand more and it'll look just like every other XK8, of which there are literally tens of thousands.

PORSCHE CARRERA 996
Another top-end charger with the same sort of stunning performance, but pricier, much more commonplace and doesn't feel anything like as special as the Maser. Likely to be as reliable as a Golf GTi though.

ASTON MARTIN DB7
Feels as exclusive as the 3200 GT, but will cost almost twice as much for the equivalent year and mileage. Running costs are in the same league and most Astons suffer the same sort of quality glitches too.

Spyder Fan

PHOTOGRAPHY MITCH PESHAVRIA

Despite some familiar failings, you could learn to love Maserati's Gransport

I knew I'd forgotten something and, worse, it was too late to do anything about it. Our Boeing 737 had left the Gatwick terminal building, and as it taxied towards the runway, I was patting pockets and rifling through bags, looking for that which I knew I didn't have. Passport, check; mobile phone, present (and switched off, captain); soporific tome with which to render myself unconscious during transit, got it.

However, the European road atlas I'd just bought from the newsagents wasn't to be found. It was, in fact, still in its plastic bag on a chair by the departure gate, and that meant we were about to throw ourselves at the mercy of the satellite navigation system fitted to Maserati's new Gransport Spyder.

A minor hitch in an otherwise pretty straightforward plan. It was Sunday night, and we were on our way to Modena to collect Maserati GB's Gransport Spyder

press car. On the following Wednesday morning it had to be at Maserati's UK headquarters in Slough to be prepared for its first official duty: an appearance in the Supercar Run at the Goodwood Festival of Speed. For the next 48 hours we were delivery drivers doing it for the kicks – but when the car you're transporting is a brand new, hand-built Maserati, and your route to your destination includes some of the finest Alpine roads ever laid down, you don't mind being taken advantage of.

SHOWROOM GRANDEUR

Modena town centre is calming down after the morning rush hour when the taxi driver drops us outside the showroom of Maserati's glassy multi-storey factory. We're ushered into the clean, air-conditioned grandeur of the place, nosing around the collection of Quattroportes, Coupés and Spyders within. Then Maserati PR manager

Which way to the thrills: Saunders seeks his route to Maserati nirvana

'I'm not aesthetically pleasing enough to go anywhere near the car'

Spyder, says **Matt Saunders**. At least, you could if you live near the Alps

Clara Magnanini emerges and leads us to the car park. An ice blue Maserati Gransport Spyder waits for us there, right-hand drive, on British plates and ready for departure.

My initial impression is that neither myself nor snapper Mitch is aesthetically pleasing enough to be allowed anywhere near it. The Spyder's basic outline has remained largely unchanged since 2001, yet it's still got the power to bowl you over with its elegant good looks. The extra chrome added to the Gransport version looks like designer jewellery on a supermodel. To get in and motor the roof down is to agree to be gawked at from the kerbside; you feel obliged to suck in your paunch, stick out your chin, don your Gucci shades and pretend that you just don't care.

Alternatively, if you're more concerned about scaring the local schoolchildren with your unconventional features, you can leave the roof up and scarper pronto. And that, →

The hills are alive with the sound of the Maserati V8 at over 4000rpm

Open her up and let her go: Matt gets the full Gransport Spyder experience

Lines have change little since 2001 but Spyder is still breathtaking

Maserati caused a stir in company's Bologna birthplace

← after squeezing our bags into the Maser's modest boot, is what we did.

Our destination at the end of day one was over the border to Switzerland. Having bought a fold-out map of the Alps from a pavement cabin, we plot a route north-west from Modena, past Brescia and Milan, and up through the Simplon Pass – but first we detour 30 minutes south to Bologna.

In a quiet side street here, 82 years ago, brothers Carlo, Bindo, Alfieri, Mario, Ettore and Ernesto Maserati founded the family company, renting a garage on the Via del Pepoli. They spent 12 years making cars for Italian race team Diatto before creating their own grand prix machine in 1926 – the first car to carry the Maserati name.

Most of the brothers were engineers, but Mario was the arty one. It fell to him to design a company badge, and he took his inspiration from the statue of Neptune in Bologna's Piazza Maggiore. So this is where we head, past the buses, scooters and city cars that fill the town's picturesque streets.

We arrive to find the piazza teeming with shoppers, and pause for just long enough to grab a few photos of the car before being moved on by the city police, with whom the Maserati curries surprisingly little favour. It's certainly a hit with the locals, though; for 10 minutes on a Monday lunchtime near Maserati's birthplace, its latest creation receives dignified approval. That's one box ticked; it's time to move on.

TOUGH TEST

Autostrada A1 is humming with traffic as we aim the Spyder north-west. This must be one of Italy's hardest-working stretches of road; its surface is rutted and scarred by a multitude of repairs, and you fight for lane space with a mixture of articulated lorries and little white vans driven without regard for the consequences. It's a tough test for the Maser's mile-munching credentials.

It isn't easy to get comfortable in this car if you're tall. There's just not enough room for a six-foot-something driver to get his legs onto the pedals easily. The driver's seat and the steering wheel have enough adjustment to allow you to find a tolerable compromise, but you have to choose between being too close to the pedals or too far from the controls. That apart, the Spyder's cabin is great for continent-crossing, covered as it is in Frua leather and carbonfibre.

As we head towards Milan, the Spyder rides with a heavy lope that betrays a car loaded up to its gills. In the softer of its two Skyhook damping modes, it makes less of a fuss over sharp bumps and ridges, but tends to amplify the larger peaks and troughs. In sport mode, body control is much better but you feel every rut and pockmark jolt through the seat and scuttle. Between these two chassis presets is the perfect long-distance set-up for this car, but Maserati is evidently still searching for it.

After a couple of hours we've passed Milan, the traffic's thinning out and the hills of Lombardy are beginning to look like mountains. We stop to refill the car's generous 88-litre tank just as the tripmeter ticks past 300 miles, then follow the signs for Sempione. The road steepens, narrows and begins to snake. An unmanned border station appears, which we roar through without pause, before finding a manned one another quarter of a mile further on.

The Swiss guard glances at our passports.

With just over two turns from lock to lock, correcting a slide is effortless

"British?" he asks from behind a pair of gold-rimmed aviators. "Yes," I reply.

He simply nods, smiles and waves us onward. It's all going according to plan. Next comes the fun part; only hope the Maserati will be up to it.

DON'T BE SCARED OF THE SPYDERS

THE MASERATI Spyder looks a little long in the tooth in comparison with the latest convertibles, but that means you can pick up a secondhand one reasonably. We have four used models here, all of which are about half the price of a new Gransport Spyder. So if you thought this car was great value at Porsche 911 prices, how does paying less than for a new BMW 330Ci sound?

Maserati Spyder
Cambiocorsa, 02/51, 25,000 miles, £32,999
Metallic silver model complete with satellite navigation and a full service history. They don't come much cheaper. Call Alfanet Cars, Bristol (0117 9520444).

Maserati Spyder
Cambiocorsa, 02/02, 23,000 miles, £33,994
A rare mix of metallic blue with beige leather and Skyhook suspension. Also comes with an anti-theft tracker. Call Imperials of Redbridge (08700 928320).

Maserati Spyder
Cambiocorsa, 03/03, 25,000 miles, £34,990
Whoever ordered this had reserved tastes; it's very smart in Grigio Alfieri metallic, and is warranted until June '07. Call Nuvola London (020 7603 3900).

Maserati Spyder GT
02/02, 4000 miles, £37,995
If the ad for this metallic blue Spyder is correct, it's a manual, and they're very rare. It also has very few miles. Call the Classic Horsepower Company, St Albans(01727 817100).

'Turn off the electronics and you can coax this rear-drive into a gentle powerslide'

ROOFLESSLY QUICK CABRIOS

We must be climbing at a rate more readily associated with a cable car than an open-top, but thanks to the amazing V8 engine we can call upon, it's incredibly easy going. You have to keep this flat-crank 4.2-litre V8 spinning above 4000rpm to get the best from it, but that's now easier to do using the Gransport's faster-acting paddle-shift gearbox, and your reward for doing so is remarkable progress, even up steep inclines, accompanied by a stirring soundtrack.

We tackle chicane after chicane and tunnel after tunnel, all the time with that luscious Maranello thrum reverberating into the cabin off concrete and rockface, and for mile after mile we see only a handful of other cars. The Swiss have obviously recently resurfaced most of this famous route, and the Maser is in its element. Its steering rack is very fast paced. There are only 2.1 turns between maximum right and left-hand lock, so you barely need a half a turn to angle around the tightest kink. If you turn off the electronics and coax this rear-driver into a gentle powerslide, you can collect it with minimal steering effort, too.

Then, without warning, we blast over a crest and past the lodge that marks the top of the pass. We stop to take in the view and a few snaps. On one side of us is the snow-capped tip of Mount Rosa and, beyond it, the Matterhorn. Scenery doesn't get much more spectacular; neither do journeys. While other convertibles could have conveyed us here just as effectively, none could have done so with the same blend of style, sound and potency. Every new Gransport Spyder owner should be made to drive their car home through the Simplon Pass; that way they'd gain the knowledge they'd bought a car to really stir the soul.

As we stood admiring the tinkling Maserati, the remaining 800 miles between us and our ferry back to Dover didn't seem to matter; our epic drive had already been delivered, and flawed as it is, the Gransport Spyder had hit its high point. From here on, it may be all downhill. ◢

VITALS		MASERATI GS SPYDER	JAGUAR XKR CONV
	Price	£69,040	£73,495
	On sale in UK	Now	Now
	0-62mph	4.95sec	5.0sec
	Top speed	177mph	155mph (limited)
	Engine	V8, 4244cc	V8, 4196cc, s'charged
	Layout	Front, longitudinal, rwd	Front, longitudinal, rwd
	Power	396bhp at 7000rpm	420bhp at 6250rpm
	Torque	333lb ft at 4500rpm	413lb ft at 4000rpm
	Power to weight	229bhp per tonne	245bhp per tonne
	Transmission	Six-speed paddle shift	Six-speed auto
	Brakes front	330mm vented discs	355mm vented discs
	Brakes rear	310mm vented discs	330mm vented discs
	Weight	1730kg	1715kg
	Suspension	Double wishbones, coil springs, electronically adjustable dampers, anti-roll bar	Double wishbones, coil springs, adaptive dampers, anti-roll bar

MASERATI **GRANSPORT SPYDER**

More is definitely not better when it comes to the new Maserati convertible

STORY **JESSE TAYLOR**

Come the Geneva motor show in March next year there'll be an all-new Coupe and Spyder from Maserati, but as a last hurrah they've released a hardcore GranSport version of the Spyder.

Like the tin-lid version (which we drove in the May 2006 issue), the GranSport Spyder gets a 295kW, 452Nm variant of the 4.2-litre Ferrari-built V8 engine. According to Maserati, the charming and glorious-sounding motor will push the Spyder all the way to 285km/h assuming you keep the lid up. We didn't quite see those speeds but the Maser is certainly not short of straight line urge – and they claim a sub-five second 0-100km/h.

Although there's been on-going improvements to the shift of the six-speed sequential manual CambioCorsa 'box, it's hardly a paragon of refinement. Full throttle shifts thump through to the rear-mounted transaxle with a disconcerting lack of mechanical sympathy. Worse still it's slow and slurry in auto mode and three-point turns are a nightmare of clutch slip and fried friction plate. Maserati knows that this system is the worst of its kind and are working on a long term improvement. And the fix can't come soon enough, especially as Head of Vehicle Development Paul Fickers, said "90 percent of Maseratis are CambioCorsa."

When the road gets twisty – especially if you add bumps to the mix – the Spyder becomes less convincing. The adaptive Skyhook suspension is a horror movie right there on your TV failing to cope with either sharp-edged, high-frequency hits or low-frequency, high-amplitude yumps. The former crash through the superstructure of the convertible and the latter cause an oscillation that takes a long time to settle. Add the flimsy torsional rigidity of the open top GranSport and you've got a recipe for an ill-handling fast car.

On bumpy broken tarmac – the kind you'd typically find in Australia – the Maser works against you, forcing you to knock the pace back a notch. The alternative is to keep fighting the car at every corner and risk it spitting you into the scrub should it strike the wrong type of bump.

The challenging chassis set-up is not a huge drama on smooth roads where the GranSport possesses limpet-like levels of grip from its 19-inch Pirelli P Zero rubber. There's plenty of turn-in grip (though the steering is dead and there's a bit of kickback) and powerdown through the 265/30 ZR19 rear rubber is scarcely believable for a 295kW car. On bumpy roads though, both the front and rear ends are hopping all over the place and an FPV Typhoon would cover ground more quickly. And given how stiff and crashy the ride is, there's also a surprising amount of bodyroll.

Thankfully the brakes are positive with the four-piston Brembo calipers clamping down on cross-drilled rotors (330mm front, 310mm rear).

But for all of its considerable faults, the Maserati has plenty of

The open top GranSport is a recipe for an ill-handling fast car

On smooth tarmac the GranSport is a god, on rough stuff it's rubbish

Ergonomics are typically Italian – long arm, short leg. JT's funereal air is an option

charms. The engine is powerful, smooth and produces one of the best notes anywhere in the automotive world. The interior, though a bit of an ergonomic lottery, is a pretty special place to be and the whole car exudes a sense of occasion that cannot be matched by the more capable Porsche 911 cabriolet.

The first cars have just arrived in Australia wearing a $260,000 price tag – that's $12k more than the GranSport coupe and about $35k more than the regular Spyder, which it replaces. Whether you can see the value depends on what price you put on exclusivity. ⚙

FAST FACTS

ENGINE 4.2-litre, DOHC 32-valve V8
POWER/WEIGHT 295kW/1750kg
DRIVE rear-wheel
ON SALE now
PRICE $260,000

Looks like a loaf of bread, sounds amazing and belts out 295kW

passing glances

Maserati Quattroporte Sport GT

When the Quattroporte debuted in 2004, it proved to be one of the sportiest large sedans available. The new Sport GT version gives it even more of an edge.

"PLEASE, WE DO NOT RECOMMEND left-foot braking. Some driving techniques are better left for the track." So went the plea from Maserati's chief test driver at the launch of the new Quattroporte Sport GT model. It was a polite way of telling the assembled gathering of international motoring scribes that this is indeed a serious car, while trying to contain the hooligan element present. Yet the word Sport to an existing model, and just watch a journalist's veil of restraint slip away.

The performance-oriented Sport GT ($112,200) now lines up alongside the standard Quattroporte ($103,700) and more luxurious Executive GT ($115,900) version. While the new package does not bring more power, it makes up for that with significant upgrades in the transmission and handling departments, giving a new twist to the Quattroporte's already sporty nature.

In terms of visual messages, the Sport GT gives little away, in keeping with its missive as a classy, seductive beauty. The traditional trident badge now pouts from a black mesh grille rather than the chromed strakes, and there are new 20-inch alloys (up from the standard 18-inchers) that fill out the shapely wheel arches in a pleasingly menacing way. The only other obviuos distinguishing feature is the subtle Sport GT lettering on the front door window frames, though if you peer closely enough, you can also spot the new cross-drilled front brakes (with braided steel lines) that address an issue few owners ever raised.

Inside, the sports theme is represented by cool carbon-fiber trim in place of the warm touchy-feely wood. The steering wheel incorporates perforated leather trim and a more chunky grip, and the accelerator and brake pedals are now drilled aluminum, with an aluminum kick panel up against the transmission tunnel. The rest of the interior remains unchanged from the sumptuous, yet understated, original.

The other modifications concocted by the Viale Ciro Menotti engineers are even less obvious. First and foremost is the adoption of faster-shifting, Sport GT-specific gear-change software for the DuoSelect paddle shifter. Already upgraded since the car's launch in 2003, the fully automatic mode on the latest QPs has seen the slightly hesitant lift-off effect on up-shifts all but banished; it's now unlikely to upset your cornering attitude by shifting up mid-bend.

Powering away from a standstill, it's still a bit jerky slicing into second gear, but you learn to drive around that little foible by feathering the accelerator gently before getting back on the power. That perhaps continues to represent the appeal or, depending on your perspective, the drawback of the electro-hydraulic manual transmission: It remains a driver's gearbox, with cog-swaps responding best to the flex of your right foot, rather than emulating a torque-converter automatic's utter indifference to a pedal pinned to the firewall. (Maserati will be offering such an automatic in 2007.)

The truth of the matter is that changing gears manually with the paddles becomes so instinctive and is so effortless, you rarely think to use the auto mode beyond the urban crawl. On the open road, this latest incarnation of the QP begs to be driven spiritedly while using the paddles, and that's where the Sport GT upgrade comes into its own. A mere stretch of your right index finger away on the fascia is the Sport button; pushing it has a much more noticeable effect on gear changes than before, with 7,000-rpm shifts occurring 33 percent faster than the previous Sport mode.

Can you feel the difference? Well, we're talking about eye-blink fractions of a second here, but the Sport button plays other tricks, too. Like other QP models, pushing the Sport button on the Sport GT also switches the Skyhook electronic damping control system into a stiffer setting; it's just that the Sport GT's setting is that bit more, well, sporty.

In terms of ride, the Sport setting does firm things up, aided and abetted by the ultra-low profile 20-inch Pirelli P Zeros. The rims are no wider, so the rubber is the same width (245/285 front/rear), but the aspect ratios drop considerably from 45 and 40 to 35 and 30, respectively. Any role the tires might play in suspension compliance on other QP models has all but vanished with the Sport GT.

The combined effect of the stiffer sidewalls and more aggressive shock valving is better body control, allowing you to carry more speed through corners in the Sport GT than in the other QPs. The lack of brake dive also allows you to carry more speed into tight corners, which we found plenty of on our test loop in the hills south of Modena. It's all the encouragement you need to stand on the stoppers just that little bit later going into a bend.

However, the real moment to savor comes once you're back on the accelerator, for the creamy snarl emitted by the dry-sumped V8—now even more soulful at high revs thanks to a new exhaust system—is one of the Sport GT's biggest feel-good factors. This two-ton four-door feels surprisingly alive; its level of driver involvement puts the majority of full-sized sport sedans to utter shame.—*Johann Lemercier*

20-inch wheels and ultra-low profile tires don't leave a lot of rubber between the rims and the road.

Specifications

ENGINE	4.2-liter DOHC V8
POWER (hp)	400 @ 7000 rpm
TORQUE (lb/ft)	326 @ 4500 rpm
TRANSMISSION	6-speed manual
Weight (pounds)	4375
0-60 MPH (sec.)	5.2
BASE PRICE	$112,200

MC HAMMER

Too extreme for racing or road use, the 755bhp Maser MC12 Corsa is the ultimate rich man's plaything ➔

Words: Harry Metcalfe | **Pictures:** Antony Fraser

Quiz Maserati Corsa's technical director, Giorgio Ascanelli, on what exactly is the point of building the MC12 Corsa – a car that can only be driven on a track, yet which can't be raced as it doesn't meet any current race regulations – and his response is refreshingly honest: 'Izza toy.'

Well that's that sorted then.

It's a very expensive toy, though, with each of the planned 12 cars costing a cool one million euros a pop. Plus local taxes, of course (which, for UK-based buyers, equates to a list price of around £800,000 at current exchange rates).

Oh, and should you wish to participate in next year's factory-organised MC12 Corsa

events as well, then you'll have to stump up a further £206,000 (give or take) for the privilege. That's an awful lot of money – especially when you realise that there will be just six events in total, and that at each one owners will get just three 30-minute sessions behind the wheel. To save you doing the maths, that works out at just shy of £23,000 an hour – or £381 *per minute* – for the privilege of driving your own car on track.

It may sound crazy, but there's clearly a demand for such an exclusive, expensive trackday car – Maserati has already taken five deposits.

The official explanation for the MC12 Corsa's existence is that it has been created to celebrate Maserati winning both the FIA GT

Manufacturers' Cup and the Spa 24-hours in 2005 with its MC12 GT1 race car. The Corsa is not just a cunningly marketed excuse to shift a few more MC12s, though. In fact, the Corsa owes little to the road car. Instead it has been based on the much more extreme GT1 race car, with only minimal changes to make it a little more civilised for its wealthy owners.

From the outside, the most obvious difference between the Corsa and the road car is the more aggressive aero package. The front air dam is considerably deeper for a start, and is finished off with a protruding splitter set at a height that'll make getting too close to a kerb a very expensive business. The new nose also houses the larger grille of the race car, lending the Corsa an even more menacing look than the

'The aero changes give the Corsa 1400kg of downforce at 155mph'

MC12 *ordinaire* when viewed head-on.

Move around to the rear, and the road car's delicate, full-width boomerang spoiler has disappeared, to be replaced by an enormous, two-metre-wide aero wing that was originally conceived for the racer before being outlawed by the regulators for being simply too big.

The original road car ran a bigger rear diffuser than was allowed for racing, too. In reality, though, due to the six-speed gearbox sitting right where the airflow was meant to go, it never produced the downforce you might have expected, so the GT1 – and now the Corsa

– happily run a smaller diffuser.

According to Ascanelli, all the aero changes borrowed from the race car really do work, together giving the Corsa a massive 1400kg of downforce at 155mph – more even than the Corsa's official kerbweight of 1150kg, and comparable with a mid-'90s F1 car.

An extra seat has been squeezed inside the Corsa's spartan, race-style cabin to enable you to treat a passenger to a few hot laps, but even the seemingly simple task of adding a second chair turned out to be more involved than you'd imagine because nearly all the electronics for

the racer's engine were originally located in the space vacated by the removal of the road-going MC12's passenger seat.

Some of those components have now been moved into the passenger footwell, so if you're considering taking passengers for a ride in your new toy, it's best if they're slightly challenged in the leg department. They will at least get the same beautifully trimmed race seat as the driver, along with a five-point race harness to clasp them in place.

Even though the fixed race seats have the usual deep side bolsters, Ascanelli was keen to

'Mechanically, the Corsa shares most of the race car's components'

Kenny P

THE INSIDE STORY ON THE MC12

SO WHY EXACTLY did Maserati think that building the flamboyant MC12 supercar would be a good idea?

Giorgio Ascanelli explains that it was Ferrari president Luca di Montezemolo's idea to build the ultimate Maserati supercar.

Despite having to share some components with the Enzo (which was under development at Ferrari at the same time), di Montezemolo wanted the Maserati to be noticeably different to the top Ferrari, so he tasked Giorgio with creating an open-topped supercar similar in style to the Ferrari F50.

The car would also form the basis of an Endurance GT1 race car, as di Montezemolo was keen to see Maserati return to long-distance racing – the last time the company had participated as an official factory team was way back in 1957.

With this brief in mind, a separate division called Maserati Corsa was formed in March 2002, headed by Giorgio Ascanelli, and exactly two years later the finished MC12 was revealed to the public at the 2004 Geneva motor show. Originally just 25 were to be built, but this was soon doubled to 50 after Maserati received 234 official expressions of interest in the car.

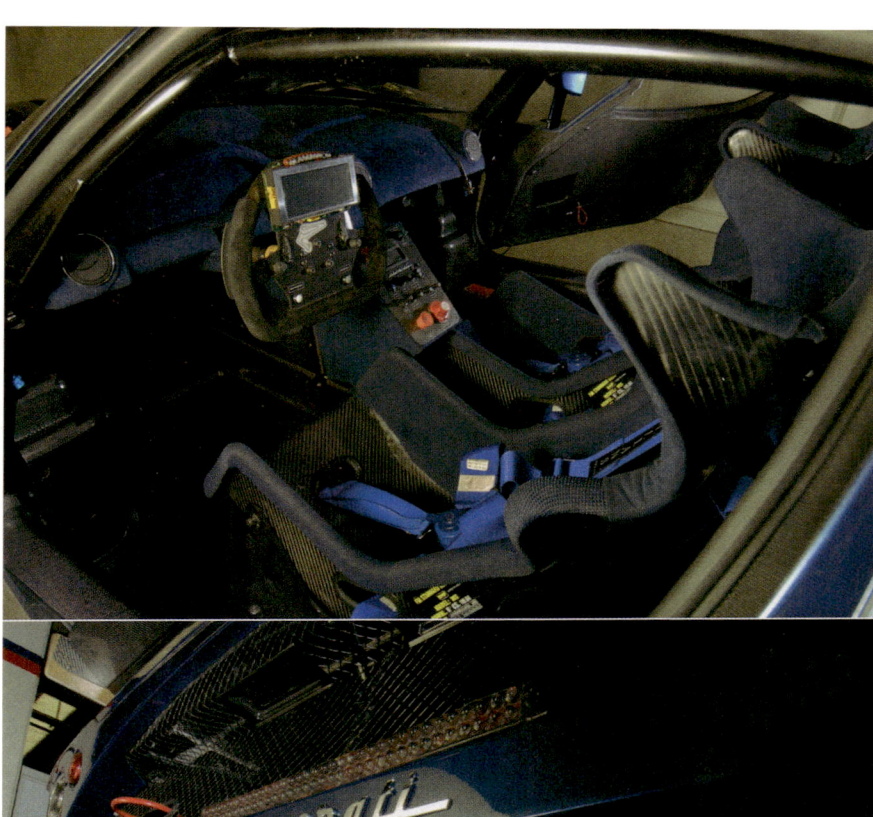

make ingress to the cabin as easy as possible. To achieve this he dispensed with the obstructive door bar of the race car's roll-cage, which was possible partly thanks to the enormously strong, deep carbonfibre sills, and partly by increasing the Kevlar re-enforcement engineered into the otherwise lightweight carbon doors.

The crosswork of tubes above the driver's head in the race car have been done away with too, so owners can place the driver's seat higher than in the racers without their crash helmet meeting with the cage. This also means that, once the still-removable roof panel is taken off, the view out to the skies is relatively unimpeded.

Mechanically, the MC12 Corsa shares most of the race car's components, although the sequential gearbox fitted to the racer has been swapped for the more user-friendly Cambiocorsa gearbox found in the road car. It was also necessary to uprate the clutch to enable it to handle the extra power produced by the engine in its enhanced

state of tune – peak power is now up from the road car's 621bhp to a more fulsome 755bhp, produced at a heady 8000rpm, making the MC12 Corsa even more powerful than the racer, which has restrictors in the intake system limiting it to 600bhp at just 5750rpm.

The exhaust system on the Corsa is different as well, with each manifold on either side of the big, midships V12 having the look of six serpents flowing from the cylinder heads down into a large drainpipe on each side of the gearbox, eventually exiting just above the rear diffuser. Disappointingly, they couldn't start the car during our visit, but I'm told that the screaming 6-litre engine possesses one of the finest exhaust notes this side of a Ferrari FXX. Strange that…

Talking with Giorgio Ascanelli later, it's clear that he has strong views on the current stance of the FIA and especially the Le Mans race regulations. He was particularly frustrated when the rules were changed to state that manufacturers ➔

GIORGIO ASCANELLI

GIORGIO ASCANELLI started his career on the machine-shop floor at an engineering firm in Bologna in 1985.

His lucky break came in 1987 when he landed a job at Ferrari as a design engineer for the F1 team.

During 1987 he was briefly involved as a test engineer with the Abarth rally team (who won the World Rally Championship that year), before returning to Ferrari at the end of the season.

In 1988 he became Head of Race Operations at Ferrari, but in '89 he was tempted away by the offer of the same post at Benetton.

In 1991 he moved again, to McLaren, where he played a part in Ayrton Senna's championship win of that year.

1995 saw Ascanelli back at Ferrari, first as Head of Operations, then as Head of R&D, during which time he was instrumental in getting the F1 team back to its winning ways.

In March 2002, di Montezemolo asked Ascanelli if he would set up a new company called Maserati Corsa, with the aim of returning Maserati to world-class endurance motor racing. Ascanelli still holds the post of Technical Director today.

Above left: MC12's version of the Enzo engine has gear-driven camshafts – the most reliable solution for endurance racing. Corsa has no fans for the radiators, so you need to keep a close eye on the temp gauge

'Producing a track-only car like this gives gifted engineers a chance to show off'

have to build 100 road-going versions of a GT car in order to take it racing – a change that came just as he had finished building (and selling) the 25 MC12s required under the old rules…

But it's clear that Ascanelli is still in love with the idea of endurance racing, despite his background being in F1 (see panel, left).

'My ideal form of racing would be where you take a fabulous road car to the racetrack, remove the number plates and go out and prove the durability of the car over four, six or 24 hours,' he says. 'That, to me, is the perfect form of endurance racing, and that was what the MC12 was meant to be. But then they outlawed it. It's a joke.'

He would have liked to have seen the MC12 competing with cars like the Porsche Carrera GT at Le Mans, rather than having diesel Audi prototype racers that bear no relation to any road car gliding to victory.

He views last year's beautiful Maserati Birdcage concept car as a wasted opportunity, too, saying that he would love to see creations such as this racing in their own separate class for concept cars. That's something which, you have to agree, would make a spectacular sight.

As things stand, though, the MC12 Corsa is as far as Giorgio's Le Mans-winning road/race car

dream will go. We'll never know how successful the MC12 would have been at la Sarthe, but at least this Corsa version has given Ascanelli the chance to let his race-engineered mind run free and Maserati the opportunity to demonstrate the MC12's full potential given freedom from some outside body's rulebook and the noise and pollution limits set by Brussels: no silly air restrictors strangling the mighty V12 engine, no need to omit the big rear wing that produced so much downforce in the wind tunnel, no requirements for the exhaust to meet any conditions other than having to sound absolutely fantastic. In other words, the MC12 as Ascanelli originally intended.

Producing a track-only car like the MC12 Corsa may initially seem like a completely pointless exercise, but actually we need to thank those enthusiasts wealthy enough to buy into such things, as they give gifted engineers like Giorgio a chance to show off. The MC12 may not have achieved its true potential on the racetrack, but 12 lucky owners are about to find just what it could really do.

Sounds like the perfect big boy's toy to me, and, as we all know, at the end of the day, the man with the most toys wins.

SPECIFICATION

MC12 CORSA

■ Engine	V12
■ Location	Mid, longitudinal
■ Displacement	5998cc
■ Cylinder block	Aluminium alloy
■ Cylinder head	Aluminium alloy, dohc per bank, four valves per cylinder
■ Fuel and ignition	Bosch ignition with sequential electronic fuel injection
■ Max power	755bhp @ 8000rpm
■ Max torque	n/a
■ Transmission	Six-speed 'Cambiocorsa' sequential manual gearbox, rear-wheel drive, limited-slip differential
■ Front suspension	Double wishbones, pushrod links, coil springs, dampers
■ Rear suspension	Double wishbones, pushrod links, coil springs, dampers
■ Brakes	Vented and cross-drilled discs, 380mm front, 335mm rear
■ Wheels	18in front and rear
■ Tyres	Pirelli P Zero slicks
■ Weight (kerb)	1150kg
■ Power-to-weight	667bhp/ton
■ 0-62mph	sub-3sec (est)
■ Top speed	215mph+ (est)
■ Basic price	c£800,000
■ On sale	Now

SEISMIC SHIFT

The Maserati Quattroporte was crying out for an auto 'box and thankfully you can now get one. But how much difference can a gearbox really make? **Chris Harris** sticks it in 'D' to find out

PHOTOGRAPHY STAN PAPIOR

7840VJ75

Seven thousand is the key number in the story of the Maserati Quattroporte Automatic's gestation. The Italian manufacturer with perhaps the finest sounding name of all was keen to point out why it had taken over three years to apply an automatic transmission to its most popular car. The answer was simple: until this latest version of ZF's now ubiquitous six-speed automatic gearbox appeared, there was no self-shifting transmission capable of revving beyond 7000rpm.

That sounded like a dubious excuse to me. So I thought hard for an example to disprove the theory. And you know what? Those Maser engineers appear to have a point. The Alpina B10 V8S I smoked in 2002 liked to work a bit, but never beyond 6750rpm. Mercedes owns the DNA blueprint to the two-pedal, superheated sedan, but its motors are no keener to spin above 6500rpm than the civil service is to buy John Reid a birthday pressie. DB9? All spent in the late sixes, I'm afraid. In fact, there appears to be only one high-revving automatic on the market: the Audi S6.

Well, now there are two. The Quattroporte needed a decent slushbox the way fresh strawberries need warm balsamic vinegar (trust me, it's amazing). But adapting the world's most elegant saloon to take this new transmission was not the matter of a moment. The Quattroporte Duo Select (as the paddle shifter will henceforth be known) couldn't have had a less helpful mechanical layout: it uses a dry-sump 4.2-litre V8, with a transaxle out at the back. Study the two versions' respective cutaways and but for the shared silhouette, they might as well be different models.

For starters, the gearbox is now nestled right behind the motor, leaving the limited slip differential at the rear axle. Naturally this required some major structural surgery, and for a company not blessed with much of a development pot, phrases like 'new transmission tunnel' are big game.

The motor has come in for many detail modifications. Some of them are designed to increase torque and reduce the crank speed at which it can be released (there's an extra 7lb ft and it arrives 250rpm lower). The biggest change is the move to wet-sump lubrication. This was taken to increase the mechanical refinement of a motor not best suited to a luxury saloon. Removing the separate oil tank released some engine-bay space, but also got rid of the external oil pumps that created much unwanted racket.

Even with these changes, the Quattroporte remains a completely different proposition to any other large saloon on sale. We collect ours from the foyer of some swanky Monaco hotel, and just seeing it stationary in pearlescent white is enough to confirm as much. A BMW M5 has more menace, a Mercedes S-class is undoubtedly more talented, but the Quattroporte has both glamour and interest on its side.

Cabin and boot space are not QP specialities. The fuel tank still robs so much boot space that you wonder if there isn't a smuggler's hold between the rear seats and the firewall for Russian clients. Equally, a six-footer can just about sit behind

'The Quattroporte is more vocal than any rival but that's in keeping with its character'

someone of similar size, but there isn't much lounging to be done. However, for the current Quattroporte owner, the new driving experience will be much more relaxing.

From a company renowned for extravagant flashes of interior design, the new selector lever is unremarkable. But so what: I've been waiting to select a computer-controlled gear setting in a QP for some time, and not have my neck slap the head rest for the next hour. Finally it has come.

There are smoother gearboxes than this one; it can be a touch harsh in terms of step-off response, and it holds on to gears longer than you'd expect when cold. But the car is now Monaco-friendly, and given that this hellish principality provides about the most unpleasant urban driving experience in Europe, we can safely say that it'll be good enough elsewhere.

This wouldn't be an Italian car if much of the praise heaped on it wasn't tempered by some objective negatives, so I'll drop the first one in now. Even though the ZF is hugely more capable of selecting gears than the Duo

Exquisitely stitched gear lever works like a proper sequential shift

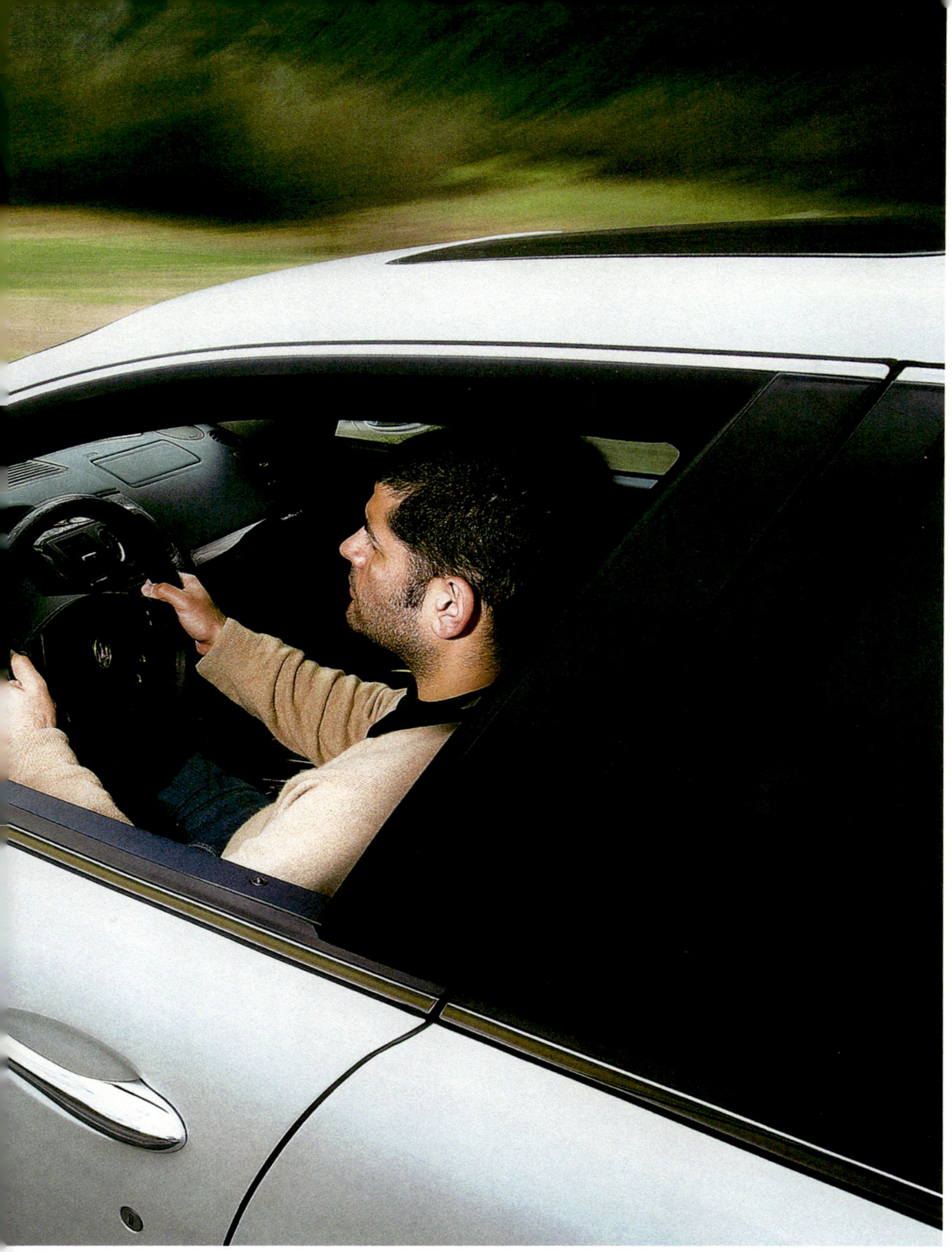

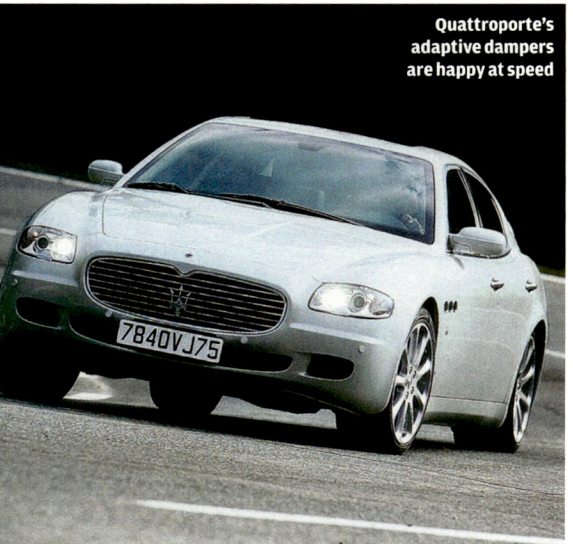

Quattroporte's adaptive dampers are happy at speed

Select in Auto mode, the QP still has a silly turning circle standing between it and town supremacy. The steering isn't what you'd call light either.

Neither of these points matters when the road clears, though, and despite its new-found low-speed decorum, the QP is happier at speed. Again, there are multiple quirks to the way it operates. The Skyhook adaptive dampers take longer to adjust than expected; accelerate hard from a toll booth and something in the electronic brain clearly sends the message that the dampers need to be stiff, despite a lack of lateral load. At this point ride comfort is borderline dreadful.

Then, about a minute later, the dampers relax and give the car a very pleasant lope indeed – easily a match for a 7-series, better than any A8 and not far short of an S-class. Wind noise is hushed, the suspension and tyres are barely heard and the engine is silent enough. By that I mean it is more vocal than any other supposedly rival car, but that is in keeping with the QP's character. Because, in reality, it doesn't have any rivals. →

IF I WERE IN CHARGE...
Other cars that could be improved

STEVE SUTCLIFFE
JAGUAR XKR MANUAL
"The autobox doesn't live up to the rest of the car; we've been missing a fast, manual Jag for years."

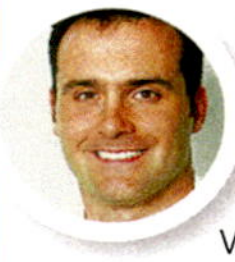

ADAM TOWLER
911 GT3-RIVALLING NISSAN 350Z
"It would be so easy: combine Infiniti's 4.5-litre V8 with a couple of turbos for 500bhp and 200mph performance. I've even got a name for it: 450Z-R."

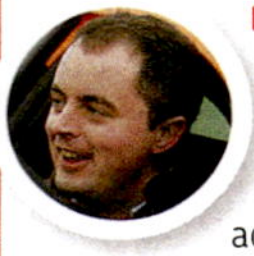

MIKE DUFF
REAR-WHEEL-DRIVE SUBARU IMPREZA
"Maybe more of a subtraction than an addition - but how sweet would a lightweight £17,000 Impreza with the centre diff removed and 250bhp channeled through the rear wheels be?"

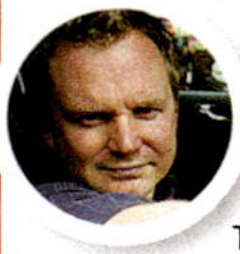

CHAS HALLETT
BMW M3 TOURING
"It's the car they should have made a long time ago, and now there's an M5 Touring on the way there just isn't an excuse not to..."

STEVE CROPLEY
LUXURY SUPERMINI
"I'd love to see someone spend proper money developing variable air suspension for a supermini; we've not had a small car with truly luxurious ride since the Citroen GSA. Toyota could do it with the Yaris, maybe even give it a Lexus badge."

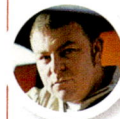

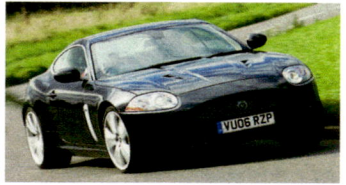

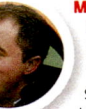

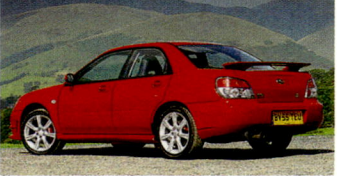

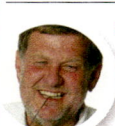

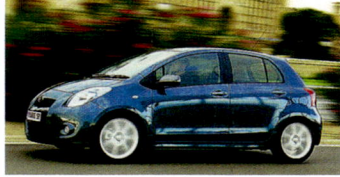

'Individuality is the hardest commodity to find in the market and the QP is rarer than Atlantic cod'

← This is the car that bridges the gap between the German muscle saloons and the accepted prestige whales. Both classes are bursting with talent, but what amazes me is that many customers still can't find the car they want. They love the M5's pace, but can't abide the transmission or the inadequate range. They find the AMG Mercedes too anodyne and don't want an S8 because it just isn't much fun to drive.

For these people, the QP automatic might be the perfect car. Individuality is the hardest commodity to find in the marketplace, and the QP is rarer than Atlantic cod.

And sometimes those qualities add to a driving experience immeasurably. I don't really care if the Skyhook dampers like to have a prolonged think now and again, or that a Mercedes E63 would ingest, digest and defecate the remains of a QP in one autobahn sitting.

But the QP is a wonderful thing to behold – all those weird angles and challenging details. I intend to reach a ripe old age, if only so I can sup whiskey and ruminate on the front headlights, and whether they are too small or perfectly sized. I doubt I will ever reach a satisfactory conclusion. With these treats available to the owner, the level of competence doesn't need to be as high as it would in a German thunder-box. Luckily it is more than good enough.

Torque, or the lack thereof, is a slight problem. You have to punch the QP hard in first to make sharp getaways, and it doesn't surge past traffic the way you might expect. Still, the power delivery is completely in line with the chassis; this is a sharp handling car. One whose heavy mechanicals are contained within the wheelbase and yet retains a 49/51 per cent weight distribution. The steering is as well weighted and accurate as could be expected in a 1990kg saloon car; it changes direction and resists understeer better than most. But the most telling aspect to the way the QP drives is that it is a car to enjoy, not a blunt instrument whose thuggish pace feels naughty. You can carve through bends, lean on it the way you would a much smaller car. It's a different take on the super-saloon, and

THINKING OUTSIDE THE 'BOX

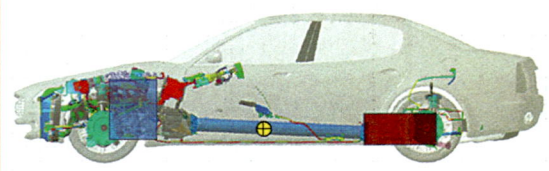

Maserati had to change the QP's layout for the Automatic because ZF doesn't make an auto for a transaxle layout (as used in the DuoSelect, top). The smaller auto 'box (above) is moved to the front and the engine is nudged back by 9mm. As a result, front/rear weight distribution moves from 47/53 to 49/51.

QP changes direction pretty well for a saloon car weighing two tonnes

Auto helps Maserati in town; poor turning circle doesn't, though

4.2-litre V8 makes a glorious noise but lacks low-down torque for 'auto cruising

as the rest of the world aims to make four-seaters that will out-thrust a Boeing 777, I think it's a clever move.

The QP is moving into junior Bentley Arnage territory. It has the same slightly bespoke feel. There are elements to its chrome and rubber-ware that are less than perfect, but show clear evidence of having been finished by hand. I like that. The paintwork on the test car was stunning too – so voluminous it looked like liquid metal.

But back to that gearbox briefly. Maserati tried to explain how many different shift programmes were available, but I couldn't understand a word they said. This is both helpful and unhelpful. On the one hand, I feel the whole point of a decent automatic is the facility to simply leave it in drive and not think about different modes and such nonsense. On the other, I can't talk you through the various shift maps.

But there are times when it's good to hold onto a gear, and here the QP has one special trick: its lever works like a proper sequential's should. Push forward to go

down, pull back to shift up. Steering wheel paddles are standard on the Sport, but optional on the standard car and the GT. The version we drove (the basic car) wouldn't blip the throttle on downshifts, though.

As if to confirm the obvious, Maserati is expecting 80 per cent of QP sales to be automatics this year, and the car is available almost immediately with no premium over the Duo Select model, which continues unchanged.

The company is understandably proud of the car the Quattroporte has become with this new transmission: something to savour when the time is right, but now entirely amenable to the everyday grind. But for those still worried about having money in a Maserati, try these numbers for size. A 53-plate QP which cost £69k new is still worth £44,500. A BMW 745Li that left the showroom for £63k the same week would only fetch £25k. Maserati has the whole class licked for residual strength. I think it's the most desirable saloon car on sale; clearly the marketplace agrees. **A**

HOW THEY COMPARE

		MASERATI QUATTROPORTE	AUDI S8
VITALS	Price	£77,000	£70,000
	On sale in the UK	Now	Now
	0-62mph	5.6sec	5.1sec
	Top speed	167mph	155mph (limited)
	Power	396bhp at 7000rpm	444bhp at 7000rpm
	Torque	339lb ft at 4250rpm	398lb ft at 3500rpm
	Power to weight	199bhp per tonne	228bhp per tonne
	Torque to weight	170lb ft per tonne	205lb ft per tonne
	Emissions (CO2)	345g/km	322g/km
THIRST	Urban	12.9mpg	14.3mpg
	Extra urban	26.9mpg	29.1mpg
	Combined	19.2mpg	21.1mpg
	Real world range	380 miles	418 miles
DIMENSIONS	Length	5052mm	5062mm
	Width	1895mm	1897mm
	Height	1438mm	1424mm
	Wheelbase	3064mm	2944mm
	Track (front/rear)	1582/1595mm	1620/1607mm
	Weight	1990kg	1940kg
	Fuel tank	90 litres	90 litres
	Boot	450 litres	500 litres
ENGINE	Engine layout	V8, 4244cc, petrol	V10, 5204cc, petrol
	Made of	Alloy	Alloy
	Installation	Longitudinal, front, rwd	Longitudinal, front, 4wd
	Specific output	93bhp per litre	85bhp per litre
	Bore/stroke	92.0/79.8mm	84.5/92.8mm
	Compression ratio	11:1	12:5
	Gearbox type	6-spd auto	6-spd auto
AT EACH CORNER	Front suspension	Double wishbones, Skyhook anti-dive system	Multi-link, double wishbones, anti-roll bar
	Rear suspension	Double wishbones, Skyhook anti-dive system	Multi-link, wishbone, anti-roll bar
	Brakes (f/r)	Ventilated discs, 330mm Ventilated discs, 330mm	Ventilated discs, 381mm Ventilated discs, 356mm
	Wheels	18in	20in
	Tyres (f/r)	235/40 R18, 265/35 R18	265/35 R20, 265/35 R20

'This car is going to be fast: 0-62 in 5.2secs, and a top speed of 180. The engine revs to 7,250 – that Maser howl is an aural treat'

CURVES IN ALL THE RIGHT PLACES

A PRICE TAG OF £70K PUTS MASER'S SEXY GRANTURISMO UP AGAINST THE XKR. WATCH OUT, JAGUAR...

"IT'S A BIG HUNK OF METAL," SAYS Guglielmo Cartia, the chief designer at Pininfarina, the studio responsible for this new Maserati GranTurismo. 'A big hunk of metal' may not sound like designer-speak, but he's got a point. This is no pared-back dinky coupe. It's for people who like having it large. And it's meant to look that way. "It creates the significant size impression we wanted," Cartia goes on.

The GranTurismo will replace the Coupe, a car that was designed by rival Italdesign. For the Quattroporte, Maserati went back to tradition and appointed Pininfarina, a house that tends to draw a more flamboyant Italian shape. The QP hit everyone's emotional buttons, so you can understand why Pininfarina's initial sketches won the GranTurismo gig.

Under the skin, we find Maserati's delicious 4.2-litre V8 at its most powerful yet, 405bhp. The platform and suspension are basically the same as the Quattroporte Automatico, so it's a

six-speed ZF automatic transmission, one of the best autos around – it serves well in BMWs, Astons, the Bentley Continental GT and the Jag XK, but it won't feel the same because Maserati has done its own driver-adaptive programming.

It's certainly going to be fast: 0-62 in 5.2secs, and a top speed nudging 180mph. The engine revs to 7,250, which is stratospheric for an auto, and that Maserati howl is a treat for the ears. You'll be grateful for the big six-piston Brembo brakes. Weight distribution is 49 front, 51 rear, which is right where you'd want it for friendly handling and decent traction, aided by a limited-slip diff. Suspension is set up more sportily than in the QP, we're told. But it has to deal with a car weighing 1,880kg, so if it's super-nimble, there's some kind of Italian magic going on.

You might guess those wheels are 18-inchers. They're actually 20s, which puts the car in some sort of proportion. The overall size has been used to good advantage. This is a genuine 2+2, not a

car with two front seats and rears that are a glorified parcel shelf. Our Creative Director Charlie, six feet and more, fits the back seat.

Pininfarina has worked miracles to make sure such a big car doesn't come across as brutish. There's a voluptuous bulge over front and back wheels, a nod to the Birdcage concept car. (The inward-chamfered sills are like the Birdcage's too, and the wheels are dead ringers.) The concave grille – which echoes coachbuilt cars by Pininfarina on Maserati's mid-Fifties A6GCS chassis – scoops back into the bulbous front wings, creating a giant mouth that seems to draw you in.

The small, snarky glasshouse and thunder-thighed haunches tell you a lot about the power within. At the back, the sharp-cut boot is softened by rear lights that melt around the rear corners. Light flows over the curves and straight lines, creating a powerful sense of movement.

So the basics are elegant and sculptural. But Maserati wanted to go further, to add some

Pininfarina design flair is evident, even in the rear lights

Red leather overload... A little goes a long way, guys

PHOTOGRAPHY: JOE WINDSOR-WILLIAMS. WORDS: PAUL HORRELL

Maserati's trident emblem features heavily through the cabin

The projector elements in the lights insinuate a pseudo-scowl

'If you want the Cambiocorsa transmission, you'll have to wait. But you might get a tasty car in reward for your patience'

character, but not a dose of the uglies. To that end, sharp geometric detailing has been melded in to offset the fluid forms. The result is an intriguing balance between hard and soft visual cues, and some clever tweaks that allow the car to look its size without seeming to have run to fat. For instance, the very sheer lower body-sides don't reflect as much light as the curved upper sections, so the bottom of the bodywork is de-emphasised and looks trim and lean.

The angular headlights use small projector elements pushed into the corners to create an expression that Guglielmo Cartia likens to a frown. The base of the A-pillars dive down into curved flanks, keeping the car looking low. The soft curves of the boot are offset by sharp lateral cut-lines that draw the eye towards the rear wheels.

The creative tension between the curved and angular forms makes the car visually engaging. The more you look at it, the more you see. And the more you see, the more you want to look at it.

Cartia explains his thinking: "Today, many cars do one thing well. They are either straight and geometric, or sculptural and voluptuous. This car is both. There is a constant interplay. The sculptural surfaces at the front and the rear transmit the Italian-ness that every Maserati should have, while the clean flanks and geometric details convey restraint and control and hint at the advanced technical aspects of the car."

Compare photos and you can easily trace a direct line of Pininfarina's philosophy from the Birdcage and even the one-off Ferrari P4/5 (both based on the MC12-slash-Enzo chassis), through the Ferrari 599 and into the GranTurismo. Look at the 599's proportions and basic graphics in the section from the headlights back to the rear wheels, and you'll find strong echoes in the GranTurismo. But the Ferrari has more strongly-angled cut-lines, harder shapes, more bulges and vents and scoops. You can see it's the hardcore two-seater, the Maserati the languid 2+2.

The sculptural surfaces of the Maserati's exterior are mirrored in the convex fascia which bulges towards the driver, and in the arm rests and door handles that are picked out in aluminium. The whole interior is leather-lined, crafted like some subtle but monumentally expensive piece of Italian luggage. On second thoughts, maybe 'subtle' ain't the word for the photo car's bloodbath colour scheme.

In effect, the GranTurismo replaces the current Coupe, even though it's bigger and will be a touch more expensive at around £70,000 when UK deliveries start in the autumn. But then at first glance £70,000 doesn't seem so steep for a car like this. In fact, while Maseratis have had their flaws, they've always been cheaper than people tend to guess. Maserati did some research and found that people thought their cars were in

the Aston DB9 or Bentley Continental price league, not the XKR level – which was sort of a compliment, but sort of a disadvantage because very few people can afford £100k-odd. So people who could actually afford a Maserati were ruling it out because they thought they couldn't.

At the moment Maserati is talking about just this one model: auto 'box, hard roof. If you want the Cambiocorsa transmission, with its attendant rear-mounted gearbox and even sportier weight distribution, you'll have to wait a year or two. But you might get a very tasty car in reward for your patience, as it's likely the Cambiocorsa will be paired with a higher-powered 4.7-litre version of the engine. As for a convertible, well, it might be a short-wheelbase two-seater or it might be a 2+2. Apparently it's not signed off yet. But we also hear word of a shorter two-seat coupe. Think Aston Vantage size. But that's years away, and susceptible to changes of plan.

Meanwhile, this car is enough to be getting on with – something about it makes us imagine ourselves behind the wheel. There's a feelgood aspect to modern Maseratis that comes from the fact they always seem to have something new to say. The design chief says that's the aim here too: "The GranTurismo is like a person with a varied and interesting character," says Cartia. "It evolves in front of your eyes over time – just as a compelling person does during a relationship."

Dawn. again

After its success with the Quattroporte, Maserati continues its re-invention with this, the 399bhp GranTurismo coupe ➲

Despite

the film-star looks and intriguing concept, it's hard not to approach the spectacular new Maserati GranTurismo without a certain sense of déjà vu. Not because it looks familiar – we've not seen anything quite so gob-smacking in years – but because it would appear that the more things change at Maserati, the more they stay the same.

Rewind almost eight and a half years to issue 001 of **evo** and you may remember the cover was adorned with the then-new Maserati 3200GT. The first fruits of a partnership with Ferrari – which saw Maserati's decrepit factory fully modernised at vast expense – the 3200GT was billed as the car to take Maserati back into the big time. Except it didn't.

To give credit where it's due, the 3200 and subsequent 4200GT models generated more than enough interest (and sales) to keep the bailiffs from the factory gates. However, it wasn't until Maserati introduced the all-new Quattroporte in 2004 that the Trident truly began to regain its lustre.

Encouragingly, while the future of Maserati genuinely does pivot on this brave new coupe, this time around the circumstances appear more favourable. Developing a new model knowing that the car on which it is based has won many plaudits has boosted Maserati's morale, and this newfound confidence is abundantly clear in the design and execution of the new coupe.

Dressed in boldly-sculpted couture curves that shame a Ferrari 612 Scaglietti, built on a shorter wheelbase (by 126mm) version of the Quattroporte's acclaimed front-mid-engined, rear-wheel-drive chassis and powered by the familiar 4.2-litre V8 – with power increased from 394bhp to 399 – the new Maserati GranTurismo is exotic and glamorous, inspiringly original and deliciously unconventional.

Concealing four full seats behind two gracefully swooping doors, and stretching an imposing 4.9 metres from its striking concave chrome grille to its pinched, streamlined tail, the GranTurismo combines the opulent accommodation of a Bentley Continental GT with the price of a well-specified BMW M5, while promising a carefully honed poise, balance and deftness either German can only dream of. It may lack their humungous firepower, but as Quattroporte owners already appreciate, deft dynamism reaps the richest rewards for discerning drivers.

Ironically, last year was the best year for the 4200GT – doubtless a result of the positive exposure generated by the Quattroporte and

Styling is the work of Pininfarina; many details and styling themes are shared with Quattroporte saloon, including vents in front wings (above)

GranTurismo is a full four-seater and therefore a bigger car than the outgoing 2+2 Coupe. Front-mid-engined layout results in a weight distribution of 49/51 front/rear. Below: head of vehicle engineering Paul Fickers talks of retaining Maserati DNA

the MC12 racer's success in the FIA GT Championship. Though heartened by this unexpected final flourish, no one at Maserati is wearing rose-tinted glasses: the ageing Coupe is more than ready for retirement.

Most people, including us, had originally expected Maserati to deliver a direct replacement for the 4200GT: a two-door 2+2 coupe to tempt a few thousand discerning enthusiasts a year from their default purchase of a Porsche 911. The GranTurismo is emphatically not that car, and for good reason, as Maserati technical director Jean-Luc Brossard and head of vehicle engineering Paul Fickers explain when we meet them at Maserati's Modena HQ.

'Right now we have a unique challenge and a unique opportunity at Maserati,' says Brossard. 'When I joined the company in 2003 it was a time to reflect on the company's position, and to define our objectives for the GranTurismo. We knew from our customers that the new coupe needed to be elegant and sporty, but that it should also offer comfort and space, so we decided on a bigger, full four-seater car.

'We had also found that where our customers used to drive 5000 miles per year or less, they now cover 20 or even 30,000 miles in a year. Consequently we've been working very hard on improving durability and quality so that we are a genuine alternative for customers who previously would only consider a Mercedes or BMW.'

Of course, the introduction of the Quattroporte Automatic (see page 82) is also playing a significant role in Maserati's re-invention, and laying the foundations for the GranTurismo, as Fickers explains: 'Our whole objective, not just with the GranTurismo but also with the Quattroporte, has been to retain Maserati's unique DNA but also attract those Mercedes and BMW customers. Many of our customers love the added edge and aggression of the Quattroporte's DuoSelect paddle-shift transmission, but for others it has been a barrier. Some customers felt intimidated by it, thinking it was somehow more complicated because they couldn't simply slot a lever into "D" and drive. Now we're hearing those same customers say how much they love the Quattroporte Automatic's gearshift paddles!'

Since the introduction of the 4200GT, it has always struck me that Maserati is deliberately kept a few steps behind Ferrari when it comes to the high-tech stuff. While the engineers in the red corner enjoyed the benefits of cutting-edge technical partnerships, the engineers in the blue corner seemingly had to make do with outdated hardware and software. This much was obvious when I attended both the Ferrari 612 and Maserati Quattroporte launches in 2004 and couldn't believe how much better the

transmission was in the F1 paddle-shift Ferrari compared with the DuoSelect paddle-shift Maser.

It's a situation Brossard guardedly acknowledges, adding that while it's inevitable that technical partners choose to develop and pioneer genuinely advanced technology with Ferrari, they do so with the knowledge that the hardware and software

will filter down to Maserati, which increases component volumes to a level that makes the development cost-effective for the supplier as well as Ferrari and Maserati. The trick, and this is something Brossard and Fickers are clearly pushing for, is to accelerate that filtration process.

'It's vital,' says Brossard, 'for a niche brand like Maserati to be close to a big group to maximise the manufacturing efficiency. We have this with Fiat and also with Ferrari. The best way I can explain it is to say that we are sufficiently independent to be able to develop our own cars, but sufficiently close to have the resources with which to do so. We also have our shareholders to thank, which is why any new product range has to justify the investment, and demonstrate Maserati's place in the automotive world.'

But where does the GranTurismo fit into our world? Right at the heart of it, judging by the looks and the promise of sharpened and more sporting dynamics. Tipping the scales at 1880kg, the GranTurismo is 50kg lighter than the Quattroporte, a couple of hundred kilos lighter than a Mercedes CL and a massive 500kg lighter than a Bentley Continental GT. Fitted with the

'The GranTurismo is exotic, glamorous and inspiringly original'

The GranTurismo's unveiling at the Geneva show comes 60 years after the first Maserati road car, the original Gran Turismo, made its debut at Geneva. Above right: technical director Jean-Luc Brossard

latest generation of Sachs' Skyhook active damper technology, the GranTurismo has switchable suspension settings – Normal and Sport – and Fickers says that the spring and damper settings are some 30-40 per cent firmer than on the Quattroporte. The initial production run – which starts in the summer – will be of GranTurismo Automatics (with paddle-shift), with a DuoSelect version to follow soon after.

Dutch by birth, Fickers grew up close to the Nürburgring, and relishes the fact that Maserati is now a member of the Ring's 'manufacturer pool', for it enables the company's test and development drivers to use the circuit for eight weeks per year. Amongst this team of drivers is Jean-Philippe Vittecoq, a crack tester who can count Michelin and Bugatti amongst his former employers. Fickers likens him to Loris Bicocchi, which tells you all you need to know about his skills and experience.

The team's task has been to effect a delicate but distinct shift of emphasis on the GT's QP-based chassis. Fickers explains: 'The Quattroporte is a car that is focused on comfort with agility built-in, whereas the GranTurismo is an agile and sporty car that's also comfortable and refined. Like the Quattroporte, the GT is a big car, but we have worked hard to increase the feel of compactness. We want the GT to be a more driver-focused car, a car that shrinks around the driver but still offers real comfort for four occupants.'

Bigger but cheaper than an Aston Martin DB9, classier, lighter and more exclusive than a Bentley or Benz, the GranTurismo is a hard car to pigeonhole. A pre-emptive strike on Porsche's forthcoming Panamera perhaps? Mention Porsche's meteoric rise from a struggling marque with an ageing model-range and feeble sales to the most profitable car company in the world, and Brossard's eyes spark with respect and admiration.

'Porsche's turnaround is one of the industry's great success stories, isn't it?' he says. 'But such success doesn't happen overnight. Everything came from a clear and detailed strategy, some of which would have been initially conceived ten, perhaps fifteen years earlier. Of course, markets and economic climates change along the way, but Porsche made the right early decisions and preparation, and now they are enjoying the success.

'I wouldn't say that we are like Porsche – Maserati is a very different brand and a very different company – but we have looked at what we need to do, the resources – both human and financial – we need to expand, the kind of cars we should make. And now we're working to that plan.'

So what of the future? Where does he see Maserati's sales, and what does the company need to achieve them?

'Our sales are growing by roughly 30 per cent per year,' says Brossard. 'We expect to produce between 7000 and 7500 units by the end of 2007: 5000 QPs, the rest GTs. The capacity of our Modena factory is 10,000 units, which we hope to reach by 2009. To continue growing, and to make Maserati a truly healthy company, a third model is essential… [cue tantalising pause] …although obviously I'm not going to tell you what that is just yet!'

And on that cryptic note it's time to finish the interview. Brossard has an appointment with Gus Gregory's Hasselblad. Little does he know it's on the factory roof. So while Brossard does his best not to look down, we leave to meet one more member of the GranTurismo's development team. He's a man with a fascinating story to tell… ●

New Quattroporte
gives a foretaste of
the GranTurismo's
powertrain, with the
4.2-litre V8 mated to
new ZF-auto gearbox

QP AUTOMATIC

Maser saloon gets a conventional auto 'box

Given the requirement for four seats and the wherewithal, who wouldn't choose a Maserati Quattroporte? It is, after all, the only limo-sized saloon that truly cuts it as a work of art and surrogate supercar.

But there's a catch. While, according to Maserati, most QP owners love the clutchless, paddle-shift DuoSelect transmission – aggressive, no-prisoners cog-swapping and all – for some potential customers it's been a

deal breaker, an unnecessary hardcore affectation at odds with what should be a luxurious big car remit. The sales figures seem to bear this out. Just 470 QPs were sold in the UK in 2006.

Maserati's confidence that more will be sold this year is founded, not unreasonably, in the belief that the new £77,000 Quattroporte Automatic is the fix the sorely tempted have been waiting for. And it's been worth the wait.

In simple terms, it's the QP we know and love, but with a conventional

torque converter auto instead of the F1-derived electro-mechanical transmission. Better news still, the auto in question is the latest version of the deliciously up-for-it ZF 6HP 26 six-speeder that does such an effective job in the Jaguar XKR. And, thanks to further co-tweaking between ZF and Maserati, for the first time it can boast sizzling 7200rpm upshifts.

It's not quite that simple, of course. Re-engineering has involved ditching the rear-mounted transaxle of the DuoSelect-equipped car and mounting the gearbox conventionally on the back of the engine. The knock-on is a new rear-suspension subframe and propshaft to replace the lengthy torque tube that locked the engine and transaxle

together as a single unit. Another switch is from dry- to wet-sump lubrication, done because it makes the engine quieter, says Maserati. This, in turn, has meant redesigning the engine block to accommodate the new oil supply system and crankcase breathing demands. Despite the changes, the QP's favourably rear-biased weight distribution has been largely preserved, dropping from 53 to 51 per cent.

There's no need to lose the paddle-shifters with the new transmission, of course; cutting-edge torque converter 'boxes, as typified by the ZF, aim to offer the best of all worlds. But they're standard only on the Sport GT version. Our regular QPA hasn't been specified with them and has to make do with the chunky gear selector on the centre console which, in manual mode, shifts up when pulled back and down when pushed forward – a more intuitive way of doing things than the opposite arrangement adopted by Porsche and Audi among others.

We start our drive through the streets of Monte Carlo and are somewhat shocked by the new exuberance with

which the QPA sets off from rest unless you're super-smooth with the throttle. The auto doesn't make much effort to cushion the razor-sharp fly-by-wire throttle-response of the gloriously musical 4244cc, 394bhp V8, but the problem requires only a little driver finesse and, once rolling, upshifts are impressively clean and smooth.

But it's when we break free from the town's narrow, Zonda-clogged streets that the ZF self-shifter shows its true mettle. No, in its QP application, it doesn't blip seductively on downshifts, but the beautifully judged part-throttle kickdown and super-snappy full-throttle upshifts more than compensate. It suits the car's fiery character well because, despite some judicious tweaking to liberate an extra 7lb ft of torque (making 340 at 4250rpm), kidney-thumping wallop simply isn't in the repertoire.

We won't hold the shortfall against it. Not with a shape like that. Not with such a direct, biddable and grippy chassis. Not with that exquisitely-crafted and comfortable cabin. And not with a transmission so worthy of the car. Finally, the Quattroporte adds up.

IT'S 1954, AND FIVE-YEAR-OLD Ivano Cornia is waiting on the Viale Ciro Menotti, the road that runs past the Maserati factory. It's a familiar routine for the little boy, for every day he makes the same short walk from his home to the spot where he waits to catch a glimpse of the latest Maserati as it embarks on or returns from a test drive in the hills above Modena.

One day a Maserati stops next to him. It's an A6GCS, Maserati's beautiful racing Berlinetta, an example of which would finish third in that year's Mille Miglia. Its driver is Guerino Bertocchi, Maserati's chief test driver. Bertocchi has become intrigued by the boy who is always waiting and waving on the pavement, and decides to reward him by taking him for a blast up the road. That magical day was to shape little Ivano's life.

It's 1968, and a 19-year-old Cornia graduates

from engineering college to start his job as a technical designer at De Tomaso. Two years later his role has grown to include some test-driving, and by 1976 he's moved to Maserati as a full-time test driver. His mentor is Guerino Bertocchi…

It's 2007, and Cornia is entering his fourth decade as a Maserati test driver. In a career that has seen him play a part in the development of every Maserati since the Kyalami, Cornia has become part of Maserati mythology. Perhaps that's why his young colleagues refer to him affectionately as *Il Drago* (The Dragon).

Cast from the same die as Ferrari's legendary tester, Dario Benuzzi, Cornia is a test driver from the old-school: happy to regale us with tales of high-speed driving and the odd high-speed crash, all with an unmistakable glint in his eye. Put simply he loves his job, as he explains while driving us to lunch in a Quattroporte Automatic.

'I'm nearly 60, but I never think of retiring. Why should I? I've got the best job in the world. Only a test pilot's job is more exciting. Of course, I've had a few big crashes in my time. I remember the largest, for it really dented my confidence. It was a big one. Fortunately I wasn't hurt, but I was scared that I'd lost my nerve. The next day I took out another car and drove through the same fast corner, just to see if I had the courage. I did…'

As you'd expect, Cornia has seen many changes in his time at Maserati; from the dark days immediately after the partnership with Citroën was dissolved, though the turbulent De Tomaso-owned years and regenerative Ferrari era to the current Alfa-Maserati restructure instigated by parent company Fiat.

Back in those early days there were just four people in Maserati's research and development team, two of those being the test drivers. Up until 1990, race tracks didn't play any part in the development programme. Now Maserati's R&D team totals around 70 people, with four dedicated ➔

test drivers and eight engineers who work on effecting changes to the test cars. The test and development regime has also altered out of all recognition.

In his role as Maserati's chief test driver, Cornia has been involved in every aspect of the GranTurismo's development, from pounding the autostradas towards the Brenner Pass and scratching up and down the hills near Serramazzoni, to lapping at Fiorano, the Nürburgring Nordschleife and Fiat's Balocco proving ground, or conducting air-conditioning tests in South Africa and signing-off ABS and ESP systems on a frozen lake in Scandinavia.

Maserati is a relative newcomer to the Nürburgring, having incorporated it into the test regime only four years ago, but it's now an important element of every new model's development. Some manufacturers play down the significance of high-speed lapping, preferring to emphasise the Nordschleife's value as a

durability-testing venue. Frankly this all makes the most exciting circuit in the world sound a bit worthy. Encouragingly, this isn't a line you'll hear from Cornia.

'We don't go to the Nürburgring to test for durability so much as to fine-tune the handling. During development of the GranTurismo we wanted to create a better performing, more driver-focused car than the Quattroporte. It still has four seats, but we never forgot we were creating a sports car. Our main goal was to achieve the best possible performance from the car, but in the most accessible way. The Nürburgring Nordschleife is perfect for this.'

After all the trouble and strife, false dawns and internal wrangles, it feels as though Maserati's latest revival has some genuine momentum behind it. The Quattroporte and recently introduced QP Automatic have deservedly won praise and created a healthy foundation on which to rebuild the brand. The company's management is implementing an increasingly confident and adventurous product strategy, and its engineers are exploiting the unique benefits of a technical partnership with Ferrari and the vast support network of Fiat.

More tellingly, while Brossard, Fickers and Cornia openly acknowledge that the GranTurismo has to work if Maserati's long-term survival is to be secured, they do so with the kind of nervous anticipation born from the heartfelt belief that they have a great car on their hands. We'll know if they have in July, but if the dynamics live up to the spectacular aesthetics, the Trident's future looks bright in their hands.

SPECIFICATION

GRANTURISMO

■ Engine	V8, 4244cc, 32v
■ Location	Front-mid, longitudinal
■ Max power	399bhp @ 7000rpm
■ Max torque	340lb ft @ 4250rpm
■ Weight (kerb)	1880kg
■ Power-to-weight	216bhp/ton
■ 0-62mph	5.0sec (est)
■ Top speed	175mph (est)
■ Basic price	c£70,000 (est)
■ On sale	July 2007

Above: chief test driver Ivano Cornia has been with Maserati since 1976. All those years of experience have been put into the development of the GranTurismo's chassis

MERCEDES-BENZ CL-CLASS
MASERATI QUATTROPORTE
MITSUBISHI LANCER GTS
ASTON MARTIN VANTAGE ROADSTER
BMW X5
PORSCHE CAYENNE TURBO
SMART FORTWO
CHEVROLET CORVETTE Z06

Maserati Quattroporte Automatica
Proper self shifter? Pure luxury...

THEORETICALLY, the Maserati Quattroporte has always been an Italian alternative to the big Germans that rule the world of full-sized performance luxury cars. Realistically, it has been let down by a fidgety, jerky manual gearbox with an automatic clutch that has stood in the way of the refinement expected from a $260,000-odd sedan.

Until now that is, because a real auto – that's one with a torque converter – has been wedged into Maserati's flagship. It might sound like an easy retro-fit but it has involved plenty of re-engineering. That's because the Quattroporte's original transmission was via a rear-mounted transaxle. The new gearbox mounts in a conventional position behind the Ferrari-supplied 4.2-litre V8, achieved without widening the transmission tunnel (or, conversely, narrowing the front footwells), and while the engine itself has switched from dry to wet-sump lubrication, the complex redesign of the Quattroporte's guts has been achieved with remarkable lack of compromise.

Weight distribution has gone from a rear-biased 47:53 to a more balanced 49:51 front/rear and kerb weight has risen 20kg to a surprisingly hefty 1990kg. The V8 itself has been retuned to drop peak revs so the torque converter doesn't spin so hard. The bonus is more torque, with 460Nm (up 10Nm) arriving 250rpm lower in the rev range at 4250rpm. Performance has dropped slightly, with Maserati claiming 5.6 seconds to 100km/h compared with 5.2sec for the sequential manual, which will still be offered on the Sport GT model.

The ZF six-speed has certainly made driving a much less frustrating and more effortless experience. The auto works brilliantly

in drive mode, changing efficiently and smoothly hanging onto a gear between corners when it senses intent of purpose from the driver.

The extra refinement adds to the beguiling charm of the Quattroporte. The engine might not match the capacity of the latest Mercedes AMG models, but it barks at full throttle, moans on the over-run and has an astounding amount of top-end urge. The ride might be more solid than expected from a supposed luxury car, even if suspension rates have been softened slightly. But then, the light and accurate steering, massive rear grip and general eagerness to attack corners also sets the Quattroporte apart.

But all is not rosy with the car's packaging: the interior looks luxurious enough, but rear leg room is ample rather than extraordinary, and the boot is still too small for the car's size.

Maserati has always claimed the Quattroporte represents a real alternative for the driver seeking greater individuality than the obvious German alternatives can provide. Now that the drivetrain has been sorted to provide real refinement while barely harming the performance, it means Italian *appassionata* is available in a four-door package with much less compromise.

JONATHAN HAWLEY

THE AUTO

Development of the ZF auto wasn't just for the sake of the Quattroporte, even if the sedan takes 65 percent of Maserati sales and spearheads the company's charge into higher sales territory. The same platform is under the recently announced GranTurismo and making an auto available in that large coupe was seen as vital. Hence the effort that went into eradicating the transaxle.

Model	Maserati Quattroporte
Engine	4244cc V8, dohc, 32v
Max Power	295kW @ 7000rpm
Max Torque	460Nm @ 4250rpm
Transmission	6-speed automatic
0-100km/h	5.6sec (claimed)
Prices	$258,000 (approximate)
On sale	June 2007

☑ Fluid, engaging drive; top-end squirt; individuality
☒ Terse ride; rear packaging; boot size

MASERATI Quattroporte Automatic

At long last, the stylish sedan gets the gearbox it deserves

BY PAUL FRÈRE »» PHOTOS BY ALLAN ROSENBERG

LAUNCHED IN 2003, THE NEW Maserati Quattroporte has been offered from the outset with a robotized conventional manual 6-speed transmission allowing the driver to choose between automatic or manual operation by paddles behind the steering wheel. Unfortunately, while a robotized box is a very good alternative for a sports car, it does not shift smoothly enough for a top luxury sedan. Hence, the recent debut of the new Quattroporte Automatic, which benefits from the latest ZF 6-speed torque-converter transmission with lock-up clutch. This transmission can be operated manually in the sequential mode through the console-mounted lever or, in the GT version, by paddles behind the steering wheel.

For the new Quattroporte Automatic, the powertrain has been extensively reengineered. The ZF transmission is bolted to the engine crankcase, while previously there was a rear 6-speed transaxle rigidly connected to the engine's clutch bellhousing by a tube surrounding the propeller shaft. This changes the front/rear weight distribution from 47/53 to 49/51 percent.

Less obvious are the modifications to the 4.2-liter 4-cam V-8 all-aluminum engine. The dry-sump lubrication of the other model has been deleted, saving weight. The air intake system has been changed, and the intake camshafts now benefit from a continuously operating timing variator. Moreover, the shape of the piston crown has been modified, with all changes increasing the maximum torque from 332 to 339 lb.-ft. and moving its peak down from 4500 to 4250 rpm. This makes for a better adaptation to the torque-converter transmission and without any loss of power, which remains at 400 bhp at 7000 rpm.

Thanks to the modifications, the Quattroporte Automatic's weight of 4387 lb. is only 44 lb. heavier than that of the Duo-Select model, which remains in production. Performance losses are minimal:

> **»» A new ZF automatic transmission and modifications to the Quattroporte's 4.2-liter V-8 improve its driving dynamics.**

Top speed is reduced by 3 mph and the time for the 0–100-km/h (0–62 mph) sprint is increased from 5.2 to 5.6 seconds, according to Maserati.

The Quattroporte is exceptionally agile for its size and weight. And the Italian engineers have successfully tuned the engine and exhaust to emit a pleasant sound, but not to mute it. When accelerating, you can hear where the performance comes from, but the sound is never obtrusive.

Three electronic transmission programs are provided: Snow, Normal and Sport. In Snow, the car starts in 2nd gear and up- and downshifts take place at low engine speeds. In Normal, all six ratios are used with the smooth up- and downshifts taking place depending on how aggressively the car is driven. In Sport mode, all shifts are made at higher revs and performed more quickly. In all modes, including manual, kicking down instantly selects the gear providing the best acceleration and keeps it until the 7000-rpm redline is reached. If the accelerator is lifted quickly enough, any gear selected remains engaged for some time.

I drove the car mostly on secondary and mountain roads, where the excellence of the new transmission was highly appreciated. The response to kick down or to manual selector shifts is excellent, except on occasion when the gearbox seemed to hesitate between 2nd and 3rd gear.

The mountain stretches were quite demanding on the powerful brakes, which never showed the slightest sign of fade. Hairpin turns highlighted the excellent steering lock, and the speed-sensitive rack-and-pinion power steering is precise and well weighted, but has a rather dead feel at urban speeds. Stability control is not obtrusive and can be switched off if necessary.

Not all secondary roads are well surfaced, and here the Quattroporte was really impressive for the way its double-wishbone suspension absorbs bumps and irregularities.

The quality and workmanship of the Maserati's interior are excellent and so is the fit of the wood or carbon trim. The instruments are easily legible; and the various controls are ergonomically well arranged. The automatic air-conditioning system has separate adjustments for the left and right sides of the cabin, both in the front and rear. The rear seat is electrically adjustable, and leg room is more than adequate. As for criticisms, the trunk is small, and the driver's seat needs more lateral support.

Nevertheless, to car fans with a good budget and a sense for exclusivity, I can only say: Try the Quattroporte; for me it was a real surprise. ●

online:

roadandtrack.com